EXAM✓CRAM

CompTIA® A+
220-801 and
220-802

Authorized Practice Questions
Fifth Edition

David L. Prowse

800 East 96th Street, Indianapolis, Indiana 46240 USA

CompTIA® A+ 220-801 and 220-802
Authorized Practice Questions
Exam Cram, Fifth Edition

Trademarks

All terms mentioned in this book that are known to be trademarks or service marks have been appropriately capitalized. Pearson IT Certification cannot attest to the accuracy of this information. Use of a term in this book should not be regarded as affecting the validity of any trademark or service mark.

Warning and Disclaimer

Every effort has been made to make this book as complete and as accurate as possible, but no warranty or fitness is implied. The information provided is on an "as is" basis. The author and the publisher shall have neither liability nor responsibility to any person or entity with respect to any loss or damages arising from the information contained in this book or from the use of the CD or programs accompanying it.

Bulk Sales

Pearson IT Certification offers excellent discounts on this book when ordered in quantity for bulk purchases or special sales. For more information, please contact

U.S. Corporate and Government Sales

1-800-382-3419

corpsales@pearsontechgroup.com

For sales outside of the U.S., please contact

International Sales

international@pearsoned.com

Associate Publisher
Dave Dusthimer

Acquisitions Editor
Betsy Brown

Development Editor
Box Twelve
Communications,
Inc.

Managing Editor
Sandra Schroeder

Project Editor
Mandie Frank

Copy Editor
Megan Wade

Proofreader
Leslie Joseph

Technical Editor
Aubrey Adams

Editorial Assistant
Vanessa Evans

Media Producer
Tim Warner

Interior Designer
Gary Adair

Cover Designer
Gary Adair

Compositor
Studio Galou, LLC

Table of Contents

About the Author

David L. Prowse is an author, a computer network specialist, and a technical trainer. Over the past several years he has authored several titles for Pearson Education, including the well-received *CompTIA A+ Exam Cram* and *CompTIA Security+ Cert Guide*. As a consultant, he installs and secures the latest in computer and networking technology. Over the past decade he has also taught CompTIA A+, Network+, and Security+ certification courses, both in the classroom and via the Internet. He runs the website www.davidlprowse.com, where he gladly answers questions from students and readers.

About the Technical Editor

Aubrey Adams is an electronics and computer systems engineering lecturer and Cisco Networking Academy instructor at Central Institute of Technology in Perth, Western Australia. With a background in telecommunications, qualifications in communications engineering and management, and graduate diplomas in computing and education, he teaches across a range of computer systems and networking vocational education and training areas. Aubrey has authored Networking Academy curriculum and assessments and is a Cisco Press author and Pearson Education technical editor.

We Want to Hear from You!

As the reader of this book, you are our most important critic and commentator. We value your opinion and want to know what we're doing right, what we could do better, what areas you'd like to see us publish in, and any other words of wisdom you're willing to pass our way.

As an associate publisher for Pearson IT Certification, I welcome your comments. You can email or write me directly to let me know what you did or didn't like about this book—as well as what we can do to make our books better.

Please note that I cannot help you with technical problems related to the topic of this book. We do have a User Services group, however, where I will forward specific technical questions related to the book.

When you write, please be sure to include this book's title and author as well as your name, email address, and phone number. I will carefully review your comments and share them with the author and editors who worked on the book.

Email: feedback@pearsonitcertification.com

Mail: David Dusthimer

Associate Publisher

Pearson IT Certification

800 East 96th Street

Indianapolis, IN 46240 USA

Reader Services

Visit our website and register this book at www.pearsonitcertification.com for convenient access to any updates, downloads, or errata that might be available for this book.

It Pays to Get Certified

IT is Everywhere	IT Knowledge and Skills Get Jobs	Job Retention	New Opportunities	High Pay-High Growth Jobs
IT is mission critical to almost all organizations and its importance is increasing.	Certifications verify your knowledge and skills that qualifies you for:	Competence is noticed and valued in organizations.	Certifications qualify you for new opportunities in your current job or when you want to change careers.	Hiring managers demand the strongest skill set.
• 79% of U.S. businesses report IT is either important or very important to the success of their company	• Jobs in the high growth IT career field • Increased compensation • Challenging assignments and promotions • 60% report that being certified is an employer or job requirement	• Increased knowledge of new or complex technologies • Enhanced productivity • More insightful problem solving • Better project management and communication skills • 47% report being certified helped improve their problem solving skills	• 31% report certification improved their career advancement opportunities	• There is a widening IT skills gap with over 300,000 jobs open • 88% report being certified enhanced their resume

In a digital world, digital literacy is an essential survival skill.

Certification proves you have the knowledge and skill to solve business problems in virtually any business environment. Certifications are highly-valued credentials that qualify you for jobs, increased compensation and promotion.

Certification Advances Your Career

- **The CompTIA A+ credential**—provides foundation-level knowledge and skills necessary for a career in PC repair and support.
- **Starting Salary**—CompTIA A+ Certified individuals can earn as much as $65,000 per year.
- **Career Pathway**—CompTIA A+ is a building block for other CompTIA certifications such as Network+, Security+ and vendor specific technologies.
- **More than 850,000**—Individuals worldwide are CompTIA A+ certified.
- **Mandated/Recommended by organizations worldwide**—Such as Cisco and HP and Ricoh, the U.S. State Department, and U.S. government contractors such as EDS, General Dynamics, and Northrop Grumman.

Some of the primary benefits individuals report from becoming A+ certified are:

- More efficient troubleshooting
- Improved career advancement
- More insightful problem solving

CompTIA Career Pathway

CompTIA offers a number of credentials that form a foundation for your career in technology and allows you to pursue specific areas of concentration. Depending on the path you choose to take, CompTIA certifications help you build upon your skills and knowledge, supporting learning throughout your entire career.

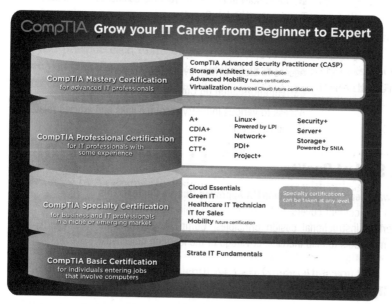

Steps to Certification

Steps to Getting Certified and Staying Certified

Review Exam Objectives	Review the certification objectives to make sure you know what is covered in the exam. http://www.comptia.org/certifications/testprep/examobjectives.aspx
Practice for the Exam	After you have studied for the certification, take a free assessment and sample test to get an idea what type of questions might be on the exam. http://www.comptia.org/certifications/testprep/practicetests.aspx
Purchase an Exam Voucher	Purchase your exam voucher on the CompTIA Marketplace, which is located at: www.comptiastore.com.
Take the Test!	Select a certification exam provider and schedule a time to take your exam. You can find exam providers at the following link: http://www.comptia.org/certifications/testprep/testingcenters.aspx

▶ **Answers and Explanations:** This section provides you with correct answers as well as further explanations about the content posed in that question. Use this information to learn why an answer is correct and to reinforce the content in your mind for the exam day.

The book also comes with a supplemental disc. It contains a simulated testing environment where you can take all seven exams on the computer in study mode or in full practice test mode.

Hints for Using This Book

Complete your exams on a separate piece of paper so that you can reuse the practice questions again if necessary. Also, plan to score 90% or higher on each exam before moving on to the next one. The higher percentages you score on practice question products, the better your chances for passing the real exam.

I am available for questions at my website:

www.davidlprowse.com

I answer questions Monday through Friday, usually in the mornings.

Need Further Study?

Consider a hands-on A+ course, and be sure to see the following sister products to this book:

▶ *CompTIA A+ Exam Cram, Sixth Edition* by David L. Prowse
(ISBN: 978-0789749710)

▶ *CompTIA A+ Cert Guide, Third Edition* by Mark E. Soper, et al
(ISBN: 978-0789749802)

CHAPTER ONE

Introduction to the 220-801 Exam

The CompTIA A+ 220-801 exam is all about PC hardware, networking, and procedures. The majority of this exam covers the nuts and bolts of computer building.

In this chapter we'll briefly discuss how the exam is categorized, give you some test-taking tips, and then prepare you to take the three 220-801 exams that follow this chapter.

Exam Breakdown

The CompTIA A+ 220-801 exam is divided up by domain. Each domain makes up a certain percentage of the test. The five domains of the A+ 220-801 exam and their respective percentages are listed in Table 1.1.

TABLE 1.1   220-801 Domains

Domain	Percentage of Exam
1.0 PC Hardware	40%
2.0 Networking	27%
3.0 Laptops	11%
4.0 Printers	11%
5.0 Operational Procedures	11%
Total	100%

The 220-801 exam concentrates on the installation and configuration of hardware and devices. It doesn't really get into troubleshooting—that is saved for the 220-802 exam.

Chances are that when you take the real CompTIA exam, you will see approximately 40 questions on PC hardware, 27 questions on networking, and so on. So it stands to reason that PC hardware should be the most important subject of your studies, due to the sheer bulk of the questions you will see.

Each domain has several or more objectives. There are far too many to list in this book (20 pages or so), but I do recommend you download a copy of the objectives for yourself. You can get them from:

http://www.comptia.org

Let's talk about each domain briefly.

Domain 1.0: PC Hardware (40%)

This domain concerns building a computer and upgrading it. The core of a PC includes the motherboard, CPU, and RAM. Those are the guts of the computer so to speak. They are installed inside a computer case.

You are required to understand motherboard form factors and compatibility concerns as well as the ports, connectors, busses, and expansion slots of a motherboard. You should also know how to access, configure, and update the BIOS and understand the relationship between the BIOS, CMOS, and lithium battery.

Then there's everything that connects to the motherboard: CPU and fan, RAM, expansion cards, hard drives, and optical drives. Plus there are all of the ports on a computer such as USB, FireWire, video, and audio ports. And finally, you should know some custom PC configurations such as gaming PCs, CAD/CAM workstations, and HTPCs and the hardware that those different types of systems require.

Domain 2.0: Networking (27%)

The Networking domain covers network standards, cabling, connectors, and tools. TCP/IP is also a big portion of this domain; you will undoubtedly see questions on IP addresses, ports, and protocols. You should be able to compare wired and wireless technologies and describe the various types of networking hardware available.

Domain 3.0: Laptops (11%)

The Laptops domain is a much smaller percentage than the PC Hardware domain. But remember that every domain is important. You should be able to demonstrate the ability to install and configure laptop hardware and software. You also should know how to operate laptops' special functions such as dual displays, wireless, and Bluetooth.

Domain 4.0: Printers (11%)

Printer technologies such as laser, inkjet, thermal, and impact will definitely present themselves as questions on the exam. You should know how to install, configure, and share printers as well as perform printer maintenance.

Domain 5.0: Operational Procedures (11%)

This domain covers safety, environmental controls, how to deal with prohibited content, how to act professionally, and how to use proper communication skills.

Test-Taking Tips

My first recommendation is to take the exams slowly. Don't rush it, especially on the first exam. Carefully read through each question. Some questions are tricky by design. Others may seem tricky if you lack knowledge in certain areas. Still other questions are somewhat vague, and that is intentional as well. You need to place yourself in the scenario of the question. Think of yourself actually installing a CPU and heat sink, or imagine that you are upgrading a video card. Picture in your head the steps you must take to accomplish what the question is asking of you. Envision what you do with computers step-by-step, and the answers will come easier to you.

Next, read through *all* of the answers. Don't just jump on the first one that seems correct to you. Look at each answer and ask yourself whether it is right or wrong. And if it is wrong, define why it is wrong. This will help you to eliminate wrong answers in the search for the correct answer. When you have selected an answer, be confident in your decision.

Finally, don't get stuck on any one question. You can always mark it and return to it later. I'll have more tips as we progress through the book, and I summarize all test-taking tips at the end of this book.

Getting Ready for the Practice Tests

The next three chapters feature practice tests based on the 220-801 exam. The first exam (Practice Exam A) is categorized by domain to help you study the concepts in order. It is also designed to be an easier exam than the other two. The other exams (Practice Exam B and Practice Exam C) are freestyle, which means the questions are mixed up to better simulate the real exam. Each exam is followed by in-depth explanations. Be sure to read them carefully. Don't move on to another exam until you have mastered the first one. And by *mastered* I mean you should be scoring 90% or higher on the exam as well as within each of the individual domains. Really understand the concepts before moving on to another exam. This will make you an efficient test-taker and allow you to benefit the most from this book.

Consider timing yourself. Give yourself 90 minutes to complete each exam. Write down your answers on a piece of paper. When you are finished, if there is still time left, review your answers for accuracy.

Each exam gets progressively more difficult. Don't get overconfident if you do well on the first exam; your skills will be tested more thoroughly as you progress. And don't get too concerned if you don't score 90% on the first try. That just means you need to study more and try the test again later. Keep studying and practicing!

After each exam is an answer key, followed by the in-depth answers/explanations. Don't skip the explanations, even if you think you know the concept. I often insert little tidbits of knowledge that are on the periphery of the concept, but they serve to build you a stronger foundation of knowledge in general. In other words, I might branch off the main topic, but this is done so you can get a clearer, bigger picture of the 220-801 exam.

So take a deep breath, and let's go!

CHAPTER TWO

220-801 Practice Exam A

Welcome to the first 220-801 practice exam. This practice exam is categorized in order of the domains. You will see 40 questions on PC Hardware; 27 questions on Networking; and 11 questions each for Laptops, Printers, and Operational Procedures, for a total of 100 questions. This is the easiest of the three 220-801 exams. The other two will get progressively harder.

Take this first exam slowly. The goal is to make sure you understand all of the concepts before moving on to the next test.

Write down your answers and check them against the answer key that immediately follows the exam. After the answer key you will find the explanations for all of the answers. Good luck!

-38   62%

Practice Questions

Domain 1.0: PC Hardware

1. Which of the following are components you might find inside a PC? (Select all correct answers.)

    Quick Answer: **27**
    Detailed Answer: **29**

    - ○ **A.** CPU
    - ○ **B.** Motherboard
    - ○ **C.** Keyboard
    - ○ **D.** Printer
    - ○ **E.** RAM
    - ○ **F.** Cable modem

2. Which device stores data over the long term?

    Quick Answer: **27**
    Detailed Answer: **29**

    - ○ **A.** CPU
    - ○ **B.** RAM
    - ○ **C.** Hard drive
    - ○ **D.** Video card

3. You would normally plug speakers into what type of port?

    Quick Answer: **27**
    Detailed Answer: **29**

    - ○ **A.** Parallel
    - ○ **B.** DVI
    - ○ **C.** 1/8-inch TRS
    - ○ **D.** 1/4-inch TRS

4. To which type of expansion slot would you install an x16 card?

    Quick Answer: **27**
    Detailed Answer: **29**

    - ○ **A.** PCI
    - ○ **B.** PCIe
    - ○ **C.** AGP
    - ○ **D.** PCI-X

5. What part of the computer checks all your components during boot?

    Quick Answer: **27**
    Detailed Answer: **29**

    - ○ **A.** CMOS
    - ○ **B.** POST
    - ○ **C.** BIOS
    - ○ **D.** EEPROM

6. Tim installs a new CPU in a computer. After a few hours, the processor starts to overheat. Which of the following might be the cause?

Quick Answer: 27
Detailed Answer: 29

- ○ **A.** The CPU is not locked down.
- ○ **B.** The CPU is not properly seated.
- ○ **C.** Thermal compound was not applied.
- ○ **D.** The CPU is not compatible with the motherboard.

7. If you have a flat-panel monitor, what type of technology is most likely being used? (Select the best answer.)

Quick Answer: 27
Detailed Answer: 29

- ○ **A.** LCD
- ○ **B.** CRT
- ○ **C.** RGB
- ○ **D.** DVI

8. Which of the following could cause the POST to fail? (Select all correct answers.)

Quick Answer: 27
Detailed Answer: 29

- ○ **A.** CPU
- ○ **B.** Power supply
- ○ **C.** CD-ROM
- ○ **D.** Memory
- ○ **E.** Hard drive

9. Which expansion bus uses lanes to transfer data?

Quick Answer: 27
Detailed Answer: 30

- ○ **A.** PCI
- ○ **B.** PCI-X
- ○ **C.** PCIe
- ○ **D.** IDE

10. Which of the following are 64-bit CPUs? (Select all correct answers.).

Quick Answer: 27
Detailed Answer: 30

- ○ **A.** Core i5
- ○ **B.** Phenom II
- ○ **C.** Pentium IV
- ○ **D.** x64

11. Which kind of socket incorporates "lands" to ensure connectivity to a CPU?

- ○ **A.** PGA
- ○ **B.** Chipset
- ○ **C.** LGA
- ○ **D.** Copper

Quick Answer: **27**
Detailed Answer: **30**

12. How should you hold RAM when installing it?

- ○ **A.** By the edges
- ○ **B.** By the front and back
- ○ **C.** With tweezers
- ○ **D.** With an IC puller

Quick Answer: **27**
Detailed Answer: **30**

13. Which device should you use to protect against power outages?

- ○ **A.** Multimeter
- ○ **B.** UPS
- ○ **C.** FedEx
- ○ **D.** Surge protector

Quick Answer: **27**
Detailed Answer: **30**

14. Which of the following uses a 24-pin main motherboard power connector?

- ○ **A.** ATX
- ○ **B.** ATX 12V 1.3
- ○ **C.** ATX 12V 2.0
- ○ **D.** ATX 5V 2.0

Quick Answer: **27**
Detailed Answer: **30**

15. What is the maximum data transfer rate of SATA revision 3.0?

- ○ **A.** 1.5 Gb/s
- ○ **B.** 150 MB/s
- ○ **C.** 3.0 Gb/s
- ○ **D.** 6.0 Gb/s

Quick Answer: **27**
Detailed Answer: **30**

16. A Compact Disc you use is rated at a speed of 48X. What does the *X* refer to?

- ○ **A.** 150 KB/s
- ○ **B.** 1.32 MB/s
- ○ **C.** 133 MB/s
- ○ **D.** 4.5 MB/s

Quick Answer: **27**
Detailed Answer: **30**

17. Which type of adapter card accepts broadcast programming?

    O **A.** FireWire card

    O **B.** Video capture card

    O **C.** Network interface card

    O **D.** TV tuner

18. Which of the following types of custom PCs requires an HDMI output?

    O **A.** HTPC

    O **B.** Gaming PC

    O **C.** Virtualization workstation

    O **D.** CAD/CAM workstation

19. How many pins are inside a SATA data connector?

    O **A.** 15

    O **B.** 7

    O **C.** 24

    O **D.** 127

20. Which of the following ports would you most likely connect a printer to?

    O **A.** USB

    O **B.** LPT

    O **C.** FireWire

    O **D.** eSATA

21. What is the delay in the RAM's response to a request from the memory controller called?

    O **A.** Latency

    O **B.** Standard deviation

    O **C.** Fetch interval

    O **D.** Lag

22. What is the minimum number of hard drives necessary to implement RAID 5?

    O **A.** 2

    O **B.** 5

    O **C.** 3

    O **D.** 4

23. A user's time and date keeps resetting to January 1, 2000. What is the most likely cause?

  ○ **A.** The BIOS needs to be updated.

  ○ **B.** Windows needs to be updated.

  ○ **C.** The Windows Date and Time Properties window needs to be modified.

  ○ **D.** The lithium battery needs to be replaced.

24. What type of adapter card is normally plugged into a PCIe x16 adapter card slot?

  ○ **A.** Modem

  ○ **B.** Video

  ○ **C.** NIC

  ○ **D.** Sound

25. To prevent damage to a computer, the computer should be connected to what?

  ○ **A.** A power strip

  ○ **B.** A power inverter

  ○ **C.** An AC to DC converter

  ○ **D.** A UPS

26. A computer has 1024 MB of RAM. It has 128 MB of shared video memory. How much RAM is available to the operating system?

  ○ **A.** 512 MB

  ○ **B.** 896 MB

  ○ **C.** 448 MB

  ○ **D.** 1024 MB

27. Which of the following components could cause the POST to beep several times and fail during boot?

  ○ **A.** Sound card

  ○ **B.** Power supply

  ○ **C.** Hard drive

  ○ **D.** RAM

28. Which of the following is the proper boot sequence of a PC?

○ **A.** CPU, POST, boot loader, operating system

○ **B.** Boot loader, operating system, CPU, RAM

○ **C.** POST, CPU, boot loader, operating system

○ **D.** CPU, RAM, boot loader, operating system

(29) Roger informs you that none of the three SCSI drives can be seen on his SCSI chain. What should you check?

○ **A.** Whether the host adapter is terminated and that the disks have consecutive IDs of 1, 2, and 3

○ **B.** Whether the SCSI adapter has an ID of 7 or 15, and whether all the disks are terminated and have consecutive IDs of 0, 1, and 2

○ **C.** Whether the host adapter has an ID of 0, and whether the disks are terminated with the same ID

○ **D.** Whether the SCSI adapter has an ID of 7, and whether both ends of the chain are terminated, and that each disk has a unique ID

30. Which of the following has the fastest data throughput?

○ **A.** CD-ROM

○ **B.** Hard drive

○ **C.** RAM

○ **D.** USB

31. Which kind of form factor is commonly found in HTPCs?

○ **A.** ATX

○ **B.** Pico-ITX

○ **C.** microATX

○ **D.** Nano-ITX

32. Which of the following CPU cooling methods is the most common?

○ **A.** Heat sink

○ **B.** Heat sink and fan

○ **C.** Liquid cooling

○ **D.** Liquid nitrogen

33. You need to store 4 GB of data to an optical disc (without using compression). Which of the following will meet your requirements? (Select the two best answers.)

Quick Answer: **27**
Detailed Answer: **32**

- ○ **A.** CD-ROM
- ○ **B.** DVD-RW
- ○ **C.** CD-RW
- ○ **D.** BD-R

34. Which of the following is not a video port?

Quick Answer: **27**
Detailed Answer: **33**

- ○ **A.** DVI
- ○ **B.** HDMI
- ○ **C.** DisplayPort
- ○ **D.** CNR

35. What does a CAD/CAM workstation require? (Select the two best answers.)

Quick Answer: **27**
Detailed Answer: **33**

- ○ **A.** Powerful CPU
- ○ **B.** HDMI output
- ○ **C.** Surround sound
- ○ **D.** High-end video

36. You need to install the fastest hard drive possible. Which port should you connect it to?

Quick Answer: **27**
Detailed Answer: **33**

- ○ **A.** USB
- ○ **B.** SATA
- ○ **C.** IDE
- ○ **D.** eSATA

37. What type of power connector is used for an x16 video card?

Quick Answer: **27**
Detailed Answer: **33**

- ○ **A.** Molex 4-pin
- ○ **B.** Mini 4-pin
- ○ **C.** PCIe 6-pin
- ○ **D.** P1 24-pin

38. Which kind of current does a typical desktop PC draw from a wall outlet?

Quick Answer: **27**
Detailed Answer: **33**

- ○ **A.** Direct current
- ○ **B.** Neutral current
- ○ **C.** Alternating current
- ○ **D.** Draw current

39. Which of the following are output devices? (Select the three best answers.)

- ○ **A.** Speakers
- ○ **B.** Keyboard
- ○ **C.** Mouse
- ○ **D.** Printer
- ○ **E.** Display
- ○ **F.** Stylus

40. A customer complains that he gets a headache when he's viewing his display for more than an hour. What should you do?

- ○ **A.** Raise the resolution to a higher setting
- ○ **B.** Install an antiglare filter
- ○ **C.** Dim the lights near the customer's desk
- ○ **D.** Upgrade the video connector from DVI to VGA

Domain 2.0: Networking

41. What does the *b* in 1000 Mbps stand for?

- ○ **A.** Megabytes
- ○ **B.** Bits
- ○ **C.** Bytes
- ○ **D.** Bandwidth

42. The IP address 192.168.1.1 uses what addressing scheme?

- ○ **A.** 64-bit
- ○ **B.** 32-bit
- ○ **C.** 128-bit
- ○ **D.** 40-bit

43. When running cable through drop ceilings, what type of cable do you need?

- ○ **A.** PVC
- ○ **B.** Category 5
- ○ **C.** Strong cable
- ○ **D.** Plenum

44. The wireless protocol 802.11n has a maximum data transfer rate of what?

- ○ **A.** 11 Mbps
- ○ **B.** 600 Mbps
- ○ **C.** 480 Mbps
- ○ **D.** 54 Mbps

Quick Answer: **27**
Detailed Answer: **34**

45. What device connects multiple computers together in a LAN?

- ○ **A.** Modem
- ○ **B.** Router
- ○ **C.** Switch
- ○ **D.** Firewall

Quick Answer: **27**
Detailed Answer: **34**

46. The IP address 192.168.1.1 should have what default subnet mask?

- ○ **A.** 255.255.0.0
- ○ **B.** 255.255.255.0
- ○ **C.** 255.0.0.0
- ○ **D.** 255.255.255.255

Quick Answer: **27**
Detailed Answer: **34**

47. What is the minimum category cable needed for a 1000BASE-T network?

- ○ **A.** Category 3
- ○ **B.** Category 5
- ○ **C.** Category 5e
- ○ **D.** Category 6

Quick Answer: **27**
Detailed Answer: **34**

48. Which of these IP addresses can be routed across the Internet?

- ○ **A.** 127.0.0.1
- ○ **B.** 192.168.1.1
- ○ **C.** 129.52.50.13
- ○ **D.** 10.52.50.13

Quick Answer: **27**
Detailed Answer: **34**

49. Which port number does HTTP use?

- ○ **A.** 21
- ○ **B.** 25
- ○ **C.** 80
- ○ **D.** 110

Quick Answer: **27**
Detailed Answer: **34**

50. What is the most commonly used network topology?

    ○ **A.** Star

    ○ **B.** Bus

    ○ **C.** Ring

    ○ **D.** Mesh

Quick Answer: 27
Detailed Answer: 35

51. What is the meaning of full duplex?

    ○ **A.** Transmitting and receiving data

    ○ **B.** Transmitting and receiving data simultaneously

    ○ **C.** Transmitting data only

    ○ **D.** Receiving data only

Quick Answer: 27
Detailed Answer: 35

52. Which of the following types of cable have a copper medium? (Select the three best answers.)

    ○ **A.** Twisted pair

    ○ **B.** Coaxial

    ○ **C.** Fiber optic

    ○ **D.** Cat 5e

    ○ **E.** Multi-mode

Quick Answer: 27
Detailed Answer: 35

53. Which types of cable can protect from electromagnetic interference (EMI)? (Select the two best answers.)

    ○ **A.** UTP

    ○ **B.** STP

    ○ **C.** Fiber Optic

    ○ **D.** Cat 6

Quick Answer: 27
Detailed Answer: 35

54. What port do you connect a network patch cable to on the PC?

    ○ **A.** USB

    ○ **B.** RJ45

    ○ **C.** RJ11

    ○ **D.** Parallel

Quick Answer: 27
Detailed Answer: 35

55. You are configuring Bob's computer to access the Internet. Which of the following is required? (Select all that apply.)

○ **A.** DNS server address

○ **B.** Gateway address

○ **C.** E-mail server name

○ **D.** DHCP server address

○ **E.** Domain name

56. Which of the following translates a computer name into an IP address?

○ **A.** TCP

○ **B.** UDP

○ **C.** DNS

○ **D.** FTP

57. One of your customers wants to access the Internet from many different locations in the United States. What is the best technology to enable her to do so?

○ **A.** Infrared

○ **B.** Cellular WAN

○ **C.** Bluetooth

○ **D.** 802.11n

58. You just configured the IP address 192.168.0.105 in Windows 7. When you press the tab key, Windows automatically configures the default subnet mask of 255.255.255.0. Which of the following IP addresses is a suitable gateway address?

○ **A.** 192.168.1.100

○ **B.** 192.168.1.1

○ **C.** 192.168.10.1

○ **D.** 192.168.0.1

59. What is the name of a wireless network referred to as?

○ **A.** SSID

○ **B.** WPA

○ **C.** DMZ

○ **D.** DHCP

60. Which of the following connector types is used by fiber-optic cabling?

- ○ **A.** LC
- ○ **B.** RJ45
- ○ **C.** RG-6
- ○ **D.** RJ11

61. Which protocol uses port 53?

- ○ **A.** FTP
- ○ **B.** SMTP
- ○ **C.** DNS
- ○ **D.** HTTP

62. Which of the following Internet services are wireless? (Select the three best answers.)

- ○ **A.** Cable Internet
- ○ **B.** WiMAX
- ○ **C.** Satellite
- ○ **D.** DSL
- ○ **E.** Cellular
- ○ **F.** FIOS

63. Which of the following terms best describes two or more LANs connected together over a large geographic distance?

- ○ **A.** PAN
- ○ **B.** WAN
- ○ **C.** WLAN
- ○ **D.** MAN

64. Which of the following devices allows wireless computers to connect to the wireless network?

- ○ **A.** WPA
- ○ **B.** WAN
- ○ **C.** WAP
- ○ **D.** VoIP

65. What device connects to the network and has the sole purpose of providing data to clients?

Quick Answer: **27**
Detailed Answer: **36**

- ○ **A.** NAS
- ○ **B.** NAT
- ○ **C.** NAC
- ○ **D.** NaaS

66. You are making your own networking patch cable. You need to attach an RJ45 plug to the end of a twisted-pair cable. Which tool should you use?

Quick Answer: **27**
Detailed Answer: **37**

- ○ **A.** Tone and probe kit
- ○ **B.** Cable tester
- ○ **C.** Crimper
- ○ **D.** Multimeter

67. Which port is used by RDP?

Quick Answer: **27**
Detailed Answer: **37**

- ○ **A.** 80
- ○ **B.** 110
- ○ **C.** 443
- ○ **D.** 3389

Domain 3.0: Laptops

68. Which is the most common type of RAM architecture used by laptops?

Quick Answer: **27**
Detailed Answer: **37**

- ○ **A.** DIMM
- ○ **B.** RIMM
- ○ **C.** SODIMM
- ○ **D.** SDRAM

69. Which key on a laptop aids in switching to an external monitor?

Quick Answer: **27**
Detailed Answer: **37**

- ○ **A.** Fn
- ○ **B.** Ctrl
- ○ **C.** Alt
- ○ **D.** Shift

70. You would most likely find this type of display on a laptop.

- ○ **A.** CRT
- ○ **B.** LCD
- ○ **C.** OLED
- ○ **D.** VGA

Quick Answer: **27**
Detailed Answer: **37**

71. What would you normally install into a Type II PCMCIA slot on a laptop? (Select all that apply.)

- ○ **A.** Hard drive
- ○ **B.** Modem
- ○ **C.** NIC
- ○ **D.** RAM

Quick Answer: **27**
Detailed Answer: **37**

72. What is the most commonly used battery type in laptops?

- ○ **A.** Lithium-ion (Li-ion)
- ○ **B.** Nickel-Cadmium (Ni-Cd)
- ○ **C.** Nickel-metal hydride (NiMH)
- ○ **D.** Fuel cell

Quick Answer: **27**
Detailed Answer: **37**

73. What does adding more RAM to a laptop that uses shared video memory do for that laptop?

- ○ **A.** Nothing
- ○ **B.** Improve video performance
- ○ **C.** Improve system performance
- ○ **D.** Increase RAM speed

Quick Answer: **27**
Detailed Answer: **37**

74. A customer can barely hear sound from the speakers on her laptop. What should you do first?

- ○ **A.** Install a new sound driver
- ○ **B.** Tap the speakers
- ○ **C.** Search for a volume wheel/key
- ○ **D.** Reinstall Windows

Quick Answer: **27**
Detailed Answer: **38**

75. Which of the following are typical names for expansion busses on laptops? (Select the two best answers.)

- ○ **A.** ExpressCard
- ○ **B.** SODIMM
- ○ **C.** PC Card
- ○ **D.** AGP

Quick Answer: **27**
Detailed Answer: **38**

76. You use your laptop often. What is a simple, free way to keep your laptop running cool?

Quick Answer: **27**
Detailed Answer: **38**

- ○ **A.** Keep the laptop on a flat surface
- ○ **B.** Put the laptop in the freezer when not in use
- ○ **C.** Direct a fan at the laptop
- ○ **D.** Keep the laptop turned off whenever possible

77. What are two important factors when purchasing a replacement laptop AC adapter? (Select the two best answers.)

Quick Answer: **27**
Detailed Answer: **38**

- ○ **A.** Current and voltage
- ○ **B.** Connector size and shape
- ○ **C.** Battery type
- ○ **D.** Inverter type

78. Eric uses an external monitor with his laptop. He tells you that his laptop will boot but the system won't display anything on the external screen. Which of the following enables the display?

Quick Answer: **27**
Detailed Answer: **38**

- ○ **A.** Connect the laptop to another external monitor
- ○ **B.** Press the Fn and Screen keys one or more times until the screen appears
- ○ **C.** Press the Enter and Esc keys while the laptop is booting
- ○ **D.** Press the Fn key while the laptop is booting

Domain 4.0: Printers

79. Which type of printer uses a toner cartridge?

Quick Answer: **27**
Detailed Answer: **38**

- ○ **A.** Ink jet
- ○ **B.** Laser
- ○ **C.** Dot matrix
- ○ **D.** Thermal

80. Which of the following should not be connected to a UPS?

Quick Answer: **27**
Detailed Answer: **38**

- ○ **A.** PCs
- ○ **B.** Monitors
- ○ **C.** Laser printers
- ○ **D.** Speakers

81. Which of the following is not a connector you might find on a printer?

   ○ **A.** RJ45
   ○ **B.** USB
   ○ **C.** PCIe
   ○ **D.** Centronics

82. Terri finishes installing a printer for a customer. What should she do next?

   ○ **A.** Verify that the printer prints in Microsoft Word
   ○ **B.** Print a test page
   ○ **C.** Restart the spooler
   ○ **D.** Set up a separator page

83. Which of the following best describes printing in duplex?

   ○ **A.** Printing on both sides of the paper
   ○ **B.** Printer collation
   ○ **C.** Full-duplex printer communication
   ○ **D.** Printing to file

84. Special paper is needed to print on what kind of printer?

   ○ **A.** Dot matrix
   ○ **B.** Thermal
   ○ **C.** Laser
   ○ **D.** Inkjet

85. Which environmental issue affects a thermal printer the most?

   ○ **A.** Moisture
   ○ **B.** ESD
   ○ **C.** Dirt
   ○ **D.** Heat

86. What happens last in the laser printing process?

   ○ **A.** Charging
   ○ **B.** Exposing
   ○ **C.** Developing
   ○ **D.** Fusing

87. This type of printer uses impact to transfer ink from a ribbon to the paper.

- ○ **A.** Laser
- ○ **B.** Inkjet
- ○ **C.** Dot matrix
- ○ **D.** Thermal

88. How can you take control of a network printer from a remote computer?

- ○ **A.** Install the printer locally and access the Sharing tab
- ○ **B.** Install the printer locally and access the spool settings
- ○ **C.** Install the printer locally and access the Ports tab
- ○ **D.** Connect to the printer via FTP

89. A color laser printer is producing images that seem to be tinted blue. What should you do?

- ○ **A.** Clean the toner cartridge
- ○ **B.** Calibrate the printer
- ○ **C.** Change the fusing assembly
- ○ **D.** Clean the primary corona

Domain 5.0: Operational Procedures

90. What tool should you use to protect a computer from electrostatic discharge (ESD) while you are working inside it?

- ○ **A.** Multimeter
- ○ **B.** Crimper
- ○ **C.** Antistatic wrist strap
- ○ **D.** PSU tester

91. While you are working at a customer site, a friend calls you on your cell phone. What should you do?

- ○ **A.** Ignore the call for now.
- ○ **B.** Go outside and take the call.
- ○ **C.** Answer the phone as quietly as possible.
- ○ **D.** Text your friend.

92. You spill an unknown chemical on your hands. What should you do?

Quick Answer: **28**
Detailed Answer: **40**

- ○ **A.** Call 911.
- ○ **B.** Call the building supervisor.
- ○ **C.** Consult the MSDS for the chemical.
- ○ **D.** Ignore it.

93. You are running some cable from an office to a computer located in a warehouse. As you are working in the warehouse, a 55-gallon drum falls from a pallet and spills what smells like ammonia. What should you do first?

Quick Answer: **28**
Detailed Answer: **40**

- ○ **A.** Call 911.
- ○ **B.** Call the building supervisor.
- ○ **C.** Get out of the area.
- ○ **D.** Save the computer.

94. While you are upgrading a customer's server hard drives, you notice looped network cables lying all over the server room floor. What should you do?

Quick Answer: **28**
Detailed Answer: **40**

- ○ **A.** Ignore the problem.
- ○ **B.** Call the building supervisor.
- ○ **C.** Tell the customer about safer alternatives.
- ○ **D.** Notify the administrator.

95. What should be done with a lithium-ion battery that won't hold a charge any longer?

Quick Answer: **28**
Detailed Answer: **40**

- ○ **A.** Throw it in the trash.
- ○ **B.** Return it to the battery manufacturer.
- ○ **C.** Contact the local municipality and inquire as to their disposal methods.
- ○ **D.** Open the battery and remove the deposits.

96. Which of the following statements is not assertive communication?

Quick Answer: **28**
Detailed Answer: **40**

- ○ **A.** "I certainly know how you feel—losing data is a terrible thing."
- ○ **B.** "Could you explain again exactly what you would like done?"
- ○ **C.** "Do your employees always cause issues on computers like these?"
- ○ **D.** "What can I do to help you?"

97. A customer has a malfunctioning PC, and as you are about to begin repairing it, the customer proceeds to tell you about the problems with the server. What should you say to the customer?

Quick Answer: **28**
Detailed Answer: **41**

- ○ **A.** Wait until I finish with the PC.
- ○ **B.** I'm sorry, but I don't know how to fix servers!
- ○ **C.** Is the server problem related to the PC problem?
- ○ **D.** I have to call my supervisor.

98. What could be described as the chronological paper trail of evidence?

Quick Answer: **28**
Detailed Answer: **41**

- ○ **A.** First response
- ○ **B.** Chain of custody
- ○ **C.** Setting and meeting expectations
- ○ **D.** Data preservation

99. What should you *not* do when moving servers and server racks?

Quick Answer: **28**
Detailed Answer: **41**

- ○ **A.** Remove jewelry
- ○ **B.** Move a 70-pound wire rack by yourself
- ○ **C.** Disconnect power to the servers before moving them
- ○ **D.** Bend at the knees and lift with your legs

100. Active communication includes which of the following?

Quick Answer: **28**
Detailed Answer: **41**

- ○ **A.** Filtering out unnecessary information
- ○ **B.** Declaring that the customer doesn't know what he or she is doing
- ○ **C.** Clarifying the customer's statements
- ○ **D.** Mouthing off

-38   62%   -15   85%

Quick-Check Answer Key

1. A, B, and E	30. C	59. A
2. C	31. C	60. A
3. C	32. B	61. C
4. B	33. B and D	62. B, C, and E
5. B	34. D	63. B
6. C	35. A and D	64. C
7. A	36. B	65. A
8. A and D	37. C	66. C
9. C	38. C	67. D
10. A and B	39. A, D, and E	68. C
11. C	40. B	69. A
12. A	41. B	70. B
13. B	42. B	71. B and C
14. C	43. D	72. A
15. D	44. B	73. C
16. A	45. C	74. C
17. D	46. B	75. A and C
18. A	47. C	76. A
19. B	48. C	77. A and B
20. A	49. C	78. B
21. A	50. A	79. B
22. C	51. B	80. C
23. D	52. A, B, and D	81. C
24. B	53. B and C	82. B
25. D	54. B	83. A
26. B	55. A and B	84. B
27. D	56. C	85. D
28. A	57. B	86. D
29. D	58. D	87. C

X **88.** C   **93.** C   **98.** B

X **89.** B   **94.** C   **99.** B

90. C   **95.** C   **100.** C

91. A   **96.** C

92. C   **97.** C

Answers and Explanations

Domain 1.0: PC Hardware

1. **Answers: A, B, and E.** Common components inside a PC include the CPU, motherboard, and RAM, along with the power supply, adapter cards, and hard drives. Keyboards (and mice) are input devices that are located outside the PC. Printers (and displays) are output devices that are located outside the PC. A cable modem is an Internet communication device that is outside of the PC. *Know the internal components of a PC!*

2. **Answer: C.** The hard drive stores data over the long term. The hard drive stores the OS and data in a nonvolatile fashion, meaning it won't be erased when the computer is turned off. The CPU calculates data and sends it to RAM for temporary storage; the RAM (which is volatile) is cleared when the computer is turned off. The video card stores temporary video data within its onboard memory, but this, like RAM, is volatile and is cleared when the computer is turned off.

3. **Answer: C.** 1/8" TRS jacks (also known as mini-jacks) are the most common for speaker connections. Speakers normally plug into a sound card or motherboard. Parallel ports are older connectors normally used for printers or scanners. DVI (Digital Visual Interface) is a type of video port. The larger 1/4" TRS connections are for instrument cables or full-size stereo connections.

4. **Answer: B.** PCI Express (PCIe) slots accept x1, x4, and x16 cards (pronounced "by sixteen"). PCIe is by far the most common expansion slot for video cards (which are usually x16). PCI is an older expansion bus that can accept video cards but, unlike PCIe, they have no particular designation. AGP works with video cards, but the cards are normally numbered as 1x, 2x, 4x, and 8x (pronounced "eight x"). PCI-X is used mostly in servers, for example, with network adapters.

5. **Answer: B.** The POST (Power-On Self-Test) is part of the Basic Input Output System (BIOS). It runs a self-check of the computer system during boot and stores many of the parameters of the components within the CMOS. EEPROM is a type of ROM chip on which the BIOS might reside. BIOS is known as firmware.

6. **Answer: C.** Without the thermal compound applied, the processor might overheat after a few hours. If the CPU is not locked down, or is not properly seated, the PC will simply fail to boot. If the CPU is not compatible with the motherboard, either it will not fit the socket or the PC will not boot.

7. **Answer: A.** Liquid Crystal Display (LCD) is most commonly the type of technology that a flat-panel monitor uses, though there is also light-emitting diode (LED)-backlit LCD, Plasma, and Organic LED (OLED). Cathode ray tube (CRT) is an older type of tube technology resulting in a much bulkier monitor. RGB simply stands for red, green, blue (the three primary colors of a CRT monitor). DVI is short for Digital Visual Interface, a port you would find on a video card.

8. **Answers: A and D.** The CPU and memory need to be installed properly for the POST to run (and to pass). The hard drive and CD-ROM might or might not be installed properly, but they are not necessary for the POST to complete. If the power supply is defective, the system will simply not boot and will not even get to the POST stage.

9. **Answer: C.** PCIe (PCI Express) uses serial lanes to send and receive data. That means one bit at a time per lane. PCI, PCI-X, and IDE are parallel technologies, which means 8 bits at a time or multiples of 8. IDE stands for Integrated Device Electronics, the predecessor to SATA hard drive technology.

10. **Answers: A and B.** Intel's Core i5 and AMD's Phenom II are both 64-bit CPUs. The Pentium IV is an older 32-bit CPU. x64 is the name given to 64-bit processor technology but is not an actual CPU.

11. **Answer: C.** LGA (Land Grid Array) is the type of socket that uses "lands" to connect the socket to the CPU. PGA sockets have pinholes that make for connectivity to the CPU's copper pins. The chipset is the combination of the northbridge and southbridge on the motherboard. LGA sockets are often a brass alloy or have gold contacts, and although copper might be a possibility for some sockets, it doesn't fit into the description of "lands" in the question. LGA is the best answer.

12. **Answer: A.** Hold RAM by the edges to avoid contact with the pins, chips, and circuitry. Touching the front and back is not advised because it will require touching the chips on the RAM module. Tools are not needed, and if they are used, metallic could be damaging to the module. Plastic tweezers are used to remove screws that fell into tough-to-reach places in the case. The IC puller is a tool that removes older integrated circuits and is not used often today.

13. **Answer: B.** The UPS is the only item listed that protects the computer from power outages like blackouts and brownouts. A multimeter is used to test AC outlets and individual wires inside the computer. FedEx is a shipping company, not a computer acronym. A surge protector (or surge suppressor) is used to protect computer equipment from surges and spikes in power, but cannot protect against power outages.

14. **Answer: C.** ATX 12V 2.0 (and higher) combined the 20-pin and 4-pin connectors used in ATX 12V 1.3 into one 24-pin connector. ATX is simply the name of the form factor; there are many types of ATX. There is no ATX 5V. Although ATX sends 12-volt and 5-volt signals, it is known as ATX 12v.

15. **Answer: D.** SATA revision 3.0 can transfer a maximum of 6.0 Gb/s (6 gigabits per second, note the lowercase *b*). This allows a peak throughput of 600 MB/s (600 megabytes per second, note the uppercase *B*). 1.5 Gb/s is the data transfer rate of SATA revision 1.0. It's maximum throughput is 150 MB/s. 3.0 Gb/s is the data transfer rate of SATA revision 2.0. It has a peak throughput of 300 MB/s.

16. **Answer: A.** The *X* in CD technology is equal to 150 KB/s. A 1X drive can read or write 150 KB/s, a 2X drive can read or write 300 KB/s, and so on. A typical speed for today's CD-ROM drives is 48X. This comes to 7.2 MB/s total. 1.32 MB/s is the 1X speed of a DVD. 133 MB/s is the maximum data transfer rate of an Ultra ATA-7 connection (IDE hard drive). 4.5 MB/s is the 1X speed of a Blu-ray disc.

17. **Answer: D.** The TV tuner card accepts television broadcast programming. It will usually have cable-in and antenna-in RG-6 ports. FireWire cards allow a computer to connect to FireWire devices such as hard drives and audio devices. Video capture cards are used to record video from a camera, VCR, or close-circuit television system. A network interface cards is also known as a NIC, or network adapter; it makes the connection to the Ethernet network for a PC.

18. **Answer: A.** A home theater PC (HTPC) requires a High-Definition Multimedia Interface (HDMI) output on the video card so that it can connect properly to the HDMI port on a television. Sure, it's possible to connect via DVI with an adapter, or even by way of VGA, but the whole point of a true HTPC is that it has the best to offer when it comes to connections. Since most theater system TVs will have one or more HDMI inputs, the HTPC should have at least one HDMI output. Gaming PCs will usually have DVI connections to connect to desktop monitors, though they might have HDMI as well. Virtualization workstations don't rely on video cards as much as the other systems listed in the answers, so HDMI is not necessary. CAD/CAM workstations require a high-end video card, but the DVI (or multiple DVI) output is usually satisfactory.

19. **Answer: B.** The SATA data connector has 7 pins. The SATA power connector has 15 pins. ATX 12V 2.0 and higher power connections have 24 pins. 127 is the maximum amount of USB devices you can connect to the computer.

20. **Answer: A.** A printer would most likely be connected to a Universal Serial Bus (USB) port. LPT is an older parallel port that is less commonly used. Though there are FireWire printers, they are much rarer than USB printers. eSATA is normally used for external hard drives or external optical drives. Printers can also connect to the network directly if they have an RJ45 port.

21. **Answer: A.** Memory latency or CAS (Column Address Strobe) latency happens when a memory controller tries to access data from a memory module. It is a slight delay (usually measured in nanoseconds) while the memory module responds to the memory controller. The memory controller (also known as the northbridge) has a specific speed at which it operates. If the CPU asks the chip for too much information at once, this might increase latency time while the memory controller works.

22. **Answer: C.** Because RAID 5 uses striping with parity, a third disk is needed. You can have more than three disks as well. Two disks are enough for plain RAID 0 striping and is the exact number you need for RAID 1 mirroring. Four disks are required by RAID 6 and RAID 10. $(R1-2)(R5-3)(R0-2)(R6,10-4)$

23. **Answer: D.** If the time and date keep resetting to a time such as January 1, 2000, chances are that the lithium battery needs to be replaced. Updating the BIOS will allow the BIOS to "see" new devices and communicate with them better but will not fix the time issue. Updating windows will not fix this problem but should be done often to keep the computer secure. Other time synchronization problems can be fixed in the clock settings within the Notification Area. Windows client computers should be configured to synchronize to a time server.

24. **Answer: B.** The PCI Express (PCIe) x16 expansion slot is used primarily for video. Modems, network interface cards (NICs), and sound cards will connect to either PCIe x1 or plain PCI slots.

25. **Answer: D.** A UPS (uninterruptible power supply) protects computer equipment against surges, spikes, sags, brownouts, and blackouts. Power strips, unlike surge protectors, do not protect against surges. Power inverters are effectively AC to DC converters; the power supply acts as a power inverter.

26. **Answer: B.** The amount of shared video memory is subtracted from the total RAM. So, if a computer has 1024 MB RAM (1 GB) and the video controller is sharing 128 MB of that RAM, the remainder for the rest of the system is 896 MB. This is common with motherboards that have integrated video cards and laptops.

27. **Answer: D.** RAM is one of the big four (RAM, CPU, motherboard, and video) that can cause the POST to fail. Different RAM errors can cause the POST to make a different series of beeps. Consult your motherboard documentation for more information about the different beep codes. The sound card does not have an effect on the POST. If the power supply has a problem, either the computer will not boot at all (and not even enter POST) or it will have intermittent problems—for example, shutting down unpredictably. Hard drive problems will result in a variety of errors. While the POST will complete in these cases, the operating system will not boot.

28. **Answer: A.** The CPU must be installed correctly for the POST to begin. After the POST is successful, the boot loader then runs (for example, BOOTMGR for Windows 7/Vista or NTLDR for Windows XP), and then the operating system comes up. That is, if there are no boot loader errors. The CPU is crucial; if installed incorrectly, the system will not POST, making it more difficult to troubleshoot.

29. **Answer: D.** The adapter should use the ID 7. Both ends of the SCSI chain need to be terminated (some SCSI cards and devices auto-terminate). Each disk needs a unique ID. The particular ID you give the disks doesn't matter.

30. **Answer: C.** RAM is much faster than the rest of the options listed. For instance, if you have PC3-8500 DDR3 RAM (aka DDR3-800), your peak transfer rate is 6,400 MB/s. The rest of the following devices are listed in descending order: hard drive (typically 133, 150, 300, or 600 MB/s), USB (typically 60 or 480 MB/s), and CD-ROM (typically 7.5 MB/s).

31. **Answer: C.** Home theater PCs (HTPCs) commonly use the microATX form factor. The Mini-ITX form factor is also used for HTPCs. Less commonly used is the ATX form factor due to its large size. Pico-ITX and Nano-ITX are used in handheld computers and are much smaller.

32. **Answer: B.** The most common CPU cooling method is the heat sink and fan combination. The heat sink helps the heat to disperse away from the CPU, while the fan blows the heat down and through the fins; it is helped in escaping the case by the power supply exhaust fan and possibly additional case fans. Heat sink and fan combinations are known as active cooling. The heat sink by itself is called passive cooling. It requires no power but is not enough to cool most desktop PCs. Liquid cooling is a more extreme method used in custom PCs such as gaming computers and possibly audio/video workstations and virtualization machines. It uses a coolant similar to the way an automobile does. Liquid nitrogen would be plain foolish and is not a legitimate answer.

33. **Answers: B and D.** A rewritable DVD-RW and a writeable Blu-ray (BD-R) meet the requirements. DVDs can store between 4.7 and 17 GB of data. Standard Blu-ray discs can store between 25 and 50 GB of data. No CD (without compression) can store more than 1 GB of data; typical CD storage is 750 MB.

34. **Answer: D.** CNR is not a video port. It stands for Communications and Networking Riser; an adapter card slot used by audio and telephony equipment. DVI is the Digital Visual Interface, the most common output on PC video cards. HDMI is the High-Definition Multimedia Interface, common in home theaters and HTPCs. DisplayPort is another video standard used by some PCs. It is designed to replace DVI but is still not as common as DVI as of 2012.

35. **Answers: A and D.** A computer-aided design/computer-aided manufacturing workstation requires a powerful CPU, high-end video, and as much RAM as possible. The CPU is especially important to run design applications such as AutoCAD. HDMI output is necessary on HTPCs. Surround sound is needed on HTPCs and perhaps gaming computers as well.

36. **Answer: B.** You should connect the hard drive to a SATA port. SATA revision 3.0 offers 6.0 Gb/s data transfer resulting in a maximum throughput of 600 MB/s. USB 3.0 comes in a close second at 5.0 Gbps (480 MB/s). However, SATA will usually still be the preferred choice because it has less latency and is internal to the computer. IDE is the predecessor to SATA and has a maximum transfer rate of 133 MB/s. As of early 2012, eSATA is limited to 3.0 Gb/s (300 MB/s). Unless you specifically are required to use an external drive, internal SATA is the way to go.

37. **Answer: C.** An x16 card is a PCI Express card. It requires one or two PCIe 6-pin power connectors (or an 8-pin connector). Molex 4-pin power connectors are used by IDE hard drives. Mini 4-pin connectors (also known as Berg) are used by floppy drives. P1 24-pin power is the main power connection that the motherboard gets from the power supply.

38. **Answer: C.** Alternating current (AC) is the standard in the United States; your computer should be connected to a 120V AC outlet. Other countries might use 230V AC connections. Direct current (DC) works inside the computer. The power supply converts between the two! In this respect, the power supply is an inverter. *Neutral current* and *draw current* are not terms you will see on the CompTIA exams.

39. **Answers: A, D, and E.** Speakers, printers, and displays are output devices. A speaker outputs sound. A printer outputs paper with text and graphics. A display (or monitor) displays video. Keyboards, mice, and styli are input devices. A stylus is used on mobile devices that incorporate touchscreens. It is a pen-like device used to manipulate the display, similar to a mouse. However, many mobile devices now allow a person to simply use a finger and tap on the screen.

40. **Answer: B.** You should install an antiglare filter on the monitor. By reducing glare, a person's eyes react better to the display and so the customer can use the computer longer without getting a headache. Raising the resolution would make the problem worse. Lowering the resolution might help, but it is only a temporary solution, and not a good one at that. Dimming the lights will decrease glare, but studies prove that a person will develop eye strain and headaches quicker when reading a backlit screen in a dark room. Video Graphics Array (VGA) is not an upgrade from DVI—quite the reverse. Besides, changing the video connector probably won't help the problem. The only ways to fix the problem are to: install an antiglare filter; upgrade the monitor to a bigger size and consider positioning it differently, for example, farther away; and recommending that the user take breaks every 30 minutes or so.

Domain 2.0: Networking

41. **Answer: B.** The *b* in 1000 Mbps stands for bits. 1000 Mbps is 1000 megabits per second or 1 gigabit per second. Remember that the lowercase *b* is used to indicate bits when measuring network data transfer rates.

42. **Answer: B.** There are 32 bits in a standard IPv4 address. In this case, the binary equivalent of the IP numbers would be 192 = 11000000, 168 = 10101000, 1 = 00000001, and 1 = 00000001. If you count all the binary bits, you end up with 32 in total. Therefore, the address is a 32-bit dotted-decimal address. 64-bit is a term used with newer x64 CPUs. 128-bit is used by IPv6. 40-bit is a commonly used amount of bits in older encryption techniques.

43. **Answer: D.** Plenum-rated cable needs to be installed wherever a sprinkler system cannot get to. This includes ceilings, walls, and plenums (airways). The reason for this is that the PVCs in regular cable give off toxic fumes in the case of a fire. Plenum-rated cable has a protective covering which burns slower and gives off less toxic fumes.

44. **Answer: B.** 802.11n runs at a maximum of 600 Mbps. 802.11b runs at a maximum of 11 Mbps. USB 2.0 Hi-Speed runs at a maximum of 480 Mbps. 802.11g has a maximum data transfer rate (DTR) of 54 Mbps.

45. **Answer: C.** A switch connects computers together in a local area network (LAN). In SOHO networks, it is usually a part of a multifunction network device. In larger networks, the switch is an individual device that has 12, 24, 48, or 96 ports. A modem connects a PC to the Internet by way of a dial-up connection over a plain old telephone service (POTS) line. A router connects one network to another. Though a SOHO multifunction device is often referred to as a *router*, it's not the router portion of that device that connects the computers together in the LAN. A firewall protects all the computers on the LAN from intrusion.

46. **Answer: B.** 192.168.1.1 is a private Class C address and therefore should have the subnet mask 255.255.255.0, the standard default subnet mask for Class C. 255.255.0.0 is the Class B default subnet mask. 255.0.0.0 is the Class A default subnet mask. 255.255.255.255 is the broadcast address for IP. It is not usable as a subnet mask for typical computers on the LAN.

47. **Answer: C.** The minimum cable needed for 1000BASE-T networks is Category 5e. Of course, Cat 6 would also work, but it is not the minimum of the listed answers. 1000BASE-T specifies the speed of the network (1000 Mbps), the type (baseband, single shared channel), and the cable to be used (T = twisted pair). Cat 3 is suitable for 10 Mbps networks. Cat 5 is suitable for 100 Mbps networks.

48. **Answer: C.** The only public address (needed to get onto the Internet) is 129.52.50.13. All the others are private IPs, meant to be behind a firewall. 127.0.0.1 is the local loopback IP address. 192.168.1.1 is a common Class C private IP address used by SOHO networking devices. 10.52.50.13 is a Class A private address.

49. **Answer: C.** The Hypertext Transfer Protocol (HTTP) uses port 80 (by default). Port 21 is used by the File Transfer Protocol (FTP). Port 25 is used by the Simple Mail Transfer Protocol (SMTP). Port 110 is used by the POP3 e-mail protocol.

50. **Answer: A.** The star topology is the most common. This is when computers are cabled to a central connecting device such as a switch. Bus and ring don't use a central connecting device and are outdated. Mesh is when each computer connects to each other. This is an expensive and complicated configuration. What is more likely is that you will encounter a partial mesh, where a few of the computers on the network have secondary connections to other systems.

51. **Answer: B.** Full duplex means that a network interface card (NIC) can transmit and receive data at the same time. A 100 Mbps network running in full-duplex mode can transfer 200 Mbps, but this is because transmitting and receiving have been combined, not because speed has been increased. A NIC that can transmit or receive data, but not at the same time, is transmitting in half-duplex mode.

52. **Answers: A, B, and D.** Twisted pair, coaxial, and Category 5e cable are all examples of network cables with a copper medium. They all send electricity over copper wire. Multi-mode is a type of fiber-optic cable; it uses light to send data over a glass or plastic medium. Twisted pair is the most common type of cabling used in today's networks.

53. **Answers: B and C.** Shielded twisted pair (STP) and fiber optic can protect from EMI. However, unshielded twisted pair (UTP) cannot. Unless otherwise mentioned, Category 6 cable is UTP. STP is shielded twisted-pair. Unlike UTP (unshielded twisted-pair), it provides an aluminum shield that protects from EMI. UTP and coaxial have no such protection. Fiber optic uses a different medium altogether, transmitting light rather than electricity; therefore, EMI cannot affect fiber-optic cables.

54. **Answer: B.** The RJ45 (Registered Jack) is the standard connector for network patch cables. RJ11 is for modem and other telephony connections. USB is for peripherals (such as a mouse or printer), and parallel is for printers and scanners, but it's not used nearly as much as USB is.

55. **Answers: A and B.** To get on the Internet, the DNS server is required so that the computer can get the resolved IP addresses from the domain names that are typed in. The gateway address is necessary to get outside the network. E-mail server information is not necessary if the person is just looking to get onto the Internet. A DHCP server address is not necessary either. However, it is an easier method. The beauty of DHCP is that you don't need to know the DHCP server's address to acquire an IP address. The domain name for your network is normally not needed either. That will only be necessary if you want to add the computer to the organization's domain.

56. **Answer: C.** The DNS (Domain Name System) protocol translates a computer name into an IP address. Whenever you type a web server name such as www.davidl-prowse.com a DNS server translates that name to its corresponding IP address. The Transmission Control Protocol (TCP) is used to send data from one computer to another utilizing a guaranteed delivery system. User Datagram Protocol (UDP), on the other hand, sends data in a streaming format, without the need for guaranteed delivery. The File Transfer Protocol (FTP) allows you to send files between computers over the Internet.

57. Answer: B. Cellular WAN uses a phone or other mobile device to send data over standard cellular connections. By themselves, the other options don't offer a *direct* connection to the Internet. Infrared is used more often for very short distance connections, allowing data to be "beamed" from one device to another. Bluetooth is also for short distances, but not as short as infrared. Bluetooth headsets are commonly used with smartphones. 802.11n is a Wi-Fi technology for the LAN.

58. Answer: D. 192.168.0.1 is the only suitable gateway address. Remember that the gateway address must be on the same network as the computer. In this case the network is 192.168.0, as defined by the 255.255.255.0 subnet mask. As to the other answers: 192.168.1.100 is on the 192.168.1.0 network; so is 192.168.1.1. 192.168.10.1 is on the 192.168.10.0 network. Don't forget that a zero at the end of an IP address denotes the network number.

59. Answer: A. The Service Set Identifier (SSID) is the name of the wireless network. This is the name you look for when locating a wireless network. WPA stands for Wi-Fi Protected Access, a secure connectivity protocol for wireless networks. The demilitarized zone (DMZ) is an area between the LAN and the Internet that often houses web, e-mail, and FTP servers. The Dynamic Host Configuration Protocol (DHCP) is a service that assigns IP addresses automatically to computers and other devices.

60. Answer: A. The LC connector is used by fiber-optic cabling. Other fiber connectors include SC and ST. RJ45 is the connector used by twisted-pair networks. RG-6 is the connector used by cable modems and TV set-top-boxes. RJ11 is the standard phone line connector.

61. Answer: C. The Domain Name System (DNS) protocol uses port 53 by default. FTP uses port 21. SMTP uses port 25. HTTP uses port 80.

62. Answers: B, C, and E. WiMAX, satellite, and cellular are examples of wireless Internet services. Cable Internet, DSL, and FIOS all use wired connections.

63. Answer: B. A wide area network (WAN) is a network in which two or more LANs are connected together over a large geographic distance—for example, between two cities. The WAN requires connections to be provided by a telecommunications or data communications company. A personal area network (PAN) is a small network made up of short-distance devices such as Bluetooth. WLAN stands for wireless local area network. This is the name that the IEEE uses for their 802.11 standards. That is because the term *Wi-Fi*, though widely used, is copyrighted. A MAN is a metropolitan (or municipal) area network; it can connect two or more LANs together but does it in a small city-based area.

64. Answer: C. A wireless access point (WAP) connects wireless clients to the wireless network. This device also gives the wireless network its name or SSID. WPA is a secure wireless connectivity protocol. A WAN is a wide area network; it connects LANs together. VoIP stands for Voice over IP. This is a technology that allows phone calls to be made over data networking infrastructures.

65. Answer: A. Network-attached storage (NAS) devices store data for network use. They connect directly to the network. Network address translation (NAT) is used on routers to take a group of computers on a private LAN and connect them to the Internet by using a single public IP. NAC stands for network access control, a group of technologies designed to allow or deny access by authenticating users. NaaS stands for

Network as a Service, a cloud-based technology where organizations can offload their network infrastructure to a third-party. Threw in a tougher one there—have to keep you on your toes!

66. **Answer: C.** Use an RJ45 crimper tool to permanently attach RJ45 plugs to the end of a cable. A tone and probe kit is used to locate individual phone lines but can also be used with network lines. The better tool, however, for testing and locating is a continuity cable tester. A multimeter is great for testing AC outlets and for testing wires inside a computer but is not often used in networking applications.

67. **Answer: D.** The Remote Desktop Protocol (RDP) uses port 3389. This protocol allows one computer to take control of another remote system. Port 80 is used by HTTP. Port 110 is used by POP3. Port 443 is used by HTTP Secure or HTTPS, a protocol used during secure web sessions.

Domain 3.0: Laptops

68. **Answer: C.** SODIMM (small outline dual in-line memory module) is the most commonly used RAM by laptops. Regular DIMMs are normally used in desktop computers; some of those types include SDRAM, DDR, and RIMMs or RDRAM.

69. **Answer: A.** The Fn (Function) key is used for a variety of things, including toggling between the built-in LCD screen and an external monitor/TV. The Fn key could be a different color (for example, blue) and offers a sort of "second" usage for keys on the laptop. Ctrl may also have secondary functions but is otherwise used the same as on a PC's keyboard. Alt and Shift work in the same manner as they do on a PC.

70. **Answer: B.** The liquid crystal display (LCD) is the most common type on a laptop. You might also see LED-backlit LCDs. Cathode ray tubes (CRTs) were the predecessor to flat-panel monitors. They were rarely used in laptops and only way back in the 1980s. CRT monitors were more commonly used with PCs. Organic LED screens are not popular on laptops as of the writing of this book. VGA is not a type of display; it is a video standard that uses a 15-pin connector. It is the predecessor to today's standards such as DVI and HDMI.

71. **Answers: B and C.** Input/output devices such as modems and NICs (network interface cards/network adapters) are the most commonly installed Type II devices. Hard drives would normally be installed internally but could also be connected to USB and FireWire ports. RAM is installed internally.

72. **Answer: A.** Although Ni-Cd and NiMH batteries have been used on laptops, the most commonly used type as of the writing of this book is lithium-ion. Some laptops and especially other smaller mobile devices use lithium-ion polymer-based batteries. Fuel cells are used in vehicles, vending machines, and highway road signs, but not laptops.

73. **Answer: C.** Increasing the amount of RAM on a laptop or a PC improves general system performance. To improve video performance, you would need to either upgrade the video card or lower some of the video settings. The fact that the laptop uses shared video doesn't come into play. The shared video will use a finite amount of RAM on the laptop. Adding more RAM won't change the amount of shared video used. However, some laptops allow you to increase this setting within the BIOS. This, in conjunction with adding RAM, might improve video performance as well.

74. **Answer: C.** Sometimes, the volume wheel on older laptops can be hard to find and could be in the lowest position (which might still make a slight audible noise). On newer laptops the volume is usually controlled by pressing the Fn key and the volume up or volume down key simultaneously. Installing a new sound driver isn't necessary yet. Always check the physical volume first, and then check if the volume is low or the sound is muted in Windows. Tapping the speakers is an interesting idea, but it has no place in this discussion. If a speaker is loose, it will often make scratchy noises; however, speakers rarely become loose on today's laptops. Reinstalling Windows is the last thing you want to do. Check the simple solutions when troubleshooting problems such as no audio or video.

75. **Answers: A and C.** ExpressCard and PC Card (also known as PCMCIA) are expansion busses used on laptops. SODIMM is the type of RAM in a laptop. AGP is the Accelerated Graphics Port; it is the predecessor of the PCIe x16 video expansion bus. Mini-PCIe is another expansion bus that is used by laptops, but it is internal and is more difficult to install cards to then its PC version.

76. **Answer: A.** Laptops have airflow underneath them; if the unit is not on a flat surface, that airflow will be reduced or stopped altogether, leading to component damage. The freezer is not a good idea because condensation could build up inside the unit. A fan won't do much good unless the laptop is on a flat surface, and although it is plausible to keep the laptop turned off, it negates the reason for using the laptop.

77. **Answers: A and B.** Make sure to purchase an AC adapter that is a true replacement. This can be found on the laptop manufacturer's website. When you enter your model number, the website will tell you everything you need to know about current, voltage, and connector type. The battery and AC adapter do need to work in conjunction with each other; because of this, they both need to be compatible with the laptop. The AC adapter inverter is simply an inverter; it converts power from AC to DC. However, there is another inverter in the laptop; it powers the display. This question is not referring to that, but if you are ever troubleshooting a display, the inverter type is very important.

78. **Answer: B.** The Screen key (also known as the display toggle) is one of the keys available when you use the function (Fn) key. This enables you to switch between the laptop display and an external display (or if you wanted to use both). If the display toggle doesn't work, then try another external monitor. No other key combinations perform this task.

Domain 4.0: Printers

79. **Answer: B.** Laser printers use toner cartridges. Inkjet printers use ink cartridges. Dot matrix printers use a ribbon. Thermal printers use specially coated paper that is heated.

80. **Answer: C.** Laser printers use large amounts of electricity, which in turn could quickly drain the battery of the UPS. They should be plugged into their own individual power strips.

81. **Answer: C.** Printers might connect via RJ45, USB, or Centronics. However, PCIe is an internal expansion bus that printers do not use. USB is the most common for local printers, meaning ones that connect directly to the computer. Centronics is an older

printer connector; a printer cable would have a centronics connector on the printer side and a 25-pin parallel connector for the computer side (which would connect to the LPT port). If the printer is network-ready, it will have a built-in RJ45 port.

82. **Answer: B.** Print a test page after installation. If the test page prints properly, it should be unnecessary to print a page in Word. Restarting the spooler is not needed if the printer has just been installed. The spooler should already be running. If that has failed, that would be a separate troubleshooting scenario. Separator pages are not necessary; they are optional and can be configured in the Printer Properties window.

83. **Answer: A.** When printing "duplex," it means that you are printing on both sides of the paper (if the printer has that capability). Some laser printers can do this, but it creates a longer total paper path, which leads to more frequent paper jams. Collation is when documents are printed in a standard order, usually numerically. Full-duplex in networking is when information can be sent and received simultaneously. A printer can have a full-duplex connection to the network, but this question is referring to printing in duplex. Printing to file is a process that can be performed by Windows. Instead of selecting a physical printer when printing a document, Windows prints to a special file and saves that file to a location of your choice with a .prn extension.

84. **Answer: B.** Regular paper can be used on all the listed printers except for thermal printers, which use specially coated paper that is heated to create the image. A dot matrix might use tractor feed paper, but that is standard for many dot matrix printers; it is also still considered regular paper. A laser printer or dot matrix printer might use two-part paper, but two-part paper isn't necessary for laser printers or dot matrix printers to operate; thermal printers won't work unless you use specially coated paper. Inkjet printers normally use standard copy paper for printing.

85. **Answer: D.** Heat is the number-one enemy to a thermal printer. If a thermal printer or the thermal paper is kept in a location where the temperature is too high, it could cause failure of the printer and damage to the paper. Excessive moisture can cause rubber rollers and separation pads to fail over time. Electrostatic discharge (ESD) is always a foe, but only if you are working inside the printer. Dirt can clog up the works over time in any device. But by far, heat is what you have to watch for with thermal printers.

86. **Answer: D.** Of the listed answers, the fusing stage happens last. It is typically considered to be the last stage of the laser printing process before paper exits the printer. The laser printing process includes the following steps in order: cleaning, charging, writing (or exposing), developing, transferring, and fusing.

87. **Answer: C.** The dot matrix is a type of impact printer. It uses a printhead to physically impact the ribbon and transfer ink to the paper. Laser printers apply toner to paper through varying voltages. Inkjet printers spray ink from a cartridge onto the paper. Thermal paper is specially coated and forms text when it is heated properly.

88. **Answer: C.** After you install the driver for the printer locally, you can then take control of it by going to the properties of the printer and accessing the Ports tab. Then click the Add Port button and select the Standard TCP/IP Port option. You will have to know the IP address of the printer or the computer that the printer is connected to.

89. Answer: B. After installing a printer, it is important to calibrate it for color and orientation, especially if you are installing a color laser printer or an inkjet printer. These calibration tools are usually built in to the printer's software and can be accessed from Windows. Or, you can access them from the printer's display. If a toner cartridge needs to be cleaned, it probably has a leak and should be replaced. The fusing assembly needs to be changed only when it fails. Many printers will give you an indication of when the fuser is at 20% life and needs to be replaced soon. If the fuser fails, the toner will fail to stick to the paper. The primary corona wire can be cleaned; it is near the drum. This can help with other types of print quality problems such as lines and smearing.

Domain 5.0: Operational Procedures

90. Answer: C. Use an antistatic wrist strap when working inside a computer to protect against electrostatic discharge (ESD). Other ways to prevent ESD include using an antistatic mat, touching the chassis of the case, and using antistatic bags.

91. Answer: A. While on the job site, limit phone calls to emergencies or if your employer calls you about another customer. Taking a personal phone call while working at a client site is considered unprofessional. Be professional when you're on the job!

92. Answer: C. If it is not life-threatening, consult the material safety data sheet (MSDS) to determine the proper first aid (if any). If it is an emergency, call 911. If you cannot get access to the MSDS, contact the facilities department of your organization or try your building supervisor. Never ignore an unknown chemical. Take action before it becomes a problem.

93. Answer: C. If there is something that is immediately hazardous to you, you must leave the area right away. Afterward, you can call 911, the building supervisor, or your manager, depending on the severity of the situation. Computers and all other technology come second after human life. Remember that. Plus, if backup systems have been implemented properly, you have nothing to lose if a computer is damaged.

94. Answer: C. You need to explain to the customer that there is a safer way. Cable management is very important when it comes to the safety of employees. Trip hazards such as incorrectly routed network cables can have devastating effects on a person. Never ignore the problem. It is not your place to notify the building supervisor or administrator because this is not your company. However, you might opt to tell *your* manager about the event. A wise consulting company wants to protect its employees and should want to know of potential hazards at customer locations.

95. Answer: C. Every municipality has its own way of recycling batteries. But you should definitely recycle them and not throw them in the trash. Manufacturers probably won't be interested in batteries that won't charge any longer. It is more likely that you will recycle them. Be safe—never open a battery!

96. Answer: C. Asking a customer if employees always cause issues is just plain rude; this type of communication should be avoided. However, the other three statements are positive and helpful, or at least consoling. Stay away from being judgmental of the customer.

97. Answer: C. Ask if the server problem is related to the PC problem. Try to understand the customer before making any judgments about the problems. Make sure it isn't a bigger problem than you realize before making repairs that could be futile. If you find out that it is a separate problem, ask the customer which issue she would like to resolve first.

98. Answer: B. Chain of custody is the chronological paper trail of evidence that may or may not be used in court. First response describes the steps a person takes when first responding to a computer with prohibited content or illegal activity: it includes identifying what exactly is happening, reporting through proper channels, and preserving data and devices. Setting and meeting expectations deals with customer service; it is something you should do before you start a job for a customer. Data (and device) preservation is a part of first response; a person who first arrives at the scene of a computer incident will be in charge of preserving data and devices in their current state.

99. Answer: B. Don't attempt to move heavy objects by yourself. Ask someone to help you. Removing jewelry, disconnecting power, and bending at the knees and lifting with the legs are all good safety measures.

100. Answer: C. One example of active communication is clarifying a customer's statements. For instance, if you are unsure exactly what the customer wants, always clarify the information or repeat it back to the customer so that everyone is on the same page. Never declare that the customer doesn't know what he is doing. This is a surefire way to lose the customer and possibly your job. It should go without saying, mouthing off could be the worst thing you could do. Save that for the drive home on the freeway—I'm just kidding! Be professional at all times when working with customers.

CHAPTER THREE

220-801 Practice Exam B

Now let's kick it up a notch. This second 220-801 exam could be considered an intermediate practice test. I'll be mixing in some more difficult questions this time. Unlike the first exam, this one is freestyle, meaning the questions are randomized. You can expect questions from any of the domains, in any order.

Again, the goal here is to make sure you understand all of the concepts before moving on to the next test. If you didn't already, I suggest taking a break between exams. If you just completed the first exam, give yourself a half-hour or so before you begin this one. If you didn't score 90% or higher on Exam A, go back and study; then retake Exam A until you pass with 90% or higher.

Write down your answers and check them against the answer key that immediately follows the exam. After the answer key, you will find explanations for all of the answers. Good luck!

-21.   79% ☺

Practice Questions

1. Which of the following IP addresses would a technician see if a computer is connected to a multifunction network device and is attempting to obtain an IP address automatically but is not receiving an IP address from the DHCP server?

   - ○ **A.** 172.16.10.10
   - ○ **B.** 192.168.0.10
   - ○ **C.** 169.254.10.10
   - ○ **D.** 192.168.10.10

   Quick Answer: **63**
   Detailed Answer: **65**

2. 80mm and 120mm are common sizes for what type of PC component?

   - ○ **A.** Case fans
   - ○ **B.** CPUs
   - ○ **C.** Heat sinks
   - ○ **D.** Memory modules

   Quick Answer: **63**
   Detailed Answer: **65**

3. What is the total number of devices that can be daisy-chained to an IEEE 1394 port?

   - ○ **A.** 127
   - ○ **B.** 63
   - ○ **C.** 15
   - ○ **D.** 255

   Quick Answer: **63**
   Detailed Answer: **65**

4. What does a yellow exclamation point next to a device in the Device Manager indicate?

   - ○ **A.** A driver is not properly installed for this device.
   - ○ **B.** The device is disabled.
   - ○ **C.** The driver is not digitally signed.
   - ○ **D.** The device driver needs to be upgraded.

   Quick Answer: **63**
   Detailed Answer: **65**

5. Beep codes are generated by which of the following?

   - ○ **A.** CMOS
   - ○ **B.** RTC
   - ○ **C.** POST
   - ○ **D.** Windows

   Quick Answer: **63**
   Detailed Answer: **65**

6. How should you apply spray cleaner to a monitor?

   ○ **A.** Spray the cleaner directly on the monitor screen.

   ○ **B.** Spray the cleaner on the top of the monitor and wipe down.

   ○ **C.** Spray evenly on the monitor.

   ○ **D.** Spray the cleaner on a clean, lint-free cloth first.

Quick Answer: **63**
Detailed Answer: **65**

7. Which bus slot provides the highest video performance?

   ○ **A.** PCI

   ○ **B.** SCSI

   ○ **C.** AGP

   ○ **D.** PCIe

Quick Answer: **63**
Detailed Answer: **65**

8. Which of the following indicates that a printer is network-ready?

   ○ **A.** An RJ11 jack

   ○ **B.** A USB connector

   ○ **C.** An RJ45 jack

   ○ **D.** An SCSI connector

Quick Answer: **63**
Detailed Answer: **65**

9. You just turned off a printer to maintenance it. What should you be careful of when removing the fuser?

   ○ **A.** The fuser being hot

   ○ **B.** The fuser being wet

   ○ **C.** The fuser being fragile

   ○ **D.** The fuser releasing toner

Quick Answer: **63**
Detailed Answer: **66**

10. Where is the memory controller located in a Core 2 Duo system?

   ○ **A.** On the CPU

   ○ **B.** On memory

   ○ **C.** Within the chipset

   ○ **D.** Within the PCIe controller

Quick Answer: **63**
Detailed Answer: **66**

11. Which of the following connectors is used for musical equipment?

   ○ **A.** MIDI

   ○ **B.** HDMI

   ○ **C.** DVI

   ○ **D.** DisplayPort

Quick Answer: **63**
Detailed Answer: **66**

12. Although not used as often as a Phillips screwdriver, this tool is sometimes used to remove screws from the outside of a computer case or from within a laptop.

   - ○ **A.** Monkey wrench
   - ○ **B.** Torx wrench
   - ○ **C.** Channel lock
   - ○ **D.** Pliers

Quick Answer: **63**
Detailed Answer: **66**

13. What is the main advantage of selecting a 64-bit operating system over a 32-bit operating system?

   - ○ **A.** The ability to use software-based data execution prevention (DEP)
   - ○ **B.** The ability to use unsigned drivers
   - ○ **C.** The ability to access more than 4 GB of RAM
   - ○ **D.** The ability to run multiple 16-bit programs in separate memory spaces

Quick Answer: **63**
Detailed Answer: **66**

14. Moving your CPU's speed beyond its normal operating range is called _____.

   - ○ **A.** Overclocking
   - ○ **B.** Overdriving
   - ○ **C.** Overpowering
   - ○ **D.** Overspeeding

Quick Answer: **63**
Detailed Answer: **66**

15. Which port is typically known as a serial port?

   - ○ **A.** DVI
   - ○ **B.** COM1
   - ○ **C.** LPT1
   - ○ **D.** SCSI

Quick Answer: **63**
Detailed Answer: **66**

16. What is the most important piece of information needed to connect to a specific wireless network?

   - ○ **A.** Channel
   - ○ **B.** MAC address
   - ○ **C.** SSID
   - ○ **D.** Administrator password

Quick Answer: **63**
Detailed Answer: **67**

17. Which password is used in the BIOS (CMOS) to prevent end users from accessing the BIOS contents?

Quick Answer: **63**
Detailed Answer: **67**

- ○ **A.** Supervisor
- ○ **B.** User
- ○ **C.** Administrator
- ○ **D.** Local

18. Why would the display on a laptop get dimmer when the power supply from the AC outlet is disconnected?

Quick Answer: **63**
Detailed Answer: **67**

- ○ **A.** The laptop cannot use full brightness when on battery power.
- ○ **B.** Power management settings on the laptop.
- ○ **C.** To operate properly, laptop displays require an alternating current power source.
- ○ **D.** Security settings on the laptop.

19. Which tool should always be used when working on the inside of the computer?

Quick Answer: **63**
Detailed Answer: **67**

- ○ **A.** Cordless drill
- ○ **B.** Antistatic strap
- ○ **C.** Multimeter
- ○ **D.** Screwdriver

20. What are advantages of using the Dynamic Host Configuration Protocol (DHCP)? (Select the two best answers.)

Quick Answer: **63**
Detailed Answer: **67**

- ○ **A.** IP addresses can be managed from a central location.
- ○ **B.** The network speed can automatically adjust based on the type of traffic being generated.
- ○ **C.** The hosts file on the computer can be validated for proper entries.
- ○ **D.** Media access control addresses can be changed.
- ○ **E.** Computers can automatically get new addressing when moved to a different network segment.

21. On a laptop, which of the following would most likely be a pointing device?

Quick Answer: **63**
Detailed Answer: **67**

- ○ **A.** Serial mouse
- ○ **B.** PS/2 mouse
- ○ **C.** USB mouse
- ○ **D.** Touchpad

22. Which of the following storage technologies is used by traditional hard disk drives?

   ○ **A.** Magnetic

   ○ **B.** Optical

   ○ **C.** Impact

   ○ **D.** Solid-state

23. On which type of computer is RAM the most important?

   ○ **A.** Gaming PC

   ○ **B.** Virtualization workstation

   ○ **C.** AV workstation

   ○ **D.** HTPC

24. A client brings in a printer that is giving a paper-feed error. What is the most likely cause?

   ○ **A.** The separation tab

   ○ **B.** The developing rollers

   ○ **C.** The paper tray

   ○ **D.** The pickup rollers

25. Which of the following is the default port for HTTPS?

   ○ **A.** Port 25

   ○ **B.** Port 80

   ○ **C.** Port 143

   ○ **D.** Port 443

26. What is the maximum distance at which a Class 2 Bluetooth device can receive signals from a Bluetooth access point?

   ○ **A.** 100 meters

   ○ **B.** 10 meters

   ○ **C.** 5 meters

   ○ **D.** 1 meter

27. Which of the following form factors does a VGA connector comply with?

   ○ **A.** 8P8C

   ○ **B.** 15-pin D shell

   ○ **C.** microATX

   ○ **D.** RG-6

28. You and a co-worker are running network cables above the drop ceiling. The co-worker accidentally touches a live AC power line and is thrown off the ladder and onto the ground. He is dazed and can't stand. He is no longer near the AC power line. What should you do first?

   - ○ **A.** Cut the power at the breaker.
   - ○ **B.** Move the co-worker farther down the hall.
   - ○ **C.** Apply CPR.
   - ○ **D.** Call 911.

29. A customer reports that an optical drive in a PC is no longer responding. What question should you ask first?

   - ○ **A.** "What has changed since the optical drive worked properly?"
   - ○ **B.** "Did you log in with your administrator account?"
   - ○ **C.** "What did you modify since the optical drive worked?"
   - ○ **D.** "Have you been to any inappropriate websites?"

30. Which device can store a maximum of 1.44 MB on a removable disk?

   - ○ **A.** Floppy drive
   - ○ **B.** CD-ROM
   - ○ **C.** ROM
   - ○ **D.** Compact Flash

31. What wireless networking standard operates at 5 GHz only?

   - ○ **A.** 802.11a
   - ○ **B.** 802.11b
   - ○ **C.** 802.11g
   - ○ **D.** 802.11n

32. What is the PC equivalent of FireWire?

   - ○ **A.** IEEE 1284
   - ○ **B.** USB
   - ○ **C.** IEEE 1394
   - ○ **D.** ISA

33. Which type of RAM has a peak transfer of 12,800 MB/s?

Quick Answer: **63**
Detailed Answer: **69**

- ○ **A.** DDR3-800
- ○ **B.** DDR2-1600
- ○ **C.** DDR3-1600
- ○ **D.** DDR2-800

34. Which type of printer uses a print head, ribbon, and tractor feed?

Quick Answer: **63**
Detailed Answer: **69**

- ○ **A.** Laser
- ○ **B.** Impact
- ○ **C.** Inkjet
- ○ **D.** Thermal

35. What is a possible symptom of a failing CPU?

Quick Answer: **63**
Detailed Answer: **69**

- ○ **A.** CPU is beyond the recommended voltage range.
- ○ **B.** Computer won't boot.
- ○ **C.** BIOS reports low temperatures within the case.
- ○ **D.** Spyware is installed into the browser.

36. Which of the following cable types is not affected by EMI but requires specialized tools to install?

Quick Answer: **63**
Detailed Answer: **69**

- ○ **A.** Cat 6
- ○ **B.** STP
- ○ **C.** Fiber optic
- ○ **D.** Coaxial

37. A computer you are working on has a lot of dust inside it. How should you clean this?

Quick Answer: **63**
Detailed Answer: **69**

- ○ **A.** Disassemble the power supply and remove the dust.
- ○ **B.** Use a vacuum to clean up the dust.
- ○ **C.** Use a surface dust cleaning solution.
- ○ **D.** Use compressed air to remove the dust.

38. Setting an administrator password in the BIOS accomplishes which of the following?

Quick Answer: **63**
Detailed Answer: **70**

- ○ **A.** Prevents a user from rearranging the boot order
- ○ **B.** Prevents a user from reading e-mail
- ○ **C.** Prevents a virus from infecting the MBR
- ○ **D.** Prevents an attacker from opening the case

39. Which function is performed by the external power supply of a laptop?

Quick Answer: **63**
Detailed Answer: **70**

- O **A.** Increases voltage
- O **B.** Stores power
- O **C.** Converts DC power to AC power
- O **D.** Converts AC power to DC power

40. Which type of cable has only two twisted pairs?

Quick Answer: **63**
Detailed Answer: **70**

- O **A.** UTP
- O **B.** POTS line
- O **C.** Fiber
- O **D.** Coaxial

41. How many pins would you see in a high-quality printhead on a dot matrix printer?

Quick Answer: **63**
Detailed Answer: **70**

- O **A.** 24
- O **B.** 15
- O **C.** 8
- O **D.** 35

42. When it comes to computer case form factors, which of the following provides the most room for effective cooling?

Quick Answer: **63**
Detailed Answer: **70**

- O **A.** ATX
- O **B.** BTX
- O **C.** ITX
- O **D.** microATX

43. A co-worker is traveling to Europe and is bringing her computer. She asks you what safety concerns there might be. What should you tell her?

Quick Answer: **63**
Detailed Answer: **70**

- O **A.** The computer is not usable in other countries.
- O **B.** Check for a compatible power adapter for that country.
- O **C.** Use a line conditioner for the correct voltage.
- O **D.** Check the voltage selector on the power supply.

44. What is an LCD display's contrast ratio defined as?

Quick Answer: **63**
Detailed Answer: **70**

- O **A.** Power consumption
- O **B.** Display resolution and brightness
- O **C.** The darkest and lightest outputs
- O **D.** Power savings

45. Which of the following tools can protect you in the case of a surge?

Quick Answer: **63**
Detailed Answer: **71**

- ○ **A.** Torx wrench
- ○ **B.** Antistatic strap
- ○ **C.** Voltmeter
- ○ **D.** Antistatic mat

46. What connector can have audio *and* video pass through it?

Quick Answer: **63**
Detailed Answer: **71**

- ○ **A.** VGA
- ○ **B.** RGB
- ○ **C.** DVI
- ○ **D.** HDMI

47. While you are working on a computer at a customer's home, the customer informs you that he needs to leave for about 10 minutes and that his 8-year-old son can help you with anything if you need it. What should you do?

Quick Answer: **63**
Detailed Answer: **71**

- ○ **A.** Tell the customer to get back home as soon as possible.
- ○ **B.** Tell the customer that you are not responsible for the child.
- ○ **C.** Tell the customer that an adult must be home while you work.
- ○ **D.** Tell the customer that the child must be removed.

48. Which device limits network broadcasts, segments IP address ranges, and interconnects different physical media?

Quick Answer: **63**
Detailed Answer: **71**

- ○ **A.** Switch
- ○ **B.** WAP
- ○ **C.** Firewall
- ○ **D.** Router

49. You just upgraded the CPU. Which of the following can make your computer shut down automatically after a few minutes? (Select the best answer.)

Quick Answer: **63**
Detailed Answer: **71**

- ○ **A.** Wrong CPU driver.
- ○ **B.** Wrong voltage to the CPU.
- ○ **C.** Incorrect CPU has been installed.
- ○ **D.** The CPU has overheated.

50. Which of the following power connections might be used by hard drives? (Select the two best answers.)

- ○ **A.** 8-pin
- ○ **B.** 7-pin
- ○ **C.** Molex
- ○ **D.** 15-pin
- ○ **E.** Berg

51. Which of the following is a valid IPv4 address for a network host?

- ○ **A.** 127.0.0.1
- ○ **B.** 169.254.0.0/16
- ○ **C.** 172.17.58.254
- ○ **D.** 255.10.15.7

52. If a lot of data is flowing through a network card, what should the activity light look like?

- ○ **A.** Unlit
- ○ **B.** Rapid, erratic flashing
- ○ **C.** Solid green
- ○ **D.** Solid yellow

53. You want to upgrade memory in your computer. Which of the following is user-replaceable memory in a PC?

- ○ **A.** CMOS
- ○ **B.** BIOS
- ○ **C.** DRAM
- ○ **D.** SRAM
- ○ **E.** ROM

54. You are working on a very old printer, and it starts to smoke. What should you do?

- ○ **A.** Turn off the printer.
- ○ **B.** Call 911.
- ○ **C.** Unplug the printer.
- ○ **D.** Call maintenance.
- ○ **E.** Tell the printer it is bad to smoke.

55. Which technology has the fastest data transfer rate?

- ○ **A.** 802.11a
- ○ **B.** 802.11b
- ○ **C.** 802.11g
- ○ **D.** 802.11n

56. You are asked to fix a problem with a customer's domain controller that is outside the scope of your knowledge. What action should you take?

- ○ **A.** Learn on the job by trying to fix the problem.
- ○ **B.** Tell the customer that the problem should be reported to another technician.
- ○ **C.** Assure the customer that the problem will be fixed very soon.
- ○ **D.** Help the customer find the appropriate channels to fix the problem.

57. Of the following, which IP address is private?

- ○ **A.** 11.58.254.169
- ○ **B.** 169.255.10.41
- ○ **C.** 172.31.1.1
- ○ **D.** 192.169.0.1

58. How should you remain in the face of adversity?

- ○ **A.** Wavering
- ○ **B.** Decisive
- ○ **C.** Positive
- ○ **D.** Certain

59. What is the local loopback IPv6 address?

- ○ **A.** 127.0.0.1
- ○ **B.** ::1
- ○ **C.** 192.168.0.0
- ○ **D.** FE80::/10

60. Which of the following statements is correct concerning IPv6 addresses?

- ○ **A.** They cannot be used with IPv4.
- ○ **B.** They are supported by all routers.

○ **C.** They represent addressing using 128 bits.

○ **D.** They require fiber-optic connections.

61. What operating CPU temperature is typical?

○ **A.** 60° Fahrenheit

○ **B.** 60° Celsius

○ **C.** 72° Fahrenheit

○ **D.** 72° Celsius

Quick Answer: **63**
Detailed Answer: **73**

62. You need to install a printer that can be used to print payroll checks on paper forms that have a carbon backing. Which printer technology should you select?

○ **A.** Impact

○ **B.** Laser

○ **C.** Inkjet

○ **D.** Thermal

Quick Answer: **63**
Detailed Answer: **73**

63. In current motherboards, which memory bus width can be accomplished by using the dual channel technology?

○ **A.** 64-bit

○ **B.** 128-bit

○ **C.** 256-bit

○ **D.** 448-bit

Quick Answer: **63**
Detailed Answer: **73**

64. Which of the following best describes a hub?

○ **A.** Inspects traffic and accepts or declines transmission

○ **B.** Determines the best route to transmit data

○ **C.** Broadcasts data to all network devices

○ **D.** Broadcasts data to specific network devices

Quick Answer: **63**
Detailed Answer: **73**

65. Which of the following tools could a person use to test an AC outlet? (Select the two best answers.)

○ **A.** Multimeter

○ **B.** PSU tester

○ **C.** Receptacle tester

○ **D.** Loopback plug

Quick Answer: **63**
Detailed Answer: **74**

66. What maximum data transfer rate is IEEE 1394b capable of?

Quick Answer: **63**
Detailed Answer: **74**

- ○ **A.** 12 Mbps
- ○ **B.** 400 Mbps
- ○ **C.** 480 Mbps
- ○ **D.** 800 Mbps
- ○ **E.** 5 Gbps

67. Which of the following is *not* a configuration that can be made in the BIOS?

Quick Answer: **63**
Detailed Answer: **74**

- ○ **A.** Boot sequence
- ○ **B.** Temperature thresholds
- ○ **C.** Overclocking
- ○ **D.** Install drivers
- ○ **E.** Intrusion detection

68. Which of the following traits and port numbers are associated with POP3?

Quick Answer: **63**
Detailed Answer: **74**

- ○ **A.** Receives inbound e-mail on port 110
- ○ **B.** Receives inbound e-mail on port 25
- ○ **C.** Sends outbound e-mail on port 110
- ○ **D.** Sends outbound e-mail on port 25

69. When working on a computer, which of the following should you disconnect to prevent electrical shock? (Select the two best answers.)

Quick Answer: **63**
Detailed Answer: **74**

- ○ **A.** Printer
- ○ **B.** Mouse
- ○ **C.** Telephone cord
- ○ **D.** Power cord

70. Which of the following controls the connection between the CPU and the PCIe x16 expansion slot?

Quick Answer: **63**
Detailed Answer: **74**

- ○ **A.** Northbridge
- ○ **B.** Power supply
- ○ **C.** Memory
- ○ **D.** Memory controller

71. What is the recommended method for handling an empty toner cartridge?

    ○ **A.** Throw it away.

    ○ **B.** Incinerate it.

    ○ **C.** Refill it.

    ○ **D.** Recycle it.

72. Which type of cable would you use to connect a laptop directly to a PC?

    ○ **A.** Cat 5e patch cable

    ○ **B.** Parallel cable

    ○ **C.** IEEE 1394b cable

    ○ **D.** Cat 5e crossover cable

73. A customer experiences a server crash. When you arrive, the manager is upset about this problem. What should you do in this scenario?

    ○ **A.** Stay calm and do the job as efficiently as possible.

    ○ **B.** Take the customer out for a cup of coffee.

    ○ **C.** Avoid the customer and get the job done quickly.

    ○ **D.** Refer the customer to your supervisor.

74. Which of the following types of printers uses toner?

    ○ **A.** Impact

    ○ **B.** Laser

    ○ **C.** Inkjet

    ○ **D.** Thermal

75. As you are servicing a manager's PC at your company, you run across a list of names of employees who are supposedly about to be let go from the company. Some of these people are co-workers. What should you do?

    ○ **A.** Turn the sheet over.

    ○ **B.** Act as if you never saw the list.

    ○ **C.** In secret, tell everyone who was on the list.

    ○ **D.** Yell at the manager for having that list out.

Quick Check

76. In order to perform a network installation of Windows, which of the following must be supported by the computer's network interface card?

Quick Answer: **63**
Detailed Answer: **75**

- ○ **A.** PXE
- ○ **B.** PCI
- ○ **C.** PCL
- ○ **D.** PnP

77. In which of the following slots would you place an 8x video card?

Quick Answer: **63**
Detailed Answer: **75**

- ○ **A.** PCI
- ○ **B.** PCIe
- ○ **C.** AGP
- ○ **D.** AMR

78. Which of the following is the newest type of mouse connection?

Quick Answer: **63**
Detailed Answer: **75**

- ○ **A.** Serial
- ○ **B.** USB
- ○ **C.** PS/2
- ○ **D.** Parallel

79. How can you reduce the chance of ESD? (Select the three best answers.)

Quick Answer: **63**
Detailed Answer: **75**

- ○ **A.** Use an antistatic strap.
- ○ **B.** Use an antistatic mat.
- ○ **C.** Raise the temperature.
- ○ **D.** Raise the humidity.
- ○ **E.** Lower the humidity.
- ○ **F.** Work in a carpeted area.

80. Which of the following is a unique characteristic of a dual-core processor versus a single-core processor?

Quick Answer: **63**
Detailed Answer: **76**

- ○ **A.** A dual-core processor has two cores, with separate caches, on the same physical chip.
- ○ **B.** A dual-core processor has several unique cores, with the same cache, on two different chips.
- ○ **C.** A dual-core processor uses higher voltage than a single-core processor.
- ○ **D.** A dual-core processor requires more RAM to function than a single-core processor.

81. Which of the following devices is the least likely to be replaced on a laptop?

    ○ **A.** CPU

    ○ **B.** RAM

    ○ **C.** PC Card

    ○ **D.** Keyboard

Quick Answer: **63**
Detailed Answer: **76**

82. If your "bandwidth" is 1000 Mbps, how many bits are you sending/receiving? (Select the two best answers.)

    ○ **A.** 100,000,000 bits per minute

    ○ **B.** 1000 bits per second

    ○ **C.** 1,000,000,000 bits per second

    ○ **D.** 1 gigabit per second

Quick Answer: **63**
Detailed Answer: **76**

83. Which of the following is an example of a broadband connection?

    ○ **A.** Cable Internet

    ○ **B.** Ethernet

    ○ **C.** Client/Server

    ○ **D.** IEEE 802.3

Quick Answer: **63**
Detailed Answer: **76**

84. Which of the following can send data the farthest?

    ○ **A.** Multi-mode fiber

    ○ **B.** Single-mode fiber

    ○ **C.** STP

    ○ **D.** Coaxial

Quick Answer: **63**
Detailed Answer: **76**

85. You need to expand the peripherals of a computer, but the system doesn't have enough ports. Which type of card should you install?

    ○ **A.** Modem

    ○ **B.** Network adapter

    ○ **C.** USB card

    ○ **D.** TV tuner card

Quick Answer: **63**
Detailed Answer: **76**

86. Which of the following is a typical speed of a SATA hard drive?

    ○ **A.** 1000 Mbps

    ○ **B.** 3.1 GHz

    ○ **C.** 8 GB

    ○ **D.** 7200 RPM

Quick Answer: **63**
Detailed Answer: **76**

87. Which of the following should you use to clean a monitor's screen if you are not sure how to do so?

- ○ **A.** Isopropyl alcohol
- ○ **B.** Mild detergent
- ○ **C.** Water
- ○ **D.** Boric acid

88. Which of the following best describes the differences between a switch and a router?

- ○ **A.** A switch interconnects devices on the same network so that they can communicate, whereas a router interconnects one or more networks.
- ○ **B.** A router broadcasts all data packets that are sent on the network, and a switch transmits data directly to the device.
- ○ **C.** A switch broadcasts all data packets that are sent on the network, and a router transmits data directly to the device.
- ○ **D.** A switch interconnects one or more networks, whereas a router interconnect devices on a network.

89. Ray wants to install a new internal SATA hard drive in his computer. Which types of cables should he connect to the drive? (Select the two best answers.)

- ○ **A.** 7-pin data cable
- ○ **B.** 40-pin data cable
- ○ **C.** 4-pin power cable
- ○ **D.** 15-pin power cable

90. A group of users in ABC Corp. needs to back up several gigabytes of data daily. Which of the following is the best media for this scenario?

- ○ **A.** DVD
- ○ **B.** Dual-Layer DVD
- ○ **C.** External USB hard drive
- ○ **D.** DLT

91. You are required to rip the contents of a CD to a compressed file format that can be read easily on PCs, Linux computers, or Macs. Which format should you select?

   ○ **A.** .AAC

   ○ **B.** .WMA

   ○ **C.** .MP3

   ○ **D.** .MOV

Quick Answer: **64**
Detailed Answer: **77**

92. You need to replace and upgrade the memory card in a smartphone. Which type of memory does the smartphone most likely use?

   ○ **A.** SSD

   ○ **B.** CF

   ○ **C.** USB flash drive

   ○ **D.** SD

Quick Answer: **64**
Detailed Answer: **77**

93. Your organization relies heavily on its server farm for resources and is less reliant on the client computers. Which type of client computer does the organization most likely use?

   ○ **A.** Virtualization workstation

   ○ **B.** Client/Server

   ○ **C.** Thin client

   ○ **D.** Thick client

Quick Answer: **64**
Detailed Answer: **77**

94. What are the respective functions of the two corona wires in a laser printer? (Select the two best answers.)

   ○ **A.** Condition the drum to be written to

   ○ **B.** Transfer toner from the drum to the paper

   ○ **C.** Fuse the toner to the paper

   ○ **D.** Clean the drum

Quick Answer: **64**
Detailed Answer: **77**

95. Which of the following capabilities enables a printer to store multiple documents?

   ○ **A.** Buffer

   ○ **B.** Print driver

   ○ **C.** Printer pool

   ○ **D.** Spooling

Quick Answer: **64**
Detailed Answer: **77**

96. While you explain a technical concept to a customer, what is the best action for you to take?

Quick Answer: **64**
Detailed Answer: **78**

- ○ **A.** Recommend a training class.
- ○ **B.** Sit next to the customer.
- ○ **C.** Use acronyms so that the customer feels comfortable about your knowledge.
- ○ **D.** Tell the customer to read the manual.

97. You are setting up a SOHO network with DSL. Which of the following devices should you place on the phone line so that the line can be shared with a phone and the DSL modem?

Quick Answer: **64**
Detailed Answer: **78**

- ○ **A.** Line filter
- ○ **B.** Heat sink
- ○ **C.** Router
- ○ **D.** Coax splitter

98. One way to provide preventive maintenance to a hard drive is to do what?

Quick Answer: **64**
Detailed Answer: **78**

- ○ **A.** Upgrade the cache on the drive to improve performance.
- ○ **B.** Increase the amount of RAM on the PC to increase the page file.
- ○ **C.** Install a second hard drive.
- ○ **D.** Keep an area of airflow around the drive so that it doesn't overheat.

99. After a blackout, the power comes back on, causing a surge to occur on all the computers and equipment in the office. Your co-worker's laptop display doesn't come on. However, if you look closely at the display, you can see that Windows is running, but very dimly. What could be the cause of this problem?

Quick Answer: **64**
Detailed Answer: **78**

- ○ **A.** The inverter has been shorted out.
- ○ **B.** The power supply has failed.
- ○ **C.** The display is not getting power.
- ○ **D.** The display driver has failed.

100. Which tool would you use to test a 24-pin ATX 12v power connector?

Quick Answer: **64**
Detailed Answer: **78**

- ○ **A.** Torx wrench
- ○ **B.** Multimeter
- ○ **C.** Receptacle tester
- ○ **D.** Tone and probe kit

Quick-Check Answer Key

1. C	30. A	59. B
2. A	31. A	60. C
3. B	32. C	61. B
4. A	33. C	62. A
5. C	34. B	63. B
6. D	35. A	64. C
7. D	36. C	65. A and C
8. C	37. D	66. D
9. A	38. A	67. D
10. C	39. D	68. A
11. A	40. B	69. C and D
12. B	41. A	70. A
13. C	42. B	71. D
14. A	43. D	72. D
15. B	44. C	73. A
16. C	45. B	74. B
17. A	46. D	75. B
18. B	47. C	76. A
19. B	48. D	77. C
20. A and E	49. D	78. B
21. D	50. C and D	79. A, B, and D
22. A	51. C	80. A
23. B	52. B	81. A
24. D	53. C	82. C and D
25. D	54. C	83. A
26. B	55. D	84. B
27. B	56. D	85. C
28. D	57. C	86. D
29. A	58. C	87. C

88. A

89. A and D

90. D

91. C

92. D

93. C

94. A and B

95. A

96. B

97. A

98. D

99. A

100. B

Answers and Explanations

1. **Answer: C.** If the computer fails to obtain an IP address from a DHCP server, Windows will take over and apply an Automatic Private IP Address (APIPA). This address will be on the 169.254.0.0 network. All of the other addresses could possibly be obtained from a DHCP server. 172.16.10.10 is a Class B private IP. 192.168.0.10 and 192.168.10.10 are Class C private IP addresses.

2. **Answer: A.** Case fans are measured in mm (millimeters). 80mm and especially 120mm are very common. They are used to exhaust heat out of the case. This aids in keeping the CPU and other devices cool. CPUs commonly use a heat sink/fan combination. However, the two are often connected together. Memory modules don't use fans, but they can be equipped (or purchased) with heat sinks of their own.

3. **Answer: B.** An IEEE 1394 (FireWire) chain can have up to 63 devices. USB can handle up to 127 devices, though both of these numbers are outside the realm of normalcy for most individuals! 15 is the maximum amount of devices that can be on a SCSI chain. Remember this doesn't count the SCSI card. 255 is a commonly used number when it comes to maximums but doesn't apply to IEEE 1394.

4. **Answer: A.** If you see a yellow exclamation point in the Device Manager, this indicates that the device does not have a proper driver. If the device is disabled, it will have either a down arrow (for Windows 7/Vista) or a red x (Windows XP). If a driver was not digitally signed, the device might show up in the Unknown devices category until it is installed properly. If a device has a working driver, then upgrading it will be up to you, but you won't necessarily be notified of this.

5. **Answer: C.** As the POST checks all the components of the computer, it may present its findings on the screen or in the form of beep codes. The complementary metal-oxide semiconductor (CMOS) stores information such as time and date and BIOS passwords. RTC stands for real-time clock; it is the device that keeps time on the motherboard. Windows generates all kinds of error codes but not beep codes. The beep codes come from the POST, which happens before Windows boots.

6. **Answer: D.** Never spray any cleaner directly on a display. Spray on a lint-free cloth first, and then wipe the display gently. Try not to get any liquid in the cracks at the edge of the screen. A lot of companies sell products that are half isopropyl alcohol and half water. You could also make this yourself. Again, remember to put the solution on a lint-free cloth first.

7. **Answer: D.** PCI Express (PCIe) offers the highest video performance. A PCIe x16 version 3 card can transfer a maximum of 16 GB/s. Compare this to the closest competitor listed: AGP, which can do 2,133 MB/s, about 1/8 of PCIe. SCSI is used for hard drives and scanners among other things, but not for video. PCI is the predecessor to PCIe but is rarely used for video anymore; it is limited to 133 or 266 MB/s depending on the speed. Either way, it doesn't hold a candle to PCIe.

8. **Answer: C.** The RJ45 jack enables a connection to a twisted-pair (most likely Ethernet) network. Printers with a built-in RJ45 connector are network ready. RJ11 ports are used by modems and dial-up Internet connections. If a printer has this, then it is a multifunction printer acting as a fax machine. USB is the standard port for a printer.

This allows it to connect to a PC or to a print server. SCSI connectors are not often found on today's printers; regardless, they would indicate a local connection, not a network connection.

9. **Answer: A.** The fuser heats paper to around 400° Fahrenheit (204° Celsius). That's like an oven. If you need to replace the fuser, let the printer sit for 10 or 15 minutes after shutting it down, and before maintenance. The fuser is not wet or fragile, and it does not contain toner—that is contained by the cartridge.

10. **Answer: C.** On Core 2 Duo, Quad, and Extreme systems, the memory controller is located within the chipset and is known as the Memory Controller Hub (MCH) by Intel, but it is also referred to as the northbridge. On AMD systems and newer Intel systems such as the Core i5 or i7, the memory controller is located "on-die," meaning within the CPU.

11. **Answer: A.** The Musical Instrument Digital Interface (MIDI) connector is used for musical equipment such as keyboards, synthesizers, and sequencers. MIDI is used to create a clocking signal that all devices can synchronize to. The other three connectors, HDMI, DVI, and DisplayPort, are all video connectors.

12. **Answer: B.** The Torx wrench is a special tool used to remove screws from the outside of a case; often, proprietary computer manufacturers will use these screws. It can also be used to remove screws (albeit smaller ones) from a laptop. The standard is the size T-10 Torx wrench. But you might also use a T-8 and even a T-6 on laptops.

13. **Answer: C.** If you want to access more than 4 GB of RAM, you will need a 64-bit operating system. 32-bit OSes are limited to 4 GB of RAM, and in some cases 3.25 GB. Many computers today, especially custom computers such as virtualization systems and gaming computers, require more than 4 GB of RAM so a 64-bit operating system is the only choice. Data Execution Prevention (DEP) is a security feature in today's operating systems; it stops a program from executing code in a forbidden area of memory. Most of today's 32-bit or 64-bit systems offer this. Unsigned drivers are based on the operating system itself; whether that particular OS is 32-bit or 64-bit will not be a factor. You must be an administrator to allow the use of unsigned drivers. 32-bit operating systems can run older 16-bit programs, but 64-bit operating systems will have problems running 16-bit programs even in compatibility mode.

14. **Answer: A.** Overclocking is the act of increasing your CPU's operating speed beyond its normal rated speed. The rest of the terms are not used in relation to this concept.

15. **Answer: B.** COM1 (communications port 1) is a serial port; it sends or receives one bit at a time, up to 115,200 Kbps. A typical example is the 9-pin male DE9 port (inaccurately referred to also as the DB9). DVI is a video port. LPT1 is an older parallel printing port. SCSI is a parallel port used by hard drives and tape drives. The older COM port is used by dial-up modems. It is also used to program devices such as handheld terminals. You don't see COM ports on PCs today, but you might still see them as an add-on card in the field, used to access networks as an administrator fail-safe in case other Internet connectivity methods fail. In rural areas, people may still use internal or external dial-up modems. The external modem is what connects to the COM1 serial port. Though USB is also technically a "serial" port, most technicians and professionals refer to the serial port as COM1 or COM2.

16. **Answer: C.** The SSID is the most important piece of information required to connect to a wireless network; it is the name of the wireless network. The wireless channel number isn't necessarily needed; the wireless access point (WAP) might auto-negotiate the channel. Also, MAC address filtering is not enabled by default, so the MAC address might not be needed. (In fact, this would be entered by the admin at the wireless access point, not from the client computer.) The administrator password is needed only if you wanted to make configuration changes to the wireless access point. For example, if you wanted to implement MAC filtering, you would have to log in to the WAP with an admin password to configure it.

17. **Answer: A.** The supervisor (or system) password is used so that only the technician can get into the BIOS (CMOS). The user password is used to password-protect what-ever operating system is running on the computer, but it does it from the firmware level. An "administrator" password is something used in Windows or on a networking device, and a local password is something used in software.

18. **Answer: B.** The power management settings on the laptop can cause the display to automatically dim when the AC adapter is unplugged. In fact, this is the default on many laptops in order to conserve battery power. These can be configured within Power Options in Windows. You can certainly set the display to full brightness when on battery power—it just isn't recommended. Laptops can operate properly when con-nected to the AC power adapter or when using the battery only. The display brightness of a laptop isn't affected by any security settings.

19. **Answer: B.** Always use an antistatic strap to avoid ESD (electrostatic discharge). Power tools and battery-operated tools such as cordless drills should be avoided. Although multimeters and screwdrivers are tools you *might* use, they might not always be necessary, whereas the antistatic strap should *always* be worn.

20. **Answers: A and E.** Advantages of using DHCP include: IP addresses can be managed from a central location and computers can automatically get new addressing when moved to a different network segment (perhaps one that uses a different DHCP serv-er). Quality of Service (QoS) adjusts the network speed based on the type of traffic generated. DHCP has nothing to do with the Hosts.txt file; that file contains static entries of hostname to IP address conversions. Media Access Control addresses are usually not changed on a network adapter, although they can be masked. MAC filtering maintains a list of MAC addresses that are allowed to access a network, but once again, this is a different concept from DHCP.

21. **Answer: D.** The touchpad is the most likely of the listed devices. Serial devices (and the port in general) are found less and less often on laptops. (They are extinct on new laptops.) PS/2 mice are also rare. Both of these have given way to the touchpad and external USB mice.

22. **Answer: A.** The traditional hard drive is still the magnetic disk. This is because it is well known and has a low cost per MB of storage space. There are optical hard drives, but they are rare; optical drives are commonly implemented as CD, DVD, or Blu-ray drives. Impact refers to a type of printer, such as the dot matrix or the daisy wheel printer. Solid-state hard drives are gaining in popularity because they have no moving parts, are quiet, and work as fast as (if not faster than) traditional magnetic hard drives. However, they are far more expensive than the traditional drive, which slows their general acceptance.

VM

23. **Answer: B.** RAM is more essential to the virtualization workstation than any of the other types of custom PCs listed. Virtual operating systems (virtual machines or VMs) require a lot of RAM to run, much more than any other application. Plus, a virtualization workstation will often have more than one virtual machine running, increasing its need for RAM even further. Gaming PCs biggest requirements are CPU and video card. Audio/video workstations require specialized audio and video cards, fast hard drives, and dual monitors. Home theater PCs (HTPCs) require an HDMI output, surround sound, a small form factor, and possibly a TV tuner.

24. **Answer: D.** Paper-feed errors are often caused by the pickup rollers, which are in charge of feeding the paper into the printer. If a separation tab fails, it might cause more than one sheet of paper to be entered into the printer. The developing rollers transfer ink to the imaging drum. The paper tray simply holds the paper. It should not cause paper-feed errors unless the constraining tabs are too tight.

25. **Answer: D.** Port 443 is the default port for Hypertext Transfer Protocol Secure (HTTPS). This is the protocol used during online banking sessions, or if you go to checkout when shopping online. Port 25 is the default port for SMTP. Port 80 is HTTP. Port 143 is the Internet Message Access Protocol (IMAP); it's similar to POP3 but offers offline operation, and multiple clients can access the same mailbox.

26. **Answer: B.** Class 2 Bluetooth devices have a maximum range of approximately 10 meters. Class 2 devices are the most common (for example, Bluetooth headsets). Class 1 has a 100-meter range, and Class 3's range is approximately 1 meter. The maximum length of a standard USB 2.0 cable is 5 meters.

27. **Answer: B.** The VGA connector uses a D shell (also referred to as D-sub) 15-pin connector. It has three rows of five pins. The 8P8C is the technically correct name for an RJ45 networking plug. microATX is a motherboard form factor commonly used in smaller PCs and HTPCs. RG-6 is the connector used for cable TV and cable Internet connections.

28. **Answer: D.** Because the immediate danger is gone, call 911 right away. Then apply first aid and CPR as necessary. The next step would be to shut the power off at the electrical panel or call the building supervisor to have the power shut off.

29. **Answer: A.** You should first ask if anything has changed since the optical drive worked properly. Don't blame the user by asking what "you" modified; it implies that you think the user caused the issue. Always ask if anything has changed first before any other questions. Try not to accuse a user of accessing inappropriate websites because this could be considered inflammatory and harassment. Think like a robot with the single purpose of fixing the problem, but act like a professional and courteous human being!

30. **Answer: A.** The floppy disk drive (FDD) stores a maximum of 1.44 MB on a removable disk (1.38 MB of which is actual data). CD-ROM drives use removable discs; however, the maximum they can store is much greater. Note that magnetic disks are spelled with a *k*, while optical discs are spelled with a *c*. The acronym *ROM* usually refers to a chip on a circuit board that is not removable. Compact Flash comes in varying sizes (all greater than 1.44 MB) and is considered a card, not a disk.

31. **Answer: A.** 802.11a operates at 5 GHz only. 802.11b and g operate at 2.4 GHz. 802.11n operates at either 2.4 or 5 GHz. The IEEE 802.11 wireless standards are

collectively known as 802.11x. There is no actual 802.11x standard; it was not used in order to avoid confusion. 802.11x is instead a variable that you will sometimes see that refers to two or more 802.11 technologies.

32. **Answer: C.** IEEE 1394 is the PC equivalent of FireWire. FireWire was originally developed by Apple, and although the two names are often used interchangeably, the PC standard is IEEE 1394. USB is the Universal Serial Bus, a similar standard but with a different architecture and data transfer rate. IEEE 1284 is an older parallel PC standard for printer cables and connections. ISA is the Industry Standard Architecture, a legacy 16-bit adapter card slot.

33. **Answer: C.** DDR3-1600 has a peak transfer rate of 12,800 MB/s. It runs at an I/O bus clock speed of 800 MHz and can send 1600 megatransfers per second (MT/s). It is also known as PC3-12800. To figure out the data transfer rate of DDR3 from the name "DDR3-1600", simply multiply the 1600 by 8 (bytes) and solve for megabytes: 12,800 MB/s. To figure out the data transfer rate of DDR3 by the consumer name "PC3-12800", just look at the number within the name and add "MB/s" to the end. To figure out the data transfer rate when given only the I/O bus clock speed (for example, 800 MHz), multiply the clock speed by 2 and then multiply that number by 8 and solve for megabytes: 800 MHz×2×8 = 12,800 MB/s. $DR \times 8$

DDR3-800 has a peak transfer rate of 6,400 MB/s; it is also known as PC3-6400. There is no DDR2-1600. The fastest DDR2 standard is DDR2-1066, which has a peak transfer rate of 8,533 MB/s. DDR2-800 (like DDR3-800) has a peak transfer rate of 6,400 MB/s. It is commonly sold as PC2-6400.

34. **Answer: B.** The impact printer uses a print head, ribbon, and tractor feed. An example of an impact printer is the dot matrix. Laser printers are much more complex and use more parts. Inkjet printers use a print head but use an ink cartridge instead of a ribbon and don't use a tractor feed. Thermal printers use a print head and a special heating element.

35. **Answer: A.** If the CPU is running beyond the recommended voltage range for extended periods of time, it can be a sign of a failing CPU. It could also be caused by overclocking. Check in the BIOS to see if the CPU is overclocked or not. If the computer won't boot at all, another problem might have occurred, or the CPU might have already failed. Low case temperatures are a good thing (if they aren't below freezing!), and spyware is unrelated to this issue.

36. **Answer: C.** Fiber-optic cable is the only answer listed that is not affected by electromagnetic interference (EMI). This is because it does not use copper wire or electricity, but instead uses glass or plastic fibers and light. Any copper cable will be susceptible to EMI to a certain degree. Regular UTP cable such as Cat 5e or Cat 6 will be very susceptible. Coaxial slightly less, and shielded twisted-pair (STP) even less than that. STP is difficult to install and must be grounded; because of these things, it is found less commonly in networks. To truly protect from EMI, fiber-optic is the best way to go.

37. **Answer: D.** Compressed air is safe. However, you might want to do this outside and vacuum up the left over residue. Never disassemble the power supply. It is called a field replaceable unit (FRU) for good reason. Do *not* stick a vacuum cleaner inside a computer; it could damage the components. Do *not* spray any kind of solutions inside the computer; this will damage the components.

38. **Answer: A.** Setting an admin password in the BIOS prevents a user from rearranging the boot order. The idea behind this is to stop a person from attempting to boot off of an optical disc or USB flash drive. As an administrator, you should change the BIOS boot order to hard drive first. Then apply an administrative (also known as supervisory) password. That'll stop 'em right in their tracks! The admin password does not prevent any of the other listed answers. To prevent a user from reading e-mail, you would have to remove e-mail applications (such as Outlook) and probably take away the browser, too! (Doesn't sound feasible.) To prevent a virus from infecting the MBR, you could turn on boot sector scanning in the BIOS (if the motherboard supports it). To prevent an attacker from opening the case, use a case lock. To find out if someone attempted to get into the computer itself, turn on the chassis intrusion alert in the BIOS.

39. **Answer: D.** The external power supply of the laptop converts AC to DC for the system to use and for charging the battery. It is known as the power adapter, and it needs to run at a very specific voltage. In fact, different make and model power adapters will usually not work with different laptops, even if the voltages are only slightly different. The adapter does not store power; that is the responsibility of the laptop battery. It is also accomplished by a UPS, though you probably wouldn't lug one of those around with your laptop while travelling.

40. **Answer: B.** The plain-old telephone service (POTS) line has two twisted pairs of copper wire, for a total of four wires. It is used for telephone landlines. Unshielded twisted pair (UTP) has four pairs, eight wires total. Fiber-optic cable has a single glass or plastic core that sends light. Coaxial has a single core of copper.

41. **Answer: A.** High-quality dot matrix printheads can come in 9, 18, or 24 pins, with 24 being the highest quality.

42. **Answer: B.** The BTX form factor provides the most room for effective cooling in a computer case. BTX was designed as a replacement for ATX; it was expected to help cool devices that used a lot of power and created a lot of heat. However, CPUs, RAM, and video cards have new designs that allow them to use less voltage and therefore create less heat, making BTX less necessary. Still, BTX combines a large cooling area with smart design and positioning of devices that allows for more cooling than is possible with ATX and its derivatives, or the various ITX versions.

43. **Answer: D.** Some power supplies have selectors for the United States and Europe (115 and 230 volts). However, your co-worker might need an adapter, too; otherwise, the plug may not fit. Newer power supplies might auto-sense the voltage. If the power supply doesn't have one of those red switches, check the documentation to see if it can switch the voltage automatically. Line conditioners simply clean the power for a specific voltage. If your circuit has dirty power (for example, it is fluctuating between 113 and 130 volts), a line conditioner will keep it steady at 120 volts.

44. **Answer: C.** LCD contrast ratio is the brightness of the brightest color (measured as white) compared to the darkest color (measured as black). Static contrast ratio measurements are static; this done as a test with a checkerboard pattern. But there is also the dynamic contrast ratio, a newer technology in LCD displays that adjusts dynamically during darker scenes in an attempt to give better black levels. It usually has a higher ratio, but it should be noted that there isn't any real uniform standard for measuring contrast ratio.

45. **Answer: B.** Most antistatic straps come with a 1 mega ohm resistor, which can protect against surges. However, the best way to avoid a surge is to 1) make sure the computer is unplugged before working on it; and 2) don't touch any components that hold a charge. This means don't open power supplies or CRT monitors, and don't touch capacitors on any circuit boards such as motherboards. And, of course, stay away from any other electrical devices when working on computers.

46. **Answer: D.** High-Definition Multimedia Interface (HDMI), as the word *multimedia* implies, can transmit video and audio signals. VGA, RGB, and DVI are video standards only, with DVI being the newest and most commonly used on PC monitors.

47. **Answer: C.** Whenever you're working in someone's home, make sure that there is an adult available. It is not your responsibility to watch over children, nor should any company agree to have its consultants do this. If the person insists on leaving, and you can pack up your things before he goes, do so, and then call your supervisor to inform her of the event.

48. **Answer: D.** A router can limit network broadcasts through segmenting and programmed routing of data. This is part of a router's job when connecting two or more networks. It is also used with different media. For example, you might have a LAN that uses twisted-pair cable, but the router connects to the Internet via a fiber-optic connection. That one router will have ports for both types of connections. A switch connects multiple computers together on the LAN; it does not limit IP-based network broadcasts. However, the switch does not segment by IP address—it communicates with computers and segments the network, via MAC addresses. Also, the switch will normally use one type of media: twisted pair, connecting to RJ45 ports. However, it is possible that the switch might connect to another switch by way of a specialized fiber-optic connector. A wireless access point (WAP) connects the computers on the wireless LAN (WLAN). It often has only one connection, a single RJ45 port. A hardware-based firewall will usually connect to the network via RJ45; regardless, it will have only one or only a few connections. It doesn't deal with routing, or broadcasts; instead it prevents intrusion to a network.

49. **Answer: D.** The CPU could overheat if thermal compound has not been applied correctly (common) or if it is not seated properly (rare). As part of the boot process, power needs to verify the CPU. If the wrong voltage is running to the CPU, the system won't even boot. If an incorrect CPU has been installed, the system will probably not boot, especially if the BIOS doesn't recognize it. Finally, the CPU doesn't use a driver; instead the BIOS recognizes it (or doesn't, if it needs a BIOS update) and passes that information to the operating system.

50. **Answers: C and D.** Molex power connectors are used by IDE drives. 15-pin power connectors are used for SATA drives. 8-pin power connectors are used by high-end PCI Express video cards. There are several types of 7-pin connectors, such as SATA data, and S-Video, but 7-pin power connections are less common. Berg is the power connector for floppy drives. Okay, we are halfway through the exam. Take a deep breath—then continue on with power! (Pun intended.)

51. **Answer: C.** Of the answers listed, 172.17.58.254 is the only valid IPv4 address for a network host. A host on the network is any computer or network device that uses an IP address to communicate with other computers or devices (hosts). 172.17.58.254 is

a Class B private IP address so it fits the description of a valid IPv4 address for a network host. 127.0.0.1 is the local loopback address. Every computer using TCP/IP gets this address; it is used for testing. It cannot be used to communicate with other hosts on the network. 169.254.0.0/16 means an IP address of 169.254.0.0 with a default subnet mask of 255.255.0.0, indicating the network number is 169.254. It is not a valid *host* IP address because it ends in 0.0. The first IP address of a network is always reserved for the network number; it can not be used by a host. Otherwise, if the address was, say, 169.254.0.1, the address would work, but because it is an APIPA address, it would be able to communicate only with other systems using APIPA addresses. 255.10.15.7 is not valid. That address is within the Class E reserved range. Normal host IP addresses' first octet will either be between 1 and 126, or 128 and 223, but not between 224 and 255.

52. **Answer: B.** When data is flowing through the activity light, it should blink or flash rapidly, in an erratic fashion. You see solid green (1000 Mbps or 100 Mbps) or yellow (10 Mbps) on the link light (if there is a separate link light). If it is unlit, the cable is not connected properly or the device is malfunctioning.

53. **Answer: C.** Dynamic Random Access Memory (DRAM) is the modules (or sticks) of memory that you can install into a motherboard. SDRAM, DDR, DDR2, and DDR3 are all examples of DRAM. The complementary metal-oxide semiconductor (CMOS) is a chip that is soldered onto the motherboard that works in conjunction with the Basic Input/Output System, another chip soldered on to the motherboard. Static RAM (SRAM) is memory that is nonvolatile (as opposed to DRAM); it is also soldered to the circuit board. Read-Only Memory (ROM) is usually not serviceable. The BIOS resides on a ROM chip, more specifically an electrically erasable programmable ROM (EEPROM) chip.

54. **Answer: C.** Turning the printer off might not be enough. It might be seriously malfunctioning, so pull the plug. Dialing 911 is not necessary unless a fire has started. Wait at least 15 minutes before opening the printer to see what caused the smoke. Printer power supplies can fail just like a PC's power supply can. In fact, a laser printer power supply does more work because it needs to convert for high voltages in the 600 V range. If you have a maintenance contract with a printer company, and the printer is under warranty or contained in the service contract, you could call the maintenance company to fix the problem. Be ready to give a detailed account of exactly what happened. You could tell the printer that it is bad to smoke, but that would be belligerent and would probably show that you have been working too hard.

55. **Answer: D.** Of the listed answers, 802.11n has the fastest data transfer rate at a maximum of 600 Mbps. However, to achieve this, you need to have the right wireless access point, configured properly, with client computers that are also compatible with the 802.11n standard. 802.11a and g have a maximum DTR of 54 Mbps. 802.11b has a maximum of 11 Mbps.

56. **Answer: D.** Make sure that the customer has a path toward a solution before dismissing the issue. Do *not* try to fix the problem if the scope of work is outside your knowledge. Most PC technicians will not work on domain controllers because they are advanced Microsoft servers that are used in client/server networks.

57. **Answer: C.** 172.31.1.1 is the only address listed that is private. It is within the Class B range of private addresses: 172.16.1.1–172.31.255.255. 11.58.254.169 is not private because it is on the Class A 11 network. The Class A private range is within the 10.0.0.0 network. 169.255.10.41 is not private either. Microsoft's APIPA, however, uses the 169.*254*.0.0 network which is private. 192.169.0.1 is public because of the second octet: 169. The Class C private range is 192.168.0.0–192.168.255.255.

58. **Answer: C.** Always have a positive outlook. The customer will have fewer concerns, and you will be more relaxed. If you appear to be wavering when problems occur, the customer will have less confidence in your skills (as will you). When you need to make a technical decision, be certain and decisive and implement the solution immediately.

59. **Answer: B.** The IPv6 loopback address used for testing is ::1. This will determine if IPv6 is working correctly on the network card but will not generate network traffic. It exists on every computer that runs IPv6. 127.0.0.1 is the IPv4 loopback address. 192.168.0.0 is simply a private IP network number. FE80::/10 is the range of auto-assigned addresses in IPv6.

60. **Answer: C.** The only statement that is correct concerning IPv6 is that it uses 128-bit addressing. This is compared to IPv4, which uses 32-bit addresses. IPv6 and IPv4 can co-habit a computer with no problems. IPv6 is not necessarily supported by all routers. Some routers still only support IPv4. IPv6 is a logical concept. The physical cable that connects to the computer has no bearing over which IP version is used.

61. **Answer: B.** 60° Celsius is a typical operating temperature for CPUs such as the Core i5 or Phenom II. The operating range may be above or below that. However, 72° Celsius becomes less typical. 60° Fahrenheit is equal to 15.5° Celsius. A processor will not run that cold (but it would be pretty efficient if it did!). 72° Fahrenheit is excellent room temperature and is what you should set the room temperature for computers to run at their best.

62. **Answer: A.** The impact printer technology is what you want. This strikes the ribbon, and consequently the paper with a printhead. The physical hammering action causes the carbon backing to take effect and apply text to the next layer of paper. Multipart forms such as these are commonly used for receipts. Laser printers can print to special multipart forms, but not ones with carbon backing.

63. **Answer: B.** Dual channel memory combines two sticks of RAM into a bank that is 128-bit. Single channel memory is 64-bit. 256-bit is a common bit length used by the Advanced Encryption Standard (AES). 448-bit memory bus width is used by some video cards. These types of video cards have much faster RAM access than motherboards do.

64. **Answer: C.** A hub broadcasts data to all network devices connected to it. Because of this inefficient method, switches are preferred. Switches send information to specific network devices based on their MAC addresses. A firewall will inspect traffic and allow or deny it access to the network. Intrusion detection systems (IDSs) and intrusion prevention systems (IPSs) can also do this, but in a more intelligent manner. A router will determine the best route for data.

65. **Answers: A and C.** A receptacle tester and multimeter can be used (with caution) to test an AC outlet. A power supply (PSU) tester is used to test the main P1 power connection (and possibly other connections) of a power supply. There are various loopback plugs for testing ports on the back of a PC (for example, the RJ45 loopback plug), but these have nothing to do with testing an AC outlet.

66. **Answer: D.** IEEE 1394b is capable of 800 Mbps. Newer versions of IEEE 1394b can support 3,200 Mbps, but an IEEE 1394b port on a computer will often allow only a maximum of 800 Mbps. 12 Mbps is the data transfer rate of USB 1.1 Full Speed. 400 Mbps is the speed of IEEE 1394a. 480 Mbps is the speed of USB 2.0. 5 Gbps is the speed of USB 3.0.

67. **Answer: D.** You cannot install drivers to the BIOS. Drivers are software that allows the operating system to communicate with hardware; they can be configured in the Device Manager in Windows. The rest of the answers can be configured in the BIOS. The boot sequence (also known as boot priority or boot order) allows you to select which device will be booted off of first (hard drive is the most secure). Temperature thresholds allow you to set alerts and possibly shut down the system if the CPU runs too hot. Overclocking is when the CPU's voltage is raised and the speed is increased. Overclocking is not recommended, but if you do configure it, you should set temperature thresholds. Intrusion detection can be enabled and will log if a person opened the computer case.

68. **Answer: A.** POP3 is the protocol used by e-mail clients to receive e-mail. It makes use of Port 110. SMTP is used by e-mail clients to send e-mail. It uses port 25.

69. **Answers: C and D.** The power cord carries 120 volts at 15 amps or 20 amps, and the telephone cord carries 80 volts when it rings. It is important to disconnect these before servicing a computer. Now, if you were opening the computer, you would disconnect everything. However, you might be fixing something that doesn't require you to open the computer—for example, connecting a network cable. Remember to always disconnect any power, data, or telecommunications cables before working on the system.

70. **Answer: A.** The northbridge takes care of the connections between the CPU and the PCI Express (PCIe) x16 expansion slot. On older Intel systems and AMD systems, the northbridge is the first of a pair of chips in the chipset (the other is the southbridge). On newer Intel systems, the northbridge functionality is combined with the CPU.

71. **Answer: D.** Recycle toner cartridges according to your company's policies and procedures, or according to municipality rules and regulations. Do not throw away or incinerate toner cartridges. Although it is possible to refill toner cartridges, it is not the recommended way to handle an empty cartridge because it is messy and time-consuming. Most companies simply purchase new toner cartridges.

72. **Answer: D.** To connect one computer to another directly by way of network adapter cards, use a crossover cable. That cable is designed to connect *like* devices. It is wired as 568B on one end and 568A on the other. Those standards are ratified by the Telecommunications Industries Association/Electronics Industries Association (TIA/EIA). A regular (and more common) Cat 5e patch cable is known as a straight-through cable. It is used to connect *unlike* devices, such as a computer to a switch. Normally this is wired with the 568B standard on each end. A parallel cable might be used to connect an older printer to a computer or an external hard drive to a SCSI

card. IEEE 1394 cables are not used to connect computers to each other; they are used to connect external hard drives to IEEE 1394 or FireWire ports.

73. **Answer: A.** Stay calm and do the job as efficiently as possible. There isn't much you can do when a customer is upset except fix the problem! I'd be interested to see what would happen if a person asked the owner of the server out for a cup of coffee, but I'm pretty sure the reaction would be negative. You don't want to avoid the customer, but you don't have to engage in anything except fixing the problem. The customer should be referred to your supervisor only if the person gets in the way of you doing your work.

74. **Answer: B.** The laser printer uses toner. Impact printers use ribbon, inkjet printers use ink cartridges, and thermal printers use specially coated paper.

75. **Answer: B.** There isn't much you can do in a situation like this. The best thing is to ignore it and act as if it never happened. Technicians must be security-minded. In addition, the purported list might be real, but it might not be. It isn't your call to make. However, before working at a *customer* site, you should ask that all confidential materials be removed before you begin work.

76. **Answer: A.** Network installations require that the network card be configured for Preboot Execution Environment (PXE). This allows the network card to boot off of the network, locate a network installation server, and request that the installation begin. This configuration might be done in the BIOS of the computer (if the network adapter is integrated to the motherboard), within a special program in Windows, or one that boots from CD (if the network adapter is an adapter card). Peripheral Component Interconnect (PCI) is an expansion bus that accepts network adapter cards, sound cards, and so on. PCL stands for Printer Command Language, developed by HP so a computer can properly communicate with dot matrix or thermal printers. PnP stands for Plug 'n Play, a Windows technology that allows devices to be located and installed automatically.

77. **Answer: C.** Any card named with a number followed by an *x* is most likely an AGP card, (2x, 4x, 8x, 16x). AGP is the Accelerated Graphics Port, usually a brown slot on the motherboard. It is faster than PCI but slower than PCIe (PCI Express) video cards. PCIe cards place the *x* before the number (for example, x16—pronounced "by 16"). AMR stands for Audio-Modem Riser, a small expansion slot developed by Intel to be used with sound cards and modems.

78. **Answer: B.** USB is the newest type of mouse connection. It replaces PS/2 as today's standard. Serial mice were used in the early 1990s, and parallel was never really used for mice at all; it was used for printers and SCSI connections.

79. **Answers: A, B, and D.** To reduce the chance of electrostatic discharge (ESD), use an antistatic wrist strap and mat. Also, consider raising the humidity. The more humidity there is, the less friction, and ultimately, less ESD. Raising the temperature will have no effect. Lowering the humidity increases the chances of ESD. Working in a carpeted area will also increase the chance of ESD; try to work in a non-carpeted area. You should also touch the chassis of the computer before handling any components. In addition, place components in antistatic bags when they are not in use.

80. **Answer: A.** A dual-core processor has two cores, with separate caches, on the same physical chip. A processor with several cores would be known as multi-core (quad-core or hex-core). Dual-core processors are generally more efficient than older single-core processors and often use less voltage. A dual-core processor does not require more RAM than a single-core, but it usually requires more cache memory. Every core of a multi-core CPU has its own L1 and L2 cache.

81. **Answer: A.** The CPU is the least likely to be replaced. You would probably need to replace other equipment, too, in this case. Just like PCs, though, the CPU should rarely fail. However, you might upgrade, replace, or add to RAM. PC Cards (PCMCIA) are commonly implemented as network adapters, modems, and more. It is common to install and remove PC Cards. Laptop keyboards fall victim to coffee, overuse, and other damage over time and sometimes need to be replaced.

82. **Answers: C and D.** 1000 Mbps is 1000 megabits per second, otherwise notated as 1,000,000,000 bits per second, or 1 gigabit per second.

83. **Answer: A.** Cable Internet is a broadband connection. It uses multiple "channels" to transmit and receive information. All the rest of the examples are technologies that are, or use, a baseband connection (one channel on the media). Ethernet (which was originally ratified by the IEEE as the 802.3 standard) is a shared technology by default; only one computer can communicate on the network at any given time. However, Ethernet switching alleviates this by segmenting computers and redirecting information to other systems via MAC address. Client/Server is less a networking technology and more of a way that computers communicate; it has a centralized server that controls the network.

84. **Answer: B.** Single-mode fiber-optic cable can send data farther than any of the other answers—up to hundreds of kilometers. Multi-mode fiber-optic cable can send data about 600 meters. STP is a type of twisted pair; all twisted pair is limited to 100 meters or 328 feet. Coaxial cable is limited to 200 or 500 meters, depending on the type.

85. **Answer: C.** You should install a USB add-on card. This will give you more ports than the computer already has for use with peripherals. Another option would be to purchase a USB hub. Modems, network adapters, and TV tuner cards all have their own purpose and do not allow additional peripherals.

86. **Answer: D.** 7200 RPM is a typical speed of a hard drive—rotational speed, that is. Other common rotational speeds include 5400 RPM; 10,000 RPM; and 15,000 RPM. 1000 Mbps is a common network data transfer rate. SATA hard drives will commonly have a DTR of 3 Gb/s (300 MB/s) or 6 Gb/s (600 MB/s). 3.1 GHz is a common CPU frequency. 8 GB might be the amount of RAM you install in a computer or the size of a USB flash drive.

87. **Answer: C.** If you are not sure about what to clean a screen with, use water. Water will most likely not damage the screen. However, if the user manual for the monitor calls for it, you might see that you can use a half-and-half mixture of water and isopropyl alcohol. Do not use detergents on a screen; they are okay for the outside of a computer case but not the display. And boric acid would just be plain silly (and dangerous).

88. **Answer: A.** A switch interconnects devices on the same network so that they can communicate, whereas a router interconnects one or more networks. Remember that the switch is in charge of connecting devices on the LAN. But the router is in charge of connecting the LAN to another LAN, to the Internet, or to both. Multifunction network devices make matters confusing; they combine the functionality of a switch, a router, a wireless access point, and a firewall. Physically, the four-port section of the device is the switch portion and the single port that leads to the Internet is the router portion.

89. **Answers: A and D.** Internal SATA drives connect to the motherboard (or SATA card) via a 7-pin data cable and a 15-pin power cable. PATA (IDE) hard drives use a 40-pin data cable and 4-pin (Molex) power cable. Who is Ray? He's just another fictitious character in this book. You'll hear more about him later.

90. **Answer: D.** In a large corporation (or enterprise environment), tape backup such as the Digital Linear Tape (DLT) is the best media for backing up. DLTs and Super DLTs (SDLT) can have a capacity as high as 800 GB, allowing for a huge amount of backup as compared to DVD and dual-layer DVD (4.7–17 GB) and external USB hard drives (up to 64 GB or so, though this number will undoubtedly increase as time goes on).

91. **Answer: C.** The MPEG Audio Layer III (.MP3) works best when dealing with multiple platforms. Advanced Audio Codec (.AAC) is used more commonly on Apple computers and devices and gaming consoles. Windows Media Audio (.WMA) is a Microsoft format developed especially for the Windows Media Player. .MOV is a QuickTime file format meant to be used with movies and other video.

92. **Answer: D.** Smartphones typically use Secure Digital (SD) cards—more to the point, microSD cards. SSD stands for solid-state drive. This technology is implemented as flash-based hard drives or as adapter cards with DDR memory and a battery. CompactFlash (CF) cards are a bit bulkier and might be used in conjunction with PCs, laptops, and handheld computers. USB flash drives won't fit inside a typical smartphone and so are relegated to hanging on people's key chains and acting as mobile transporters of data.

93. **Answer: C.** In this scenario, the organization probably has thin-client computers for its users. These have operating systems that are embedded in flash memory, and the rest of the information they require comes from a server. Thin clients normally have no hard drive; this is why they are referred to as *diskless* workstations. Virtualization workstations definitely need a hard drive and require lots of other resources; they are not as dependent on servers. Client/server is a type of networking organizational technique. However, thin clients will often log in to a server. Thick clients are for the most part PCs, the typical desktop computer.

94. **Answers: A and B.** Know the six main steps of laser printing: Cleaning, charging, writing (also known as exposing), developing, transferring, and fusing. In the charging step, the drum is conditioned/charged by the primary corona wire (negatively charging it) and prepared for writing. In the transferring step, the paper is positively charged by the transfer corona wire, preparing it to accept the toner from the drum.

95. **Answer: A.** The printer has RAM, which acts as a buffer if you or others send multiple documents to it. It prints them one at a time according to which job entered the queue first. Don't confuse the printer's buffer with the spooler that exists on the hard drive of

the computer that controls the printer. The print driver is the software you install so , that Windows can "talk" to the printer properly; it needs to be the *exact* driver. A printer pool is a group of printers (often identical) that share the duties of printing.

96. Answer: B. Make the customer truly feel comfortable by sitting down next to her and taking the time to explain the technical concept from a simple and concise point of view. The less jargon, the better. Recommending a training class is tantamount to dismissing the customer off-hand. Telling the customer to read the manual is just downright rude. I know, I say this often to you the reader—however, you are a tech, so reading the manual is what you do. The customer is not supposed to be super-technically oriented. The acronym RTM should be kept within technical circles!

97. Answer: A. Line filters are required for DSL modems to share phone lines with a phone. A line filter shields the phone line from digital noise and interference caused by telephone devices and makes DSL communications possible. If DSL is installed in a SOHO (small office/home office), devices such as telephones, fax machines, answering machines, dial-up modems, and security alarms should have line filters. But don't install one where the DSL modem is located. A heat sink is used to disperse heat away from a CPU. A router allows access to another network or the Internet. A coaxial splitter is used to split the signal coming from a cable TV company, so that multiple TVs can be used at the same time.

98. Answer: D. Hard drives run pretty hot; keeping an area of airflow around the drive can help to keep it cool. The key is to make sure the PC has proper airflow. This can be done by adding fans or using a liquid cooling system. It isn't quite possible to add cache to a hard drive; the cache on most hard drives is hardwired, and there are no locations to add more. Increasing RAM does not necessarily increase the pagefile, and regardless, this won't prevent problems with a hard drive over the short term, but it can make the hard drive work more efficiently. A second hard drive should be treated as a completely separate device. However, installing the OS to one drive and storing data on the second drive can go a long way to making both drives last longer.

99. Answer: A. Power surges can cause the inverter to short out, after which the cold-cathode fluorescent lamps (CCFL) cannot get any power. You need to open the LCD panel to replace the inverter in this case.

100. Answer: B. When testing the main 24-pin ATX power connector that leads from the power supply to the motherboard, use a multimeter. It can test each individual wire's voltage. Better yet, use a power supply unit (PSU) tester. This tests them all in one shot. A Torx wrench is used to open computers and laptops that have special Torx screws; T-10 is a common size. A receptacle tester is used to test an AC outlet, although multimeters can be used for that as well. A tone and probe kit is used to test telephone and network connections for continuity. However, it can test only one pair of the wires in the cable. For better results when testing network cables, use a proper network cable testing kit. Testing tools are a key ingredient in a computer technician's toolkit.

CHAPTER FOUR

220-801 Practice Exam C

This time, let's turn up the gas a little further. I'll be increasing the level of difficulty once more. This third 220-801 exam could be considered an advanced practice test. This exam is also freestyle. You can expect questions from any of the domains, in any order.

This is where you prove your stuff. If you can score 90% or higher on this practice test—on the first time through—then you should be just about ready for the real exam. Still, you should thoroughly understand all of the concepts before you register for the real test. Even if you score well, read through the explanations carefully.

If you didn't already, I suggest taking a break between exams. If you just completed the first exam, give yourself a half-hour or so before you begin this one. Don't forget, if you did not score 90% or higher on the first two 220-801 practice exams, do not take this one yet. Go back and study, and then retake those exams until you pass with 90% or higher. Then come back to this exam.

Write down your answers and check them against the answer key that immediately follows the exam. After the answer key you will find the explanations for all of the answers. Good luck!

_44 56%_

Practice Questions

1. Your co-worker Patrick has a Core i5 3.1 GHz CPU. Pat wants you to tell him what the bus speed is and what the maximum multiplier is. What do you tell him?

Quick Answer: **102**
Detailed Answer: **104**

- ○ **A.** 3.1 GHz and 31
- ○ **B.** 3.1 GHz and 100
- ○ **C.** 100 and 31
- ○ **D.** 200 and 31

2. Which of the following expansion busses can transmit 1 GB/s per lane?

Quick Answer: **102**
Detailed Answer: **104**

- ○ **A.** PCI
- ○ **B.** AGP
- ○ **C.** USB 3.0
- ○ **D.** PCIe

3. A user complains that his network interface card (NIC) is not functioning and has no link lights. The weather has been changing drastically over the past few days, and humidity and temperature have been rising and falling every day. What could be the direct cause of this problem? (Select the best answer.)

Quick Answer: **102**
Detailed Answer: **104**

- ○ **A.** Thermal expansion and contraction
- ○ **B.** Thermal sublimation
- ○ **C.** Chip creep
- ○ **D.** POST errors

4. A user reports that the battery in his Windows 7 laptop is often low on power. Which of the following should you recommend to help the user conserve laptop battery power?

Quick Answer: **102**
Detailed Answer: **104**

- ○ **A.** Configure the laptop power options to restore power usage when the laptop is unattended
- ○ **B.** Configure the laptop power option to power saver plan
- ○ **C.** Have the user remove the battery and run the notebook using the electrical cord only
- ○ **D.** Have the user run the laptop using the battery until all the power is depleted and then recharge the battery

5. What is the most important consideration when installing Windows 7 Ultimate 64-bit?

Quick Answer: **102**
Detailed Answer: **105**

- ○ **A.** Memory type
- ○ **B.** Processor speed
- ○ **C.** Memory speed
- ○ **D.** Processor type

6. A help desk phone support technician is finding it difficult to understand the customer due to a heavy accent. Which action should the technician take next to help the customer resolve the problem?

Quick Answer: **102**
Detailed Answer: **105**

- ○ **A.** Repeat the problem back to the customer
- ○ **B.** Have the customer call back at a later time
- ○ **C.** Ask the customer to not speak with an accent
- ○ **D.** Tell the customer that her accent is preventing the problem from being solved

7. Which of the following is indicated by repetitive flashing lights on the keyboard during POST?

Quick Answer: **102**
Detailed Answer: **105**

- ○ **A.** A software error
- ○ **B.** A hardware error
- ○ **C.** A password is required
- ○ **D.** An external peripheral error

8. Which network type enables high-speed data communication and is the most difficult to eavesdrop on?

Quick Answer: **102**
Detailed Answer: **105**

- ○ **A.** Satellite
- ○ **B.** DSL
- ○ **C.** Fiber optic
- ○ **D.** Cable

9. Which of the following is a difference between a cellular WAN card and a WLAN card?

Quick Answer: **102**
Detailed Answer: **105**

- ○ **A.** A cellular WAN card requires a subscription to a cellular provider, while a WLAN card can work without provider payment.
- ○ **B.** A cellular WAN card will work on most public wireless access points, while a WLAN card is more proprietary.

    ○ **C.** A WLAN card generally has a range of 6 miles, while a cellular WAN card is limited in range to 1,200 feet.

    ○ **D.** A WLAN card is usually an external card, while a cellular WAN card is usually an internal card.

10. Which of the following defines the protocols associated with the following TCP or UDP port numbers, in order?

21, 22, 25, 53, 443, 3389.

    ○ **A.** FTP, Telnet, SMTP, DNS, HTTP, RDP

    ○ **B.** FTP, SSH, SMTP, DNS, HTTP, RDP

    ○ **C.** FTP, SSH, SMTP, POP3, HTTPS, RDP

    ○ **D.** FTP, SSH, SMTP, DNS, HTTPS, RDP

Quick Answer: **102**
Detailed Answer: **106**

11. Which of the following is the most appropriate question to ask a customer first when attempting to troubleshoot an input device issue over the phone?

    ○ **A.** Can you describe the steps you have taken?

    ○ **B.** Have you verified that all USB plugs are secure?

    ○ **C.** Have you tried turning it off and on again?

    ○ **D.** Are you sure that the device is plugged in?

Quick Answer: **102**
Detailed Answer: **106**

12. Which type of RAM stick is RIMM 6400?

    ○ **A.** DDR

    ○ **B.** EEPROM

    ○ **C.** SDRAM

    ○ **D.** RAMBUS

    ○ **E.** PC2-6400

Quick Answer: **102**
Detailed Answer: **106**

13. You are tasked with installing a new SATA revision 3.0 hard drive controller so that the computer can access hard drives at 6 Gb/s. Which step list will most likely prevent errors?

    ○ **A.**

       1. Install the card.

       2. Update the BIOS.

       3. Upgrade the card's firmware.

       4. Install the driver.

       5. Apply system updates.

Quick Answer: **102**
Detailed Answer: **106**

○ **B.**

   1. Apply system updates.

   2. Update the BIOS.

   3. Install the card.

   4. Install the driver.

   5. Upgrade the card's firmware.

○ **C.**

   1. Update the BIOS.

   2. Install the driver.

   3. Install the card.

   4. Upgrade the firmware.

   5. Apply system updates.

○ **D.**

   1. Apply system updates.

   2. Install the driver.

   3. Install the card.

   4. Upgrade the firmware.

   5. Update the BIOS.

14. A new video card you are installing requires a 600 W power supply. The power supply should have how many pins on the main cable?

   ○ **A.** 6 pins

   ○ **B.** 8 pins

   ○ **C.** 20 pins

   ○ **D.** 24 pins

   ○ **E.** 40 pins

Quick Answer: **102**
Detailed Answer: **106**

15. Russ's computer has a 60 GB IDE hard drive that contains his operating system. He wants to add a second IDE hard drive to his computer. How should he configure the two drives?

   ○ **A.** Russ should configure the new drive as master and set the old drive as slave.

   ○ **B.** Russ should configure both drives as slaves.

   ○ **C.** Russ should configure both drives as master.

   ○ **D.** Russ should configure the new drive as slave and the old drive as master.

Quick Answer: **102**
Detailed Answer: **106**

16. Examine the following illustration. Then answer the question that follows.

Quick Answer: **102**
Detailed Answer: **107**

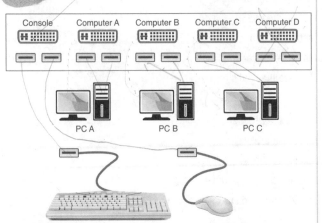

What is the minimum number of USB cables required to set up the three computers, including the keyboard and mouse?

- ○ **A.** 2
- ○ **B.** 6
- ○ **C.** 8
- ○ **D.** 10

17. Which of the following data rates are supported by PC3-10600 memory?

Quick Answer: **102**
Detailed Answer: **107**

- ○ **A.** 1333 MT/s and 1066 MT/s
- ○ **B.** 1066 MT/s and 800 MT/s
- ○ **C.** 1600 MT/s and 1333 MT/s
- ○ **D.** 1600 MT/s and 800 MT/s

18. Which of the following properties of a heat sink has the greatest effect on heat dissipation?

Quick Answer: **102**
Detailed Answer: **107**

- ○ **A.** Connection type
- ○ **B.** Shape
- ○ **C.** Surface area
- ○ **D.** Proximity to the power supply

19. You are working just outside a server room that is being built, and you hear a loud popping sound from inside. As you enter the server room, you notice an electrician lying on the floor with an electrical cord in his hand. What should you do first?

Quick Answer: **102**
Detailed Answer: **107**

○ **A.** Call 911.

○ **B.** Call the building supervisor.

○ **C.** Pull the electrician away from the cord.

○ **D.** Turn off the electrical power at the source.

20. You have been asked to load a copy of the company's purchased software on a personal computer. What should you do first?

Quick Answer: **102**
Detailed Answer: **107**

○ **A.** Verify that the install is allowed under the company's licensing agreements.

○ **B.** Notify the company's owner of the breach.

○ **C.** Advise the individual that downloading unlicensed software is illegal.

○ **D.** Leave the premises and call local law enforcement.

21. After removing malware/spyware from a customer's PC for the third time, what should you do?

Quick Answer: **102**
Detailed Answer: **107**

○ **A.** Tell him you can't fix the system again.

○ **B.** Do nothing; the customer pays every time.

○ **C.** Show him how to avoid the problem.

○ **D.** Change his user permissions.

22. A PC has the memory configuration listed below. Assuming RAM is the same price per MB, which of the following answers would be the least expensive when upgrading the PC to 12 GB of RAM?

Quick Answer: **102**
Detailed Answer: **107**

Memory Slots:	2
DRAM Frequency:	667 MHz

Slot 1

Capacity:	4096 MB
Memory Type:	DDR3 (PC3-10600)
Speed:	667 MHz (DDR3-1333)

Slot 2

Capacity:	2048 MB
Memory Type:	DDR3 (PC3-10600)
Speed:	667 MHz (DDR3-1333)

○ **A.** A single 6 GB DDR3 PC3-12800 memory module

○ **B.** A single 8 GB DDR3 PC3-12800 memory module

○ **C.** A single 10 GB DDR3 PC3-10600 memory module

○ **D.** Two 6 GB DDR3 PC3-10700 memory modules

23. A user calls and complains that he cannot get onto the Internet, although he could just minutes before. What should you say to the user?

    ○ **A.** What is your IP address?

    ○ **B.** Wait 10 minutes, and then try it again.

    ○ **C.** Do you remember the last thing that you did?

    ○ **D.** Let me get my supervisor.

Quick Answer: **102**
Detailed Answer: **108**

24. Which of the following multimeter settings should be used only when there is no electrical flow through the part being tested? (Select the two best answers.)

    ○ **A.** Continuity

    ○ **B.** Wattage

    ○ **C.** Voltage

    ○ **D.** Amps

    ○ **E.** Resistance

Quick Answer: **102**
Detailed Answer: **108**

25. You need to set up a server system that will run in a VM. It will have the bulk of the network computers' resources and will supply much of the resources necessary to the client computers that will connect to it. You are also required to set up the client computers. What two types of systems (server and client) will you be implementing?

    ○ **A.** CAD/CAM workstation and PCs

    ○ **B.** Virtualization workstation and thin clients

    ○ **C.** Home server PC and thick clients

    ○ **D.** AV workstation and laptops

Quick Answer: **102**
Detailed Answer: **108**

26. Your boss can receive e-mail but can't seem to send e-mail with the installed e-mail client software. Which protocol is not configured properly?

    ○ **A.** SMTP

    ○ **B.** POP3

    ○ **C.** FTP

    ○ **D.** HTTP

Quick Answer: **102**
Detailed Answer: **108**

27. A customer's laptop LCD needs replacement. Which tool should you use to open the case?

   - ○ **A.** Pliers
   - ○ **B.** Plastic tweezers
   - ○ **C.** Flathead screwdriver
   - ○ **D.** Plastic shim

Quick Answer: **102**
Detailed Answer: **108**

28. A customer is having a hard time describing a computer problem. You are not sure what the problem is or where it is occurring. What should you do?

   - ○ **A.** Offer various different repair options
   - ○ **B.** Use computer jargon to help relax the customer
   - ○ **C.** Ask the customer to slowly repeat what the problem is
   - ○ **D.** Tell the customer that you have to leave and that the problem will be fixed soon

Quick Answer: **102**
Detailed Answer: **108**

29. Which component requires a "burn-in" period?

   - ○ **A.** CPU
   - ○ **B.** Hard drive
   - ○ **C.** Power supply
   - ○ **D.** Motherboard

Quick Answer: **102**
Detailed Answer: **109**

30. When a PC is first booted, which of the following tests the processor, RAM, video card, disk controllers, disk drives, and keyboard?

   - ○ **A.** CMOS chip
   - ○ **B.** BIOS setup
   - ○ **C.** POST
   - ○ **D.** Bootstrap loader

Quick Answer: **102**
Detailed Answer: **109**

31. What controls the data transfer between the CPU, RAM, and PCIe devices on motherboards that support Intel Core 2 CPUs?

   - ○ **A.** ICH
   - ○ **B.** MCH
   - ○ **C.** FSB
   - ○ **D.** DMI

Quick Answer: **102**
Detailed Answer: **109**

32. It seems someone has spilled a large amount of coffee in the break room and has not cleaned it up. It is seeping into the server room next door. What should you do first?

   - ○ **A.** Fill out an accident report
   - ○ **B.** Notify the network administrator
   - ○ **C.** Start mopping up the mess
   - ○ **D.** Reference the MSDS

Quick Answer: **102**
Detailed Answer: **109**

33. A laser printer's primary corona wire does which of the following?

   - ○ **A.** Puts a uniform negative charge on the drum
   - ○ **B.** Puts a uniform positive charge on the drum
   - ○ **C.** Puts the toner on the drum
   - ○ **D.** Removes static electricity

Quick Answer: **102**
Detailed Answer: **109**

34. What device on the motherboard retains variable information such as the time and date?

   - ○ **A.** BIOS
   - ○ **B.** CMOS
   - ○ **C.** CR2032
   - ○ **D.** Setup

Quick Answer: **102**
Detailed Answer: **109**

35. Which of the following is the fastest?

   - ○ **A.** Bus speed
   - ○ **B.** External clock speed
   - ○ **C.** Internal clock speed
   - ○ **D.** Expansion bus speed

Quick Answer: **102**
Detailed Answer: **110**

36. Which of the following can be used to verify settings between the computer and a connected modem?

   - ○ **A.** AT&V
   - ○ **B.** IRQ
   - ○ **C.** MBR
   - ○ **D.** QPI

Quick Answer: **102**
Detailed Answer: **110**

37. Tim wants to use a wireless mouse with short-range communications. Which of the following is the best?

   - ○ **A.** Cellular
   - ○ **B.** Bluetooth
   - ○ **C.** USB
   - ○ **D.** Ethernet

Quick Answer: **102**
Detailed Answer: **110**

38. Which of the following cables connects the parallel port of the computer to the printer?

    ○ **A.** IEEE 802.3

    ○ **B.** IEEE 1394

    ○ **C.** IEEE 1284

    ○ **D.** IEEE 802.11

Quick Answer: **102**
Detailed Answer: **110**

39. What tool is used to test all computer hardware prior to installing an operating system?

    ○ **A.** Another computer system

    ○ **B.** BIOS setting

    ○ **C.** Windows

    ○ **D.** POST card

Quick Answer: **102**
Detailed Answer: **110**

40. When explaining a technical concept to a customer, which of the following is not permissible?

    ○ **A.** Using analogies

    ○ **B.** Using visual aides

    ○ **C.** Using jargon

    ○ **D.** Limiting the amount of information to what is necessary for the user to know

Quick Answer: **102**
Detailed Answer: **110**

41. What tool would you use to test the voltage of a power supply? (Select the two best answers.)

    ○ **A.** Multimeter

    ○ **B.** Loopback plug

    ○ **C.** Cable tester

    ○ **D.** Antistatic mat

    ○ **E.** PSU tester

Quick Answer: **102**
Detailed Answer: **110**

42. One of your customers is running Windows 7 on a PC that has a 2 GHz CPU, 2 GB RAM, and a 64 MB video card. The customer tells you that performance is slow when Aero is enabled. How can you increase performance on the computer?

    ○ **A.** Increase system RAM

    ○ **B.** Upgrade the video card

    ○ **C.** Increase the hard drive capacity

    ○ **D.** Upgrade the CPU

Quick Answer: **102**
Detailed Answer: **111**

43. Why do some computers share RAM with the video card?

- ○ **A.** To make the computer faster
- ○ **B.** To make the computer run more quietly
- ○ **C.** To lower cost
- ○ **D.** To reduce temperature

44. Which socket replaces the Intel 1156 socket?

- ○ **A.** 775
- ○ **B.** 940
- ○ **C.** 1155
- ○ **D.** 1366

45. What is the data transfer rate of DMI version 2.0?

- ○ **A.** 1000 Mbps
- ○ **B.** 20 Gb/s
- ○ **C.** 3.0 Gb/s
- ○ **D.** 5 Gbps

46. You are building an HTPC. Which form factor and video output should you select?

- ○ **A.** ATX and DVI
- ○ **B.** Mobile-ITX and HDMI
- ○ **C.** Pico-ITX and RG-6
- ○ **D.** microATX and HDMI

47. Which of the following would you configure in the BIOS? (Select the four best answers.)

- ○ **A.** Time and Date
- ○ **B.** The registry
- ○ **C.** Boot sequence
- ○ **D.** Passwords
- ○ **E.** USB drivers
- ○ **F.** WOL

48. You have selected a motherboard for your new audio workstation. You have opened the computer case and are ready to install. What are the first and last things you should do? (Select the two best answers.)

   ○ **A.** Select a motherboard

   ○ **B.** Install the CPU

   ○ **C.** Test the motherboard

   ○ **D.** Put on an antistatic strap

   ○ **E.** Connect the main power cable

49. You want to test whether IPv4 *and* IPv6 are working properly on a computer. Which commands should you issue?

   ○ **A.** `ipconfig ::1` and `ping ::1`

   ○ **B.** `Ping 127.0.0.0` and `Ping :1`

   ○ **C.** `Ping 127.0.0.1` and `Ping ::1`

   ○ **D.** `ipconfig 127.0.0.1` and `Ping 127::1`

Quick Answer: **102**
Detailed Answer: **112**

50. Jim has a Core 2 Quad CPU in his desktop computer. If the base clock of his motherboard is 333MHz, what would the front side bus (FSB) be?

   ○ **A.** 1 GHz

   ○ **B.** 333 MHz

   ○ **C.** 666 MHz

   ○ **D.** 1333 MHz

Quick Answer: **102**
Detailed Answer: **112**

51. Which of the following measurements is the typical latency of a SATA hard drive?

   ○ **A.** 300 MB/s

   ○ **B.** 7200 RPM

   ○ **C.** 16 MB

   ○ **D.** 4.2 ms

Quick Answer: **102**
Detailed Answer: **112**

52. The marketing printer has been used for 4 years. What should you do for the printer?

   ○ **A.** Clean the printer

   ○ **B.** Install a maintenance kit

   ○ **C.** Clear the counter

   ○ **D.** Print a test page

Quick Answer: **102**
Detailed Answer: **112**

53. Which PC Card slot can manage all the various PC Cards?

   ○ **A.** Type I

   ○ **B.** Type II

   ○ **C.** Type III

   ○ **D.** Type IV

Quick Answer: **102**
Detailed Answer: **112**

54. What should you never expose the drum of a laser printer to?

   ○ **A.** Airflow

   ○ **B.** Cold temperature

   ○ **C.** A strong light source

   ○ **D.** Toner dust

Quick Answer: **102**
Detailed Answer: **112**

55. Which tool should you use to determine why a computer fails to boot?

   ○ **A.** Cable tester

   ○ **B.** Loopback plug

   ○ **C.** PSU tester

   ○ **D.** Tone and probe kit

Quick Answer: **102**
Detailed Answer: **112**

56. You just installed a customer's printer and tested it. What should you do next?

   ○ **A.** Recheck all connections

   ○ **B.** Bill the customer

   ○ **C.** Turn the printer on and off

   ○ **D.** Show the customer the printer's basic functionality

   ○ **E.** Install a maintenance kit

Quick Answer: **102**
Detailed Answer: **112**

57. Which of the following are AMD CPU sockets? (Select the three best answers.)

   ○ **A.** AM3

   ○ **B.** 1155

   ◉ **C.** FM1

   ○ **D.** 775

   ○ **E.** G34

Quick Answer: **102**
Detailed Answer: **113**

58. How much L1 cache does a Core i5 CPU with four cores contain in total?

   ○ **A.** 32 KB

   ○ **B.** 64 KB

   ○ **C.** 128 KB

   ○ **D.** 256 KB

Quick Answer: **102**
Detailed Answer: **113**

59. Which type of cache memory is shared by all cores of a CPU?

    ○ **A.** L1

    ○ **B.** L2

    ○ **C.** L3

    ○ **D.** DRAM

60. Which technology calculates two independent sets of instructions simultaneously, simulating two CPUs?

    ○ **A.** Hyper-threading

    ○ **B.** HyperTransport

    ○ **C.** TurboBoost

    ○ **D.** Multi-core

61. How is TDP measured?

    ○ **A.** Volts

    ○ **B.** Watts

    ○ **C.** Ohms

    ○ **D.** Amps

62. You are tasked with plugging a network patch cable into an inactive drop within a user's cubicle. Which tool enables you to find the correct network drop in the wiring closet so that you can make the port hot?

    ○ **A.** PSU tester

    ○ **B.** Multimeter

    ○ **C.** Cable tester

    ○ **D.** Tone and probe kit

63. You think that the power supply in your PC might be failing, causing issues with a SATA drive. You decide to test the SATA drive. What are the standard voltages of a SATA connection on an ATX power supply?

    ○ **A.** 3.3 V, 5 v, 12 V

    ○ **B.** -3.3 V, 5 V, −12 V

    ○ **C.** -5 V, 5 V, 12 V

    ○ **D.** 5 V and 12 V

64. You just installed a maintenance kit to a laser printer. What should you do next?

- ○ **A.** Restore the printer to factory settings
- ○ **B.** Print a test page
- ○ **C.** Refill the paper trays
- ○ **D.** Restart the printer

Quick Answer: **102**
Detailed Answer: **114**

65. Which type of external connection allows for the fastest hard drive data rate?

- ○ **A.** USB 2.0
- ○ **B.** eSATA
- ○ **C.** IEEE 1394a
- ○ **D.** 1000BASE-T

Quick Answer: **102**
Detailed Answer: **114**

66. What is the best solution for making a direct wireless connection between a laptop and a printer?

- ○ **A.** FireWire
- ○ **B.** IEEE 1284
- ○ **C.** Bluetooth
- ○ **D.** IEEE 1394

Quick Answer: **102**
Detailed Answer: **114**

67. A company has Category 5e cabling lying on the floor in several locations. Which of the following is the most appropriate action to take?

- ○ **A.** Reroute the cables using a protective material
- ○ **B.** Secure the cables to the floor with tape
- ○ **C.** Install a wireless network
- ○ **D.** Move the computers closer to the server

Quick Answer: **102**
Detailed Answer: **114**

68. You've opened a CRT. Before working on the CRT, what should you do?

- ○ **A.** Discharge the monitor
- ○ **B.** Clean the monitor
- ○ **C.** Degauss the monitor
- ○ **D.** Unplug the monitor

Quick Answer: **102**
Detailed Answer: **114**

69. You are on a service call and receive an urgent phone call. What action should you take?

- ○ **A.** Leave the site and take the call.
- ○ **B.** Talk with the person while working.
- ○ **C.** Ask to be excused, and after determining the urgency of the call, go back to work.
- ○ **D.** Ask to be excused, and after determining that it is not a truly urgent call, get right back to work while talking on the phone.

70. Which of the following is defined as the movement of electric charge?

- ○ **A.** Voltage
- ○ **B.** Wattage
- ○ **C.** Amperage
- ○ **D.** Impedance

71. What are the standard voltages in the United States for a home and for the internal workings of a PC?

- ○ **A.** 240 V AC, 12 V DC
- ○ **B.** 120 V AC, 240 V DC
- ○ **C.** 240 V AC, 5 V DC
- ○ **D.** 120 V AC, 12 V DC

72. Which of the following should be used to clean a laser printer's rubber rollers?

- ○ **A.** Soap and water
- ○ **B.** WD-40
- ○ **C.** Isopropyl alcohol
- ○ **D.** A moist cloth

73. One of your customers wishes to have broadband Internet access set up in her home office. She is on a tight budget and doesn't want to pay for additional equipment. Which of the following technologies would be the best solution?

- ○ **A.** ISDN
- ○ **B.** T-3
- ○ **C.** Cable modem
- ○ **D.** T-1

74. An administrator cannot connect to a network volume. Which of the following is the best path for the administrator to use?

   ○ **A.** \\computername\C$

   ○ **B.** \\ipaddress\sharename

   ○ **C.** //computername/C$

   ○ **D.** http://computername/C

   ○ **E.** \\computername\sharename

Quick Answer: **102**
Detailed Answer: **115**

75. A co-worker at a satellite office reports that a new replacement shared workgroup printer has arrived. It is the same model as the old one. Your co-worker replaced the old printer and connected all the cables to the new printer. What is the easiest way to ensure that all the client computers can connect to the new printer via IPP?

   ○ **A.** Name the new printer with the old printer name

   ○ **B.** Allow the printer to acquire a DHCP address

   ○ **C.** In DHCP, set a reservation by MAC address

   ○ **D.** Have your co-worker print the configuration page

Quick Answer: **102**
Detailed Answer: **115**

76. A user cannot connect to a printer with the following UNC path: \\10.10.1.5\printer1. Which of the following paths is the best solution?

   ○ **A.** ipp://10.10.1.5/printer1

   ○ **B.** https://10.1.1.5/printer1

   ○ **C.** //10.10.1.5/printer1

   ○ **D.** http:\\10.10.1.5\printer1

Quick Answer: **102**
Detailed Answer: **115**

77. Which of the following communications protocols is used to connect to websites over secure communications links?

   ○ **A.** SSH

   ○ **B.** SFTP

   ○ **C.** HTTPS

   ○ **D.** Kerberos

Quick Answer: **102**
Detailed Answer: **115**

78. Which of the following protocols can be used to configure and monitor network printer device status?

   ○ **A.** SMTP

   ○ **B.** SNMP

   ○ **C.** TCP/IP

   ○ **D.** IPP

   ○ **E.** DNS

Quick Answer: **102**
Detailed Answer: **116**

79. Your co-worker Jake is planning on using an extension magnet to pick up a screw that dropped inside a computer case. What should you recommend he do before attempting this?

    ○ **A.** Make sure the extension magnet is rubber coated

    ○ **B.** Back up the computer to prevent any potential loss of data

    ○ **C.** Turn on the computer to prevent shorts

    ○ **D.** Unplug the power cord to prevent shorts

Quick Answer: **102**
Detailed Answer: **116**

80. Which of the following are descriptions or examples of unicast IPv6 addresses? (Select the two best answers.)

    ○ **A.** An address assigned to a group of interfaces where the packets are delivered to all interfaces

    ○ **B.** An address assigned to one interface

    ○ **C.** An address assigned to a group of interfaces where the packets are delivered to the first interface only

    ○ **D.** A loopback address of ::1

Quick Answer: **102**
Detailed Answer: **116**

81. Which of the following symptoms would indicate to you that there is a power supply issue?

    ○ **A.** The CPU is overclocking.

    ○ **B.** Wi-Fi range is reduced.

    ○ **C.** Frequent failure of hard drives.

    ○ **D.** Your CD burner takes longer to write than usual.

Quick Answer: **102**
Detailed Answer: **116**

82. Which of the following custom PC configurations require powerful CPUs? (Select the three best answers.)

    ○ **A.** CAD/CAM workstation

    ○ **B.** Audio/Video editing workstation

    ○ **C.** Virtualization workstation

    ○ **D.** Gaming PC

    ○ **E.** Home theater PC

    ○ **F.** Home server PC

Quick Answer: **102**
Detailed Answer: **116**

83. You need to install a device that can read groupings of parallel lines. Which device should you select?

    ○ **A.** Biometric scanner

    ○ **B.** Image scanner

    ○ **C.** Barcode reader

    ○ **D.** Touchpad

Quick Answer: **102**
Detailed Answer: **117**

84. You are building a new PC and want to select a motherboard that will support the Scalable Link Interface (SLI) technology so that you can install two SLI video cards connected by a bridge. Which of the following expansion slots should the motherboard have for your two video cards?

Quick Answer: **102**
Detailed Answer: **117**

- ○   **A.** Two AGP slots
- ○   **B.** Two PCIe slots
- ○   **C.** A PCI and PCIe slot
- ○   **D.** An AGP and PCIe slot

85. You are building a new PC for a customer. Which of the following is the most valid reason why you would select SATA 3.0 over the original SATA 2.0?

Quick Answer: **102**
Detailed Answer: **117**

- ○   **A.** You are installing an external SATA drive.
- ○   **B.** You are attempting to implement hot-swapping functionality.
- ○   **C.** You are trying to optimize the system for audio and video.
- ○   **D.** You do not want to use jumpers.

86. Which of the following is the *best* tool to use to reach a screw that has fallen into a computer case and out of reach?

Quick Answer: **102**
Detailed Answer: **117**

- ○   **A.** Pliers
- ○   **B.** Wrist strap
- ○   **C.** Tweezers
- ○   **D.** Extension magnet

87. You need to replace RAM in a customer's PC that currently uses PC3-10600 memory. Unfortunately, you do not have any RAM meeting that exact specification. Which RAM should you install?

Quick Answer: **102**
Detailed Answer: **117**

- ○   **A.** PC3-6400
- ○   **B.** PC3-8500
- ○   **C.** PC3-12800
- ○   **D.** DDR3-1066

88. Which of the following RAID arrays is fault tolerant *and* allows you to do striping?

Quick Answer: **103**
Detailed Answer: **117**

- ○   **A.** RAID 0
- ○   **B.** RAID 1
- ○   **C.** RAID 5
- ○   **D.** RAID 10

89. Which of the following are components of dealing with prohibited content? (Select the three best answers.)

Quick Answer: **103**
Detailed Answer: **118**

   ○ **A.** First response

   ○ **B.** Maintaining a positive attitude

   ○ **C.** Preserving data

   ○ **D.** Creating a chain of custody

   ○ **E.** Avoiding distraction

90. Which of the following are two possible reasons that an optical mouse cursor erratically jumps around the screen? (Select the two best answers.)

Quick Answer: **103**
Detailed Answer: **118**

   ○ **A.** It's using an incorrect mouse driver.

   ○ **B.** The mouse trackball needs to be removed and cleaned.

   ○ **C.** There's a conflict with the keyboard.

   ○ **D.** It's on an uneven surface.

   ○ **E.** The mouse needs to be charged.

91. If you are dealing with a power issue, what should you check first?

Quick Answer: **103**
Detailed Answer: **118**

   ○ **A.** Input devices

   ○ **B.** Cabling

   ○ **C.** Wall outlet

   ○ **D.** Power supply

92. If a computer receives the IP address 169.254.127.1, what has failed?

Quick Answer: **103**
Detailed Answer: **118**

   ○ **A.** DHCP

   ○ **B.** DNS

   ○ **C.** WINS

   ○ **D.** APIPA

93. An older Core 2 Duo computer is overheating because there is very little open space within the computer case. What are two things you can do to increase proper airflow? (Select the two best answers.)

Quick Answer: **103**
Detailed Answer: **119**

   ○ **A.** Drill holes in the computer case to increase airflow

   ○ **B.** Install a passive hard drive cooler

   ○ **C.** Install an additional case fan

   ○ **D.** Install a liquid cooling system

   ○ **E.** Install rounded IDE cables

94. Emergency! Your boss forgot the password to the BIOS on a computer. Which of the following methods helps you to reset the password?

   ○ **A.** Remove the RAM from the motherboard

   ○ **B.** Remove the CMOS battery from the motherboard

   ○ **C.** Remove the RAM jumper from the motherboard

   ○ **D.** Remove the main power connection from the motherboard

Quick Answer: **103**
Detailed Answer: **119**

95. When dealing with difficult customers, what should you do?

   ○ **A.** Do not minimize a customer's problems

   ○ **B.** Report through proper channels

   ○ **C.** Track evidence through documentation

   ○ **D.** Tell the customer to remove confidential documents

Quick Answer: **103**
Detailed Answer: **119**

96. In a RAID 5 array of eight hard drives, how many can fail without losing the entire array?

   ○ **A.** 0

   ○ **B.** 1

   ○ **C.** 2

   ○ **D.** 5

Quick Answer: **103**
Detailed Answer: **119**

97. What should you do first before shipping a user's laptop to the manufacturer for repair?

   ○ **A.** Remove the LCD

   ○ **B.** Clean it thoroughly

   ○ **C.** Remove the hard drive

   ○ **D.** Remove the WLAN card

Quick Answer: **103**
Detailed Answer: **120**

98. Which of the following are the Intel and AMD names for CPU virtualization? (Select the two best answers.)

   ○ **A.** VT-x

   ○ **B.** AMD-Vi

   ○ **C.** VT-d

   ○ **D.** AMD-V

Quick Answer: **103**
Detailed Answer: **119**

99. At 12x speed, how much data can a Blu-ray drive read per second?

   ○ **A.** 50 GB

   ○ **B.** 432 Mb/s

   ○ **C.** 4.5 MB/s

   ○ **D.** 150 KB/s

100. Which of the following video connectors accepts digital and analog video signals only?

   ○ **A.** DVI-D

   ○ **B.** DVI-A

   ○ **C.** DVI-I

   ○ **D.** HDMI Type B

Quick-Check Answer Key

1. C	**30.** C	**59.** C
2. D	**31.** B	**60.** A
3. A	**32.** B	**61.** B
4. B	**33.** A	**62.** D
5. D	**34.** B	**63.** A
6. A	**35.** C	**64.** B
7. B	**36.** A	**65.** B
8. C	**37.** B	**66.** C
9. A	**38.** C	**67.** A
10. D	**39.** D	**68.** A
11. A	**40.** C	**69.** C
12. D	**41.** A and E	**70.** C
13. B	**42.** B	**71.** D
14. D	**43.** C	**72.** D
15. D	**44.** C	**73.** C
16. C	**45.** B	**74.** A
17. A	**46.** D	**75.** C
18. C	**47.** A, C, D, and F	**76.** A
19. D	**48.** C and D	**77.** C
20. A	**49.** C	**78.** B
21. C	**50.** D	**79.** D
22. B	**51.** D	**80.** B and D
23. C	**52.** B	**81.** C
24. A and E	**53.** C	**82.** A, C, and D
25. B	**54.** C	**83.** C
26. A	**55.** C	**84.** B
27. D	**56.** D	**85.** C
28. C	**57.** A, C, and E	**86.** D
29. C	**58.** C	**87.** C

88. C

89. A, C, and D

90. A and D

91. C

92. A

93. C and E

94. B

95. A

96. B

97. C

98. A and D

99. B

100. C

Answers and Explanations

1. **Answer: C.** The default bus speed (without overclocking) for a Core i5 3.1 GHz CPU is 100 MHz. The maximum multiplier is 31 times that, or 3.1 GHz. But that is only if the processor requires it. Often, a CPU such as this will hover at around 1600 MHz (1.6 GHz), for a multiplier of 16. The multiplier is variable and will only increase if the system runs more applications and requires more CPU power. Of course, many Intel CPUs also have TurboBoost technology, which allows the CPU to be raised by 10% beyond the maximum; in this case it would be up to 3.4 GHz when needed. This is a basic and fairly safe type of overclocking. Many motherboards also let you increase the system bus speed. Some boards will stop you at say 105 MHz; others let you overclock the system bus to as high as 300 MHz (not recommended). Treat overclocking with extreme caution—the increased voltage and ensuing heat can easily cause the CPU to overheat and cause damage to the CPU and other devices in the system, as well as possibly corrupt data stored on the hard drive.

2. **Answer: D.** PCI Express (PCIe) version 3.0 can transmit 1 GB/s per lane. That means it can send and receive 1 GB of data every second. And PCIe x16 slots, since they have 16 lanes, can send and receive 16 GB/s simultaneously. PCIe is the only technology listed that uses lanes. AGP maxes out at 2,133 MB/s. PCI has a maximum of either 133 or 266 MB/s. USB 3.0 sends 5 Gbps, or 480 MB/s. Neither AGP, PCI, nor USB use lanes. AGP and PCI are parallel technologies. PCIe and USB are serial technologies.

3. **Answer: A.** Thermal expansion and contraction happen when humidity changes quickly. This can lead to what some technicians refer to as "chip creep" or "card creep." Although there might have been chip creep, the direct cause of the problem was most likely thermal expansion/contraction. POST errors would not be the cause of the error but in some cases could give you diagnostic information leading to the cause. Thermal sublimation deals with a specific type of printing process and is not involved in the problem. While in the computer, you might want to check other adapter cards in case they were affected by this phenomenon as well.

4. **Answer: B.** You should recommend configuring the laptop power option to power saver plan. The power saver plan will dim the display, shut down the display and hard drives after 10 minutes or so, and put the computer to sleep soon after that. This will help to conserve battery power. You can also suggest that the user close applications when not in use and turn off Bluetooth and Wi-Fi while they are not being used. Disabling special video effects in Windows can also conserve battery power. Keeping the device stored in a dry cool area out of direct sunlight also helps. Finally, tell the user that he should charge the battery often! As for the other answers: Restoring power usage when the laptop is unattended would seem like the opposite of conserving battery power. Removing the battery will definitely conserve battery power, but at the cost of not using it anymore. Only fully discharge the battery if it will not hold a charge anymore. If that doesn't help, replace the battery. The question's scenario says nothing about the battery not charging; it simply says that the battery is often low on power.

5. **Answer: D.** The most important consideration when installing any 64-bit operating system is the processor type. The CPU needs to be 64-bit to run 64-bit Windows. 32-bit CPUs will not run 64-bit Windows. Yes, Windows 7 requires a 1 GHz CPU, but honestly, if you don't have that speed, then you don't have much of a computer. Memory type doesn't really matter much; if it's a PC, then the memory type should be fine. But the amount of memory is important. 1 GB is necessary for 32-bit systems, but once again, the 64-bit consideration becomes important again; 64-bit versions of Windows 7 require 2 GB RAM.

6. **Answer: A.** The technician should repeat the problem back to the customer to make sure that everyone is talking about the same thing and that both parties understand each other. Always clarify! Having the customer call back later is just delaying the problem. Asking a person with an accent to stop speaking with an accent is like telling a dog to stop wagging its tail; it probably will be futile. A technician needs to be culturally sensitive. If you seriously cannot understand the customer even after attempting to listen several times and repeating the problem back, you will have to get someone else involved who can help you or attempt to communicate with the person through e-mail.

7. **Answer: B.** Most likely, repetitive flashing lights on a keyboard will indicate the presence of a hardware error, probably internal to the computer. If nothing comes up on the display, and all you have to go by are flashing lights on the keyboard, you can probably ascertain that the POST has failed and that the problem lies within the big four (as I like to call them): CPU, RAM, video, or motherboard. Software errors can't occur until the operating system attempts to boot, and without the POST finishing successfully, that won't happen. Passwords are required when you see a repetitive flashing light on the screen, not on the keyboard—and even then, only if you are attempting to access the BIOS or if someone configured a user password in the BIOS. External peripherals don't need to post properly for the computer to boot to the OS. Even the keyboard isn't necessary. The POST is more interested in the guts of the computer, especially the big four and the hard drive.

8. **Answer: C.** Fiber-optic networks use fiber-optic cables that have a core of plastic or glass fibers. These are much more difficult to eavesdrop on than any copper cable. Satellite connections and cable Internet use RG-6. DSL uses a standard phone line or other twisted-pair cable.

9. **Answer: A.** The only real difference listed between cellular WAN cards and WLAN cards is that a cellular WAN card requires a subscription to a cellular provider, while a WLAN card can work without provider payment. There are plenty of free Wi-Fi (WLAN) networks out there. It is cellular WAN cards that are more proprietary. You would have to get a WAN card that matches your service: AT&T, Verizon, and so on. On to the other answers: It is the WAN card that has a range of miles, whereas the WLAN card will be limited to 820 feet outdoors (if 802.11n less for other WLAN standards). Finally, both WLAN and WAN cards can be external or internal. Remember that Wireless LAN (WLAN) technologies that are ratified by the IEEE such as 802.11n and 802.11g are commonly referred to as Wi-Fi. However, remember that Wi-Fi is a registered trademark, and the actual technologies you are using are technically known as WLAN.

10. **Answer: D.** The port numbers 21, 22, 25, 53, 443, and 3389 correspond to the protocols FTP, SSH, SMTP, DNS, HTTPS, and RDP. The Telnet protocol uses port 23. Telnet is deprecated, insecure, and outdated; plus it isn't even enabled or installed on newer versions of operating systems. Use SSH in its place for a more secure connection. HTTP uses port 80. POP3 uses port 110. Know your port numbers!

11. **Answer: A.** The key here is what you ask the customer *first*. You should first ask the customer to describe the steps taken so far. By asking this, you will probably elicit a lot of the other listed answers from the customer. Remember, you are not accusing the user of anything; you are simply asking what the customer did so far. You don't even know if the device is USB or not. Plus, some devices are not turned on and off. They simply plug into the computer and either work or don't. And when you ask what the customer has done so far, the person will probably tell you that she plugged the device in. The moral of this question is to get the whole story before asking questions that are arbitrary—and possibly unnecessary.

12. **Answer: D.** RIMMs are designed by a company called Rambus. The RIMM is a competitor of DDR; it is also known as RDRAM as opposed to SDRAM. Rambus also makes RAM for game consoles known as XDR RAM. EEPROM stands for electrically erasable programmable read-only memory; it is used by BIOS chips and is not a RAM stick. PC2-6400 is a DDR2 module name that transmits 6,400 MB/s; its standard name is DDR2-800 because it can perform 800 MT/s.

13. **Answer: B.** The process order for installing a new hard drive controller card is to: 1. Apply system updates; 2. Update the BIOS; 3. Install the card physically; 4. Install the driver; and finally 5. Upgrade the card's firmware. That's the smartest list of steps for any hardware upgrade. You want to update the BIOS before installing the card, so that the BIOS will have a better chance of recognizing it. Of course, you should have made sure that the card is compatible with the motherboard and your version of Windows before purchasing. Update the controller card's firmware last. All of the other listed orders have anomalies that could lead to errors. For example, applying the system updates last would cause Windows to recognize the card properly too late. It might also cause Windows to attempt to install a Microsoft driver when you really want the manufacturer's driver. When upgrading, think this way: Windows updates, BIOS updates, physical install, driver install, special firmware upgrades. Then test it, and if it tests true, sit back and whistle your favorite tune. All PC techs do that, right?

14. **Answer: D.** The main power connection should have 24 pins. Just about all PCs you will see will have a 24-pin power cable. So the question was more of a tricky one. It's not asking for the video power connection, which could be a single 6-pin, a double 6-pin, or a single 8-pin; that will depend on the type of video card. You have to remember that powerful video cards will require more powerful power supplies. Older systems used the 20-pin main power connector, but those are rare nowadays, even if you are upgrading an older computer. 40 pins is the amount of pins an IDE hard drive's data cable has. You might ask "Who cares about IDE?" The answer: CompTIA. It's on the objectives so you should know it. But also, you will still be dealing with IDE drives, whether it is on older computers or on systems that you are upgrading (or restoring data from).

15. **Answer: D.** The operating system should be contained within the master drive. By setting the jumper to master on the old drive and setting the jumper to slave on the

new drive, Russ will accomplish that. Selecting any other setting listed might result in problems booting to the operating system. Another option is to use the cable select jumper setting that will attempt to automatically configure the new drive as a slave. Note that this can be done only if the drive is equipped with that jumper setting.

16. **Answer: C.** Eight USB cables minimum are required for this configuration—one for the USB mouse, one for the USB keyboard, and six for the PCs that are connecting to the KVM switch (two each). A KVM switch allows you to control two or more computers with a single keyboard and mouse. The device also needs only one display. Of course, you can look at only one computer's video display at a time. This kind of device is great for training purposes and lab and testing environments.

17. **Answer: A.** If a motherboard supports it at all, the board will support PC3-10600 running at 1,333 megatransfers per second (MT/s) and at 1066 MT/s. A PC3-10600 module is DDR3-1333. The default data rate is 1333 MT/s, but it can be underclocked to 1066 MT/s. You might see this referred to as 1333 and 1066 MHz, respectively, but that is not accurate. DDR3-1333 actually has an I/O bus clock rate of 667 MHz; it's the data rate that is 1333 MT/s. Most motherboards can underclock a RAM module by at least one step if necessary. For example, if you have a motherboard that can normally only handle DDR3-1066 memory modules, you could still install DDR3-1333 memory modules, but they would be automatically underclocked to 1066. If you were to see this question expressed as the I/O bus clock rate, then PC3-10600 would run at 667 MHz (the default) and 533 MHz (underclocked). Some RAM modules and motherboards support underclocking even further; for example, in this scenario as low as 400 MHz (800 MT/s.)

   Of course, another option (though not recommended) would be to overclock the motherboard to meet the data rate of the new RAM. The key in this question is to know the various data rates of DDR. To sum up: Any particular memory module will usually run at least one step slower than its default rate.

18. **Answer: C.** It's the surface area of the heat sink that has the greatest effect on heat dispersion. The more solid the bond between the heat sink and CPU cap, the better the transition of heat out of the CPU. To aid in this, thermal compound must be used.

19. **Answer: D.** If the electrician is being electrocuted, you do not want to touch him. Because it appears that the power is still on, turn it off at the source (if it is not near the sparking wire). This will usually be the circuit breaker. Then call 911. Do not move the cord or the electrician; you could be next.

20. **Answer: A.** You should first verify that the installation is allowed under a company's licensing agreement. It probably isn't, but you should check first. Most organizations will not allow purchased software to be installed on an employee's home computer. If it is against organization policy, then you should notify your supervisor.

21. **Answer: C.** Teach the user how to avoid this problem. The customer will then be more likely to come back to you with other computer problems. 'Nuff said.

22. **Answer: B.** The best answer here is to select a single 8 GB DDR3 PC3-12800 memory module. Even though it is faster than the current RAM, it can be underclocked automatically by most PC motherboards to match the PC3-10600 speed. Note that the question stated that RAM is assumed to be the same price per MB. The current 2 GB

memory module in Slot 2 would be removed, and the new 8 GB module would replace it. When finished, that and the current memory module in Slot 1 would equal 12 GB total. The 6 GB module wouldn't work because there would be no way to achieve 12 GB mathematically (we are limited to two slots). The 10 GB module would work mathematically (if we removed the current module in Slot 1) but would be more expensive as opposed to an 8 GB module (more GB, more money). Finally, two 6 GB modules would work if we removed both current modules, but it would be even more expensive. Compatibility is quite important, but in some situations you might actually purchase a faster type of RAM to save money!

23. **Answer: C.** Questioning the user can often lead to what caused the issue. Of course, you do not want to accuse the user of anything; instead, just ask what the user did last on the computer.

24. **Answers: A and E.** Of the listed answers, continuity and resistance are the settings that should be used when there is no electrical flow through the part being tested, and you want to be sure that there is no electrical flow when doing these tests! Examples of continuity or resistance tests include testing a fuse's impedance (measured in ohms) and testing a network cable for continuity. In each example, you don't want any electricity flowing through the device or line. It would give erratic results and could possibly cause damage to your testing equipment, and even you. When testing for watts, volts, and amps, you need to have electricity flowing through the item you want to test.

25. **Answer: B.** You will be implementing a virtualization workstation and thin clients. The virtualization workstation will run virtual software that will allow you to install the server software to a virtual machine (VM). This server will provide most of the resources for the clients on the network—the thin clients. Thin clients normally have very limited resources of their own and rely on the server (be it a regular or virtual server) for the additional resources they need. A CAD/CAM workstation is used for computer-aided design and manufacturing. PCs have plenty of their own resources and do not need a server supplying those resources. A home server PC is a possibility in this scenario, if it runs in a virtual environment. However, thick clients don't meet the requirements of this scenario. Thick clients have plenty of resources and are often used as another name for PCs. An AV workstation is an audio/video workstation, not a server, and laptops are not thin clients; they also have plenty of internal resources.

26. **Answer: A.** The Simple Mail Transport Protocol (SMTP) is not configured properly. That is the protocol used to send mail. POP3 receives e-mail. FTP enables two computers to upload and download files. HTTP is the protocol used by web browsers to surf the Internet.

27. **Answer: D.** Use a plastic shim to open the display or remove the bezel that surrounds it. Pliers have many uses but could cause damage to the plastic that surrounds the display of a laptop. Plastic tweezers are used to remove hard-to-reach parts such as screws from the inside of a PC. Flathead screwdrivers are not recommended because the metal can damage the plastic case of the laptop.

28. **Answer: C.** If the customer is having a hard time describing the problem, leaving you at a loss as to what to fix, ask the person to slowly repeat what the problem is. Try to relax him and be understanding, and especially patient. The more patient you appear, the more chance the customer will paint you a good picture of what the problem is. You should not offer any repair options until you know exactly what the problem is.

Computer jargon never helps the situation; if you start using terms the customer is unfamiliar with, then you risk alienating the customer and making things more difficult. Never abruptly leave the customer. Persevere, find out what the problem is, and repair it as soon as possible.

29. **Answer: C.** Power supplies are easily damaged in transit. Because of this, it is wise to run them for a while (burn them in) as part of your final checklist when working on or building a PC. This way you will be sure that the power supply is functional.

30. **Answer: C.** The Power-on Self Test (POST) checks the CPU, memory, video card, and so on when the computer first boots and displays any error messages if any errors occur. The POST is a part of the BIOS. The CMOS chip retains settings that the BIOS records during the POST. The Bootstrap loader is within the ROM ship as well. When the computer is turned on, it automatically reads the hard disk drive boot sector to continue the process of booting the operating system.

31. **Answer: B.** The Memory Controller Hub (MCH) makes the connection between, and controls the data transfer of, the CPU, RAM, and x16 PCIe devices on older Intel motherboards that support Core 2 CPUs. This device is also referred to as the northbridge. On newer Intel systems (such as Core i5 or i7 systems), the northbridge functionality is embedded within the CPU. The ICH (I/O Controller Hub) makes the connections to secondary systems such as USB and SATA. This device is also referred to as the southbridge. The FSB (front side bus) connects the CPU to the MCH (northbridge) in motherboards that support Core 2 CPUs. The Direct Media Interface (DMI) makes the connection between the chipset and the CPU on motherboards that support Core i3, i5, and i7 CPUs. It is somewhat of a replacement for the FSB. AMD systems still use the northbridge/southbridge concept; however, like Intel, any memory controlling functionality is built in to the CPU. *Be sure to understand both Intel architectures as well as how AMD fits into the whole scheme of things!*

32. **Answer: B.** If anything is going to disturb the server room or other equipment rooms, notify the network administrator immediately. It's coffee—no need to fill out an accident report. After you notify the admin, you might choose to mop up the mess; that's your prerogative, but I would hope the person who made the mess had a hand in cleaning it up. Material Safety Data Sheets (MSDS) are available for anything that has a chemical within it. I've had some terrible coffee in my day, but nothing that required an MSDS.

33. **Answer: A.** The primary corona wire places a negative charge on the photosensitive drum. A positive charge is applied to the paper by the transfer corona wire later in the laser printing process. Toner is placed on the drum from the toner hopper. The toner is attracted to the areas that have a lesser negative charge. Static electricity is removed by a static eliminator strip.

34. **Answer: B.** The complementary metal-oxide semiconductor (CMOS) retains (stores) changing or variable information such as the time and date. It is volatile, so a lithium battery (usually a CR2032) is used to power the CMOS when the computer is off. The BIOS or setup can locate and identify devices but does not store the variable information mentioned. The term *"Setup"* is usually associated with the file (setup.exe) which installs Windows and programs to be installed to Windows.

35. **Answer: C.** The internal clock speed is the frequency of the CPU—for example, 3.1 GHz. It is normally faster than the external clock speed (FSB on older Intel systems). It is also faster than the bus speed (otherwise known as the base clock speed)—for example, 100 MHz.

36. **Answer: A.** The AT&V modem diagnostic command is used to verify connectivity and display settings between a computer and a connected dial-up modem. Most modem commands begin with AT. IRQ stands for Interrupt ReQuest, a number assigned to a device that allows it to initiate communication with the CPU. The MBR is the master boot record. A boot sector on PCs, it is 512 bytes in size and is within the first sector of the hard drive. It often holds the partition table and/or bootstrapping information. QPI stands for QuickPath Interconnect, an Intel technology that connects the chipset to the CPU. It is a more powerful version of the Direct Media Interface (DMI).

37. **Answer: B.** Bluetooth works well as a short-range wireless communication technology. Cellular is longer range and actually for sending data (for example, an ExpressCard GPRS cellular data card). USB and Ethernet are wired! And there are no Ethernet mice, except for the ones that crawl around the network looking for the exit, but they are of no consequence.

38. **Answer: C.** IEEE 1284 is the ratified standard for printer cables that connect to the parallel port (LPT1) of the computer on one end and the Centronics connector of the printer on the other end. IEEE 1284 also sets the specifications for Extended Capabilities Port (ECP). While the parallel printer connection is an older technology, it is still on the A+ objectives, and you never know when you will see a question on it or when you might stumble upon one in the field! IEEE 802.3 is the standard for Ethernet. IEEE 1394 is the PC equivalent standard of FireWire, used for external drives and AV equipment. IEEE 802.11 is the collective standard of wireless technologies.

39. **Answer: D.** A power-on self-test (POST) card can be used to test all hardware on a computer prior to installing an operating system. More often, it is used to troubleshoot computer boot-up problems. The BIOS employs its own POST, but this is limited compared to what a POST adapter card can do. If an OS hasn't been installed yet, we can't use Windows to test hardware (and probably wouldn't want to rely on that anyway).

40. **Answer: C.** Keep away from the jargon. Customers can be confused by it, intimidated by it, and sometimes even frightened by it. This means to stay away from mentioning computer acronyms, the latest technology names, TCP/IP in general, and anything more technical than "reboot the computer". Analogies and visual aids can be great when explaining technical concepts to a customer. Think along their lines and paint a picture that they can understand. You should definitely limit what the customer needs to know. For example, there is no reason for the customer to know that 802.3z is the IEEE standard for 1000BASE-X: Ethernet over fiber optic transmissions at 1000 Mbps on the LAN. In fact, there's no reason you should know it for the A+ exam, but then again, you are a techie and the customer is not.

41. **Answers: A and E.** Use a multimeter or a power supply unit (PSU) tester to test the voltage of a power supply. The multimeter will test one wire at a time, whereas the PSU tester will test the entire main power connection all at once. Loopback plugs are used to test RJ45 ports on network adapters and COM1 serial ports. Cable testers are used to test networking cables. An antistatic mat is used to reduce ESD when working on a computer.

42. **Answer: B.** The only solution listed is to upgrade the video card. This is the only way that computer performance can be increased while Aero is running. The CPU and RAM can make the system faster when dealing with applications and calculations of many kinds, but when it comes to the video configurations, a 64 MB video card is just too weak. No matter how much RAM you add or what CPU you put in, the video will still perform like an actor on the late, late, late movie—badly. Increasing the hard drive capacity will have no effect on video but can definitely help in other areas of system performance such as pagefile access and general data access.

43. **Answer: C.** By sharing the RAM, motherboards can have integrated video cards, thus making for a cheaper system in general. This will not be satisfactory if you need to design a custom PC such as a gaming PC or a CAD/CAM workstation, but it will work just fine if you are building a PC that will have the primary function of accessing the Internet. To make the computer run faster, upgrade the CPU and possibly the hard drive. To make the computer run quieter, install quieter fans and solid-state drives and consider a quieter case. To reduce temperature, install more case fans and RAM heat sinks or consider a liquid cooling system.

44. **Answer: C.** The LGA 1155 socket is the replacement for the LGA 1156 socket. Even though it is one number less, it is the newer socket type. It is commonly used with Core i3, i5, and i7 CPUs. LGA 775 is used by Intel Core 2 Duo and similar CPUs. The 940 is an AMD socket, used with Opteron and Athlon 64 FX CPUs. The LGA 1366 is used with Intel Core i7 CPUs exclusively.

45. **Answer: B.** The Direct Media Interface (DMI) connection has a data transfer rate of 20 Gb/s or 2.5 GB/s. The DMI is the high-speed point-to-point interconnection mechanism between the CPU and the chipset. 1000 Mbps is the data transfer rate of gigabit Ethernet. 3.0 Gb/s is the data rate of SATA revision 2.0. 5 Gbps is the data rate of USB 3.0.

46. **Answer: D.** You should select the microATX form factor and the HDMI video output for an HTPC. ATX is acceptable but won't fit in most HTPC designed cases. Mobile-ITX and Pico-ITX are used by ultra-mobile PCs (UMPCs) and smartphones. DVI is the standard video connector for regular PCs, but for a true multimedia experience you want HDMI—not only for its capabilities with HD formats, but also because it carries HD audio signal as well. RG-6 is the network connection on a cable modem or set-top box (STB).

47. **Answers: A, C, D, and F.** The time/date, boot priority (boot sequence), passwords, and Wake-on-LAN (WOL) can all be configured in the BIOS. However, the registry and USB drivers are configured in Windows.

48. **Answers: C and D.** The first thing you should do is put on your antistatic strap. The last thing you should do is test the motherboard. Always remember to test! You already selected the motherboard. Technically, installing the CPU isn't really part of the motherboard installation process. But you can't really test the motherboard without it. Either way, the CPU would be installed before testing. Cables need to be connected during the installation and prior to testing. But anything that deals with power or circuit boards should not be touched unless you are wearing an antistatic strap.

49. **Answer: C.** To test IPv4, use the command `ping 127.0.0.1`. To test IPv6, use the command `ping ::1`. You don't run ipconfig commands to particular IP addresses. There is no Ping :1 or Ping 127::1 commands.

50. **Answer: D.** The front side bus (FSB) is usually four times the base core clock of a motherboard that supports Core 2 CPUs. That would be 1333 MHz in this case. Remember that newer Intel motherboards do not use the FSB; it has effectively been supplanted by the DMI (on lesser Intel boards) and QPI (on more powerful Intel boards).

51. **Answer: D.** 4.2 ms (milliseconds) is the typical latency of a SATA hard drive. When dealing with magnetic drives, latency is the delay in time before a particular sector on the platter can be read. It is directly linked to rotational speed. A hard drive with a rotational speed of 7200 RPM has an average latency of 4.2 ms. 300 MB/s is the data transfer rate of a SATA revision 2.0 hard drive; it is also expressed as 3.0 Gb/s. 16 MB is a common amount of cache memory on a hard drive; it is usually DRAM.

52. **Answer: B.** A maintenance kit includes a new fuser assembly, rollers, and more. Installing a maintenance kit is like changing a car's oil (although it isn't done as often). You could also sing *Happy Birthday*, but that would just be silly. Cleaning the printer might not be necessary. If you have a toner spill or work in a dirty environment, it might be a good idea. Clearing the counter is something you might do on an inkjet printer; it clears the counter of how much ink goes through the cartridge. Printing a test page is important when first installing a printer and when you finish installing a maintenance kit.

53. **Answer: C.** The Type III PC Card slot can handle Type I, Type II, or Type III PC Cards, also referred to as PCMCIA cards. Type I cards are often flash memory cards. Type II cards might be network adapters or modems. Type III cards are usually hard drives. Type IV cards can support all of the devices mentioned as well. They are bigger than Type III cards: 16 mm as opposed to 10.5 mm thick. PC Cards generally max out at 133 MB/s. A faster solution for laptops, the ExpressCard can go as fast as 250 MB/s, if used in PCI Express mode.

54. **Answer: C.** Because light is what affects the drum, the drum should remain sealed in the toner cartridge. Keep the cartridge away from magnets, too. If a toner cartridge breaks or forms a crack, recycle it and install a new toner cartridge.

55. **Answer: C.** Use a power supply unit (PSU) tester to determine why a computer fails to boot. One of culprits could be a faulty power supply. A cable tester will check network cables only to see if they are wired correctly and have continuity. Loopback plugs are used to test network cards and serial ports. The tone and probe kit is used to test phone lines. So, the rest of the answers are all tools that are used externally from the computer, whereas the PSU tester is the only one used inside the computer.

56. **Answer: D.** After installing something for a customer, teach the customer how to use it (at least the basics). If you tested it, then there is no reason to recheck connections or turn the printer on and off. Unless you are an independent contractor or consultant, you probably won't bill the customer yourself. Even if that is your responsibility, you shouldn't do so until you have shown the basics of the new printer to the customer. Maintenance kits are not necessary for new printers. They are required when the printer reaches approximately 200,000 pages printed.

57. **Answers: A, C, and E.** The AM3, FM1, and G34 are all AMD CPU sockets. The AM3 is used to house Phenom II, Sempron, and Athlon II CPUs. The FM1 is used with the Llano CPU. G34 is a replacement of the F socket and is used with Opteron CPUs. These are all Pin Grid Array (PGA) sockets. The Intel LGA1155 works with Core i3, i5, i7, and Xeon CPUs. The older LGA775 works with Core 2 Duo, Core 2 Quad, and older Xeon CPUs.

58. **Answer: C.** 128 KB total. Every core of a Core i5 CPU contains 32 KB of L1 cache. There are two core Core i5 CPUs; they have a total of 64 KB of L1 cache. And like in the question, there are four core Core i5 CPUs, with 128 KB total L1 cache.

59. **Answer: C.** L3 cache is shared by all of the cores of the CPU. L1 cache (often 32 KB per core) is built in to the CPU. L2 cache (often 256 KB per core) is built on to the CPU; it is also known as on-die. DRAM is the memory modules you install into the slots in the motherboard. DRAM is not cache memory. Some people consider DRAM to be L4 cache, but there is an actual CPU cache known as L4 used by Xeon and other high-end processors.

60. **Answer: A.** Hyper-threading (for example, Intel HT) calculates two independent sets of instructions simultaneously, simulating two CPUs. HyperTransport is a high-speed link between various devices such as the CPU and northbridge on AMD systems. TurboBoost is a basic form of overclocking that Intel allows with many of their processors. Multi-core is the technology where a CPU physically contains two or more processor cores. Newer Intel CPU designs combine multi-core technology with hyper-threading to allow for even more processing.

61. **Answer: B.** The thermal design power (TDP) of a CPU is measured in watts. For example, a typical Core i5 CPU might be rated at 95 watts. Older single-core CPUs were rated as high as 215 watts. The less the wattage rating, the less the computer's cooling system needs to dissipate heat generated by the CPU.

62. **Answer: D.** The tone and probe kit allows you to find the network drop in the wiring closet. How this would work is you would take the tone generator portion of the tone and probe kit and connect it via RJ45 to the network port in the user's cubicle. Switch it on so it creates tone. Then go to the wiring closet (or network room or server room) and use the probe (an inductive amplifier) to find the tone. You do this by pressing the probe against each of the cables. This is an excellent method when there are dozens, or hundreds, of cables in the wiring closet. Once you find the right cable, plug it into the patch panel or directly to a network switch. When you return to the user's cubicle, the RJ45 jack should be hot, meaning it can be used to send and receive data. As for the other answers: A PSU tester tests the power supply of a computer. A multimeter can test any wire's voltage or AC outlets. Cable tester is somewhat of a vague term, but it usually either means a network patch cable tester or a LAN tester, which checks the individual wires of longer network cable runs.

63. **Answer: A.** SATA power connections have 3.3, 5, and 12-volt wires. There are no negative voltage wires on SATA power connections. Molex power connections use 5 V and 12 V only, but SATA includes the 3.3 volt line. In this scenario you should test the SATA power connector and the main power connector from the power supply with your trusty PSU tester. (Most PSU testers will have an SATA power port in addition to the main 24-pin power port.)

64. **Answer: B.** Print a test page after doing preventative maintenance to a laser printer. Normally when you maintenance a laser printer, you will power it down and unplug it before any work begins. So there is no need to restart the printer; when you finish, you simply start it. There is also no need to restore a printer to factory settings unless it fails. Your preventative maintenance will hopefully stave off that dark day. The paper trays probably still have paper in them, and regardless, part of preventative maintenance is to fill the trays. But printing the test page should be last.

65. **Answer: B.** As of the writing of this book, external SATA (eSATA) runs at 3.0 Gbps, which is the fastest of the listed answers. 6.0 Gbps eSATA is unquestionably on the horizon. USB 2.0 is limited to 480 Mbps. IEEE 1394a is limited to 400 Mbps. 1000BASE-T is a networking connection that offers 1000 Mbps. However, if you had USB 3.0, your data rate would be 5.0 Gbps, and that would be the winner. And although typical IEEE 1394*b* devices run at 800 Mbps, the full specification calls for a maximum of 3.2 Gbps, slightly edging out eSATA. But that is only if you can find an IEEE 1394 device that complies with that speed. Plus, as I mentioned, technologies are always coming out with newer versions that are faster and faster.

66. **Answer: C.** Bluetooth works best for a direct wireless connection; in fact, it is the only wireless connection listed. FireWire and IEEE 1394 are effectively the same (IEEE 1394 is the equivalent PC standard), and IEEE 1284 is the standard for wired parallel port printing.

67. **Answer: A.** Your local municipality's electrical and safety code requires that all cables be installed properly. No cables can be left hanging or lying on the floor. Rerun the cables through the walls and ceiling, or use a special conduit to run the cables in a way that is safe. This in a nutshell is known as *cable management*.

68. **Answer: A.** The CRT holds a lethal charge and needs to be discharged before working on it. Of course, you should have unplugged the monitor *before* you opened it. In the strange case that you get a question like this, only a person trained on the repair of monitors should be opening them and even they should be discharging them before commencing work. Why would you clean a monitor before working on it? I don't know, seems something to do after the work is complete. Degaussing CRT monitors eliminates stray magnetic fields; most CRTs come with a built-in onscreen degaussing utility.

69. **Answer: C.** Everyone has urgent calls sometimes. But, are they actually urgent? Determine this, and then get back to work as quickly as possible. Don't text, e-mail, or use the phone while at the job site.

70. **Answer: C.** Amperage can be defined as electric current or the movement of electric charge. It is measured in amps (A). You should know your circuits in your office. The more you know, the less chance of overloading them. For example, a standard 15-amp circuit might be able to handle three or four computers and monitors. But a 20-amp circuit can handle a computer or two more. Circuit breakers, electrical cable, and outlets all must comply with a certain amount of amps. If you connect a power strip or surge protector, make sure that it is specified to work with your circuit's amp rating. Voltage is a representation of potential energy, measured in volts (V). Wattage is electric power, the rate of electric energy in a circuit, measured in watts (W). Impedance is the amount of resistance to electricity, measured in ohms (Ω).

71. **Answer: D.** Homes in the United States are wired for 120 volts alternating current (AC). The wires inside a PC might be 12 volts direct current (DC), 5 volts, or 3.3 volts.

72. **Answer: D.** Use a simple moist cloth, not too wet; you don't want to get any liquid inside the printer. Alcohol will be too strong, and WD-40 will cause damage in the long run. Soap and water can be used to clean the outside of a computer case.

73. **Answer: C.** Installing cable Internet would be the best solution given the parameters of this scenario. It is the cheapest of the four technologies listed above, and it is a broadband Internet solution. ISDN is generally known as a narrowband technology. Although there is a type of Broadband ISDN, that is designed to handle high-bandwidth applications and is quite expensive. T-1 and T-3 lines are dedicated high-speed connections that will not fit the customer's tight budget.

74. **Answer: A.** The universal naming convention (UNC) \\computername\C$ or \\ipaddress\C$ would be the best option. This allows the administrator to connect to the hidden share for the root of C. If the administrator has issues connecting to a network volume with a particular share name, they should use the hidden share. This can be done by computer name or by IP address. It would not be necessary to connect utilizing HTTP. Also, it is not wise to share the C: drive with a share name called "C."

75. **Answer: C.** In DHCP, set a reservation by MAC address. In this scenario it is most likely that the clients are connecting to the printer by IP address. The Internet Printing Protocol (IPP) will often be used in this manner. By default, the moment the new printer is connected to the network, it will acquire an IP address from the DHCP server—a new IP address, different from the one used by the old printer. This will cause the clients to fail when attempting to connect, and print, to the new printer. To prevent this, we go to the router (or other DHCP device) and configure a MAC address reservation. The MAC address of the printer (which might be on a label or can be accessed from the onscreen display) can be plugged into the DHCP server and reserved to a specific IP address. Of course, a better option would be to simply configure the printer to use a static IP address. As to the other answers, renaming the printer with the old name won't help because the client computers are most likely connecting by IP, not by name. Printing the configuration page is great and might help you to figure out what the problem could be, but it doesn't actually solve the problem!

76. **Answer: A.** IPP stands for the Internet Printing Protocol. It is a common standard used for remote printing. IPP paths are similar to HTTP paths, but instead they begin with the letters ipp. IPP supports access control, authentication, and encryption enabling secure printing. Some organizations prefer to use IPP instead of UNC paths. Although answer B could be a possibility, it would be more likely to use IPP instead of HTTPS. However, the IP address in answer B is also incorrect; the second octet is a 1 instead of a 10. Answer C isn't correct syntax; two slashes should be preceded by some kind of protocol such as IPP or HTTP. Or if this was meant to be a UNC, the slashes should be backslashes; however, a UNC was the original path that failed, so it is incorrect either way. Answer D is showing backslashes in the path instead of the proper slashes.

77. **Answer: C.** Hypertext Transfer Protocol Secure (HTTPS) is used to make secure connections to websites. It uses the Secure Socket Layer (SSL) or Transport Layer Security (TLS) protocols to encrypt the connection and make it safe for logins, purchases, and so on. HTTPS relies on port 443. SSH stands for Secure SHell; this is

used to make secure remote connections between computers for the purposes of command execution and remote control, and it replaces the deprecated Telnet protocol. It uses port 22. SFTP is the SSH File Transfer Protocol, a more secure version of FTP that is built on SSH. Kerberos is a network authentication protocol used by various systems including Microsoft domains. It uses port 88.

78. **Answer: B.** The Simple Network Management Protocol (SNMP) can be used to monitor remote computers and printers. This requires the installation of SNMP on the appropriate hosts. SMTP is the Simple Mail Transfer Protocol, which deals with the sending of e-mail. TCP/IP is the entire suite of protocols that we use when we connect to an IP network. IPP is the Internet Printing Protocol, which allows hosts to print documents to a remote printer without the need for UNC paths. DNS is the Domain Name System, which resolves domain names to their corresponding IP addresses.

79. **Answer: D.** You should recommend to your co-worker that he unplug the power cord to prevent shorts. Always unplug the computer before working on it. There are other tools that you can use as well—for example, the 3-prong parts grabber or, for something nonmetallic, the plastic tweezers. You could also try turning the computer upside down and letting gravity do its thing (if the computer is light enough). Backing up the computer's data is not necessary if you take the right precautions. Definitely do not turn on the computer. Make sure the computer is off and unplugged.

80. **Answers: B and D.** Unicast IPv6 addresses are addresses assigned to one interface on a host. Examples of unicast IPv6 addresses include Global unicast addresses that begin at 2000, link-local addresses that begin at FE80::/10, and the loopback address ::1. Addresses assigned to a group of interfaces where the packets are delivered to all interfaces are known as multicast addresses. Addresses assigned to a group of interfaces where the packets are delivered to the first interface only are known as anycast addresses.

81. **Answer: C.** An indication of a power supply issue is frequent failure of hard drives. If the power supply fails to provide clean power to the 3.3 V, 5 V, and 12 V lines to the hard drives, then they will fail frequently. These are often the first devices to fail when a power supply starts having intermittent problems. You should test this with a power supply tester or multimeter. If the power supply fails, the CPU would not overclock—quite the reverse, it might lose power and turn the computer off altogether. Overclocking is controlled in the BIOS, and there are thresholds in place to stop the CPU from overclocking too far. The wireless adapter would either work or not work. Reduced range could be due to obstruction or distance from the wireless access point. If the CD burner takes longer to write data than usual, it could be because the system is busy doing other tasks, or perhaps the burn rate setting was lowered.

82. **Answers: A, C, and D.** CAD/CAM workstations, virtualization workstations, and gaming PCs all require powerful CPUs with multiple cores—as many cores as possible. The other custom PCs are not nearly as reliant on CPUs. Audio/Video editing workstations rely most on specialized audio and video cards, dual monitors, and fast hard drives. Home theater PCs (HTPCs) require surround sound audio, HDMI output, compact form factors, and possibly TV tuners and video capture cards. Home server PCs rely on RAID arrays and powerful network cards.

83. **Answer: C.** You should select a barcode reader. This will read barcodes such as UPC barcodes that have groupings of parallel lines of varying widths. A biometric scanner authenticates individuals by scanning physical characteristics such as fingerprints. There are many types of image scanners; multifunction printers have these and allow you to scan in photos or make copies of documents. The touchpad is a device that takes the place of a mouse. It is often used in laptops but can be purchased as an external peripheral for PCs as well.

84. **Answer: B.** For SLI to work properly, you will need two identical PCIe (PCI Express) slots. Although older SLI cards were available for PCI, the technology cannot span different expansion slots.

85. **Answer: C.** SATA Revision 3.0 (maximum transfer rate of 6 Gb/s or 600 MB/s) can send and receive twice as much data as SATA Revision 2.0 (maximum transfer rate of 3 Gb/s or 300 MB/s). This makes it the better choice for audio and video applications and would be the most valid reason why you would select it for a new computer. When building a new computer, you would most likely start with an internal drive. You might add an external drive later, but regardless, just having an external drive is not a reason to use SATA 3.0 over SATA 2.0. In fact, as of the writing of this book, most eSATA drives are limited to 3.0 Gb/s data rates. SATA drives are not hot-swappable by default, whether they are internal or external. Special drive enclosures can be purchased to make a SATA drive hot-swappable, however. Neither SATA 2.0 nor SATA 3.0 uses jumpers. IDE drives are the most well-known for their use of jumpers.

86 **Answer: D.** The extension magnet is the best of the listed answers. Just remember to turn off power and disconnect the power cable before attempting this. Pliers are too big and bulky a tool to use in this situation. They can too easily damage components on a motherboard or other device. The antistatic wrist strap should always be worn, but it is not meant to pick up items. Because it is not specified, we have to assume that the answer "Tweezers" means metal tweezers. It is better to use an extension magnet—a tool more conforming to the job—than a metal object. However, if you have plastic tweezers or a three-prong pickup tool, you should use those before the extension magnet.

87. **Answer: C.** You should install a PC3-12800 memory module. If you don't have the exact speed RAM, go with a memory module that is one step higher. That RAM should underclock to match the motherboard. However, the best thing to do is to get the closest compatible RAM to the motherboard! Anyways, it's better to go up one level first. If the PC works without any errors, then all is good. If you install slower RAM such as PC3-8500 (which is DDR3-1066 by the way) or PC3-6400, the customer will end up with a slower computer than they originally started with.

88. **Answer: C.** RAID 5 is fault tolerant and allows for striping *with parity* (given you have three disks minimum to dedicate to the array). It's the parity information that makes it fault tolerant. RAID 0 is simply striping of data. It is not fault tolerant, meaning that it cannot recreate data after a failure or continue to function after a failure. RAID 1 is mirroring; it requires two disks and is fault tolerant. (An advanced version of RAID 1 is called disk duplexing when each hard drive in the mirror is connected to its own hard drive controller.) RAID 10 is a stripe of mirrors. It requires fours disks and is fault tolerant.

89. **Answers: A, C, and D**. When dealing with prohibited content, there will always be a first responder who is required to identify the issue, report through proper channels, and preserve data and possibly devices used. This person will be in charge of starting the documentation process which includes a chain of custody, the tracking of evidence and maintaining a chronological log of that evidence.

90. **Answers: A and D**. The mouse can move erratically due to an incorrect driver or an uneven surface. Remember to visit the manufacturer of the device to get the latest and greatest driver. That should fix the problem. But optical mice are very sensitive and need to be on an even, flat surface. Also, it helps if that surface is nonreflective. Optical mice don't have a trackball. Older ball mice had these, and they would have to be cleaned to fix this problem. The mouse should not conflict with the keyboard. Older PS/2 mice would not because they used a separate IRQ from the PS/2 keyboard. Newer USB mice won't either. Every USB device gets its own resources; this is taken care of by the USB controller. Finally, if the mouse needs to be charged, it should simply stop working. Some mice use double AA batteries that simply need to be replaced.

91. **Answer: C**. You should check the wall outlet first if you are dealing with a power issue. Since power comes from the AC outlet, it should be foremost on your mind. Now, if you already deduced that the wall outlet is not causing a problem, check the power supply next. Input devices won't often cause a power issue unless they are active devices, meaning they plug into an AC outlet. But once again, you would unplug them and check the AC outlet that they are plugged into. Phone and network cabling can carry power surges and spikes, especially if they are not installed or grounded properly. However, it is less likely that the power issue emanates from a cable. After checking the wall outlet and power supply, unplug these from the computer when troubleshooting power issues.

92. **Answer: A**. If a computer is attempting to obtain an IP address automatically and it receives the IP address 169.254.127.1, or any other IP address starting with 169.254, then DHCP has failed either at the client or the server. When this happens, Windows will automatically assign an APIPA address. The computer will be able to communicate only with other computers on the 169.254 network, which is pretty worthless if that is not your main network number. What went wrong? It could be one of several things. Perhaps the DHCP client service on the client computer needs to be restarted. Or maybe the computer is not connected to the right network. Still yet it could be a problem with the server: lack of IP addresses, the DHCP service failed, the DHCP server is down, and so on. DNS deals with resolving domain names to IP addresses; it doesn't affect DHCP address assignment. The Windows Internet Naming Service is an older Microsoft service that resolves NetBIOS names to IP addresses; like DNS, it doesn't affect DHCP. Both DNS and WINS could fail and a computer could still obtain an IP address from a DHCP server. If APIPA failed, then the computer wouldn't be able to get an address on the 169.254 network. If DHCP and APIPA were both to fail, the client computer would effectively have an IP address of 0.0.0.0. (or nothing would be listed in the ipconfig screen) placing the computer in the twilight zone.

> **NOTE**
>
> If you did not understand any of the acronyms used in that explanation, or you are having any trouble with any of the concepts listed (besides the twilight zone), then it is a strong indicator that you need to study more.

93. **Answers: C and E**. You should install an additional case fan and rounded IDE cables. The liquid cooling system answer might have jumped out at you, but the question states that there is *very* little open space within the computer case. Liquid cooling systems require space for their various components. Regardless, liquid cooling is a pretty advanced solution, where cheaper and easier solutions will probably suffice. An additional case fan almost always fixes the problem of overheating, especially if there was no case fan installed besides the power supply exhaust fan. By default, IDE data cables are flat ribbon cables that take up a lot of space. By using rounded cables for IDE and for other equipment, you can create some open space. The IDE cables are a cheap solution. However, newer power supplies use rounded power cables for other devices as well, but this would require more time, effort, and money. Drilling holes in a case is never a good idea. In fact, the more holes you drill, the tougher it will be for hot air to exhaust out of the case properly. A passive hard drive cooler is basically a heat sink. While it might help a little bit, it would be better to create more open space around the hard drive—for example, with the rounded cables.

94. **Answer: B**. Remove the CMOS battery from the motherboard. Normally, this will reset any variable settings in the BIOS such as the password and time/date. Some systems also have a BIOS configuration jumper that must be moved to another position in addition to removing the battery. Removing the RAM doesn't do anything. When the computer is turned off, RAM contents are emptied. There are usually no RAM jumpers on today's motherboards. Removing the main power connection from the motherboard will have no effect if the computer was already turned off and unplugged. By the way, RAM and power connections should not be removed unless the power *has* been shut off and the AC cable has been unplugged.

95. **Answer: A**. Not minimizing a customer's problems is one way to deal with a difficult customer. Other ways include avoid arguing, avoid being judgmental, and clarify customer statements. As for the other answers, reporting through proper channels is part of the fundamentals of first response. Tracking evidence and documenting is part of the concept of chain of custody. Finally, you should *ask* the customer to remove confidential documents; this is one method of dealing with customers' confidential materials appropriately.

96. **Answer: B**. One hard drive can fail in a RAID 5 array, and the array will be able to rebuild that drive's data from the remaining drives. However, if a second drive fails, the array is toast. That is because the array requires the parity information from all the other disks. Now, if you had a RAID 6 array (which includes another parity stripe), you could lose as many as two disks and still continue to function.

97. **Answer: C.** Remove the hard drive before releasing a computer to a third party. There could very well be confidential company data on the drive. Store the drive in a locking cabinet. Don't worry, the manufacturer of the laptop has plenty of hard drives to make it work! There is no need to remove the LCD or WLAN card because these do not contain confidential information. You could clean it if you want, but do you really have time for that?

98. **Answers: A and D.** Intel CPU virtualization is named VT-x. AMD CPU virtualization is named AMD-V. AMD-Vi is the name for AMD chipset virtualization. VT-d is the name for Intel chipset virtualization.

99. **Answer: B.** 432 Mb/s is the answer at 12x speed. The default 1x speed of Blu-ray allows a data rate of 36 Mb/s (4.5 MB/s). 50 GB is the maximum storage capacity of a standard size dual layer Blu-ray disc. 150 KB/s is the 1x data rate of a CD-ROM drive.

100. **Answer: C.** DVI-I accepts analog and digital video signals. All DVI ports are video only. DVI-D is digital only as you would guess from the *D*, and DVI-A is analog only. HDMI can accept video *and* audio signals. HDMI type B is known as double bandwidth; it supports higher resolutions.

CHAPTER FIVE

Review of the 220-801 Exams

Phew! That was a lot of questions. But if you are reading this, you survived. Great work!

Now that you have completed the three practice exams, let's do a little review of the 220-801 domains, talk about your next steps, and give you some test-taking tips.

Review of the Domains

Remember that the 220-801 is divided into five domains, as shown in Table 5.1.

TABLE 5.1   220-801 Domains

Domain	Percentage of Exam
1.0 PC Hardware	40%
2.0 Networking	27%
3.0 Laptops	11%
4.0 Printers	11%
5.0 Operational Procedures	11%
Total	100%

PC hardware has the majority of questions on the exam, but remember there are so many kinds of PC hardware: motherboards, CPUs, RAM, power supplies and cases, hard drives and optical drives, input/output devices, and peripherals. So, for example, you will get more networking questions than you will questions about just CPUs. But PC hardware questions in general should outweigh any of the other domains. Laptops, printers, and operational procedures collectively make up a third of the exam. That comes to 33 questions you will see on those subjects. This is what really can make or break a test score. Many technicians are great with PC hardware and networking. But if a tech is weak in the other three areas, the final exam score could be in jeopardy. Study all the concepts in each of the domains!

Everyone who takes the exam gets a different group of questions. Because it is randomized, one person may see more questions on, say, printers than the next person. Or one person might see more questions on laptops. It differs from person to person. To reduce your risk, be ready for any question from any domain, and study all of the objectives.

In general, this exam deals with installation and configuration methods, and it is hardware-based. The bulk of troubleshooting and Windows is reserved for the 220-802 exam, as is security and mobile devices.

Review What You Know

At this point you should be pretty well versed when it comes to the 220-801 exam. But I still recommend going back through all of the questions and making sure there are no questions, answers, concepts, or explanations you are unclear about. If there are, then additional study is probably necessary. If something really just doesn't make sense, is ambiguous or vague, or doesn't appear to be technically correct, feel free to contact me at my website (www.davidlprowse.com), and I will do my best to clarify.

Here are a couple great ways to study further:

▸ **Take the exams in flash card mode**—Use a piece of paper to cover up the potential answers as you take the exams. This helps to make you think a bit harder and aids in committing everything to memory.

▸ **Download the A+ 220-801 objectives**—You can get these from www.comptia.org. Go through them one-by-one and checkmark each item that you are confident in. If there are any items in the objectives that you are unsure about, study them hard. That's where the test will trip you up. There are 20 pages of objectives, so this will take a while. But it really helps to close any gaps in your knowledge and gives that extra boost for the exam.

▸ **Take the CompTIA A+ Practice Exam**—This can also be found at www.comptia.org. Re-take that exam until you get 100% correct. If any questions give you difficulty, contact me at my website so that I can help you understand them.

▸ **Study the 220-802 questions, and then return to the 220-801 tests!**—This might sound a bit crazy, but I have found that if an A+ candidate has a strong grasp of *all* A+ topics, he or she is more likely to pass *either* one of the exams. My recommendation is for you to go through the 220-802 practice exams, then return to the 220-801 exams for a review, and then go take the actual 220-801 test. It's a big extra step, but it has proven very effective with my students and readers.

More Test-Taking Tips

The majority of questions have four multiple-choice answers, but some have more. These answers are usually connected within the same concept. For example, a question about video connectors might provide four answers—DVI, HDMI, DisplayPort, and VGA—all of which are video ports. But some of the questions are not as synergistic; they might have a group of answers that seem at odds with each other. For example, a question about hard drive technologies might provide four answers: SATA, PATA, DVD-ROM, and solid-state. While SATA and PATA are definitely hard drive technologies, DVD-ROM is not and solid-state is a type of long-term memory storage that *might* be used as a hard drive technology. This will be true on the real exam as well.

Regardless of the type of question, there is often one answer that is just totally wrong. Learn to identify it; once you have, you will automatically improve to at least a 33% chance of getting the answer right, even if you have to guess.

No single question is more important than another. Approach each question with the same dedication, even if you are not interested in the topic or don't like how the question is worded. Remember that the CompTIA tests are designed and double-checked by an entire panel of experts.

NOTE

You may also see hands-on, scenario-oriented questions that test your knowledge by asking you to click on items, click and drag, or navigate through a system. These scenario-based questions are new to CompTIA exams and will probably be limited in quantity, but you should be ready and know how to do these things hands-on!

When you take the exam, remember to slowly read through the questions and each of the answers. Don't rush it. Let's list a couple more smart methods you can use when presented with difficult questions:

- Use the process of elimination.

- Be logical in the face of adversity.

- Use your gut instinct.

- Don't let one question beat you!

- If all else fails, guess.

I'll expand on these points in the final chapter. If you finish the exam early, use the time allotted to you to review all of your answers. Chances are you will have time left over at the end, so use it wisely. Make sure that everything you have marked has a proper answer that makes sense to you. But try not to overthink! Give it your best shot and be confident in your answers.

Taking the Real Exam

Do not register until you are fully prepared. When you are ready, schedule the exam to commence within a day or two so that you won't forget what you learned! Registration can be done online. Register at Pearson Vue (www.vue.com). They accept payment by major credit card for the exam fee. First-timers will need to create an account with Pearson Vue.

Here are some good general practices for taking the real exams:

- Pick a good time for the exam

- Don't over-study the day before the exam

- Get a good night's rest

- Eat a decent breakfast

- Show up early

- Bring earplugs

- Brainstorm before starting the exam

- Take small breaks while taking the exam

- Be confident

I'll embellish on these concepts in the final chapter.

Well, that's about it for the 220-801 portion of this book. Good luck on your exams!

CHAPTER SIX

Introduction to the 220-802 Exam

The CompTIA A+ 220-802 exam covers Windows operating systems, computer and network security, mobile devices such as tablets and smartphones, and troubleshooting. The largest percentage of the exam will focus on troubleshooting: repairing Windows, fixing computer hardware problems, mending networking issues, and repairing printers.

In this chapter I briefly discuss how the exam is categorized, give you some test-taking tips, and then prepare you to take the four 220-802 practice exams that follow this chapter.

Exam Breakdown

The CompTIA A+ 220-802 exam is divided by domain. Each domain makes up a certain percentage of the test. The four domains of the A+ 220-802 exam and their respective percentages are listed in Table 6.1.

TABLE 6.1   220-802 Domains

Domain	Percentage of Exam
1.0 Operating Systems	33%
2.0 Security	22%
3.0 Mobile Devices	9%
4.0 Troubleshooting	36%
Total	100%

Chances are that when you take the real CompTIA exam, you will see approximately 33 questions on Operating Systems, 22 questions on Security, 9 questions on Mobile Devices, and a whopping 36 questions on Troubleshooting. So it stands to reason that troubleshooting should be the most important subject of your studies, due to the sheer bulk of the questions you will see. Without good troubleshooting skills and experience, you have very diminished hopes of passing the exam.

Each domain has several or more objectives. There are far too many to list in this book (20 pages or so), but I do recommend you download a copy of the objectives for yourself. You can get them from:

http://www.comptia.org

Let's talk about each domain briefly.

Domain 1.0: Operating Systems (33%)

We've hardly talked about Windows up until this point. But now that we're here, you'll see lots of questions on Windows—I guarantee it. Domain 1.0 deals with Windows 7, Vista, and XP, in all their forms and versions. It covers how the operating systems can be installed, how they are configured, and how they are utilized. You should understand how to: configure Windows networking technologies such as HomeGroup, create shares, map network drives, and work with firewalls. This domain also covers how to maintain the computer, user accounts and groups, permissions, and virtualization. It's a lot of information to cram into one domain, but remember that this domain does not cover Windows troubleshooting—that is left for Domain 4.0.

Domain 2.0: Security (22%)

Security takes on a bigger role every year. This domain deals with common security threats, physical and digital prevention methods, how to secure a workstation, how to dispose of hard drives properly, and how to secure a small office/home office (SOHO) network. Basically, nowadays careful consideration for security should be applied to anything technology-oriented.

Domain 3.0 Mobile Devices (9%)

Mobile devices such as tablets and smartphones have become so popular that they earned themselves a spot in the 220-802 exam. You should know the differences between Android and iOS operating systems and understand the basics when it comes to navigating those systems. This domain expects you to demonstrate how to configure wireless and Bluetooth connections, synchronize data, and of course secure the devices.

Domain 4.0: Troubleshooting (36%)

Here it is: we left the best for last. It's the troubleshooting methodologies that make the ultimate computer tech. And it's those skills that will make you or break you on this exam. Many people agree that the 802 exam is more difficult than the 801 exam, and a lot of that can be attributed to this domain. CompTIA has its own six-step troubleshooting process that you should know. I'd like you to try to incorporate this six-step process into your line of thinking as you read through the practice exams, and whenever you troubleshoot a PC, mobile device, or networking issue:

Step 1: Identify the problem.

Step 2: Establish a theory of probable cause. (Question the obvious.)

Step 3: Test the theory to determine cause.

Step 4: Establish a plan of action to resolve the problem and implement the solution.

Step 5: Verify full system functionality and, if applicable, implement preventative measures.

Step 6: Document findings, actions, and outcomes.

This domain covers it all: from troubleshooting PC hardware and networking issues, to troubleshooting Windows, malware, and printers. It's the most difficult section and, unfortunately in the IT field, the most insidious. Issues can look or act like one thing, yet be another. Stay really focused when dealing with troubleshooting questions. You'll know them when you see them—they include real-world scenarios and often end in a phrase such as "what should you do to fix the problem," or "how can this be resolved," and so on.

Master this domain, and you will be well on your way to passing the A+ 220-802 exam, attaining your A+ certificate, and becoming a true expert at troubleshooting.

Test-Taking Tips

Just like with the 220-801 exams, I recommend you take it slow. Carefully read through each question. Read through *all* of the answers. Look at each answer and think to yourself whether it is right or wrong. And if it is wrong, define why it is wrong. This will help you to eliminate wrong answers in the search for the correct answer. When you have selected an answer, be confident in your decision.

Be ready for longer questions. On the average, a reader needs 60 minutes to take a 220-801 exam but 90 minutes to take a 220-802 exam. This is due to the complexity of some of the scenarios. You will need to imagine yourself within the situation and think how you would approach the problem step-by-step. Be prepared to write things down as you look at the question. This can help you to organize your thoughts. It's allowed on the real exam as well.

Finally, don't get stuck on any one question. You can always mark it and return to it later. I'll have more tips as we progress through the book, and I summarize all test-taking tips at the end of this book.

Getting Ready for the Practice Tests

The following four chapters (Ch 7–10) have practice tests based on the 220-802 exam. The first exam (Practice Exam A) is categorized by domain to help you study the concepts in order. It is also designed to be an easier exam than the other three. The other exams (Practice Exam B, Practice Exam C, and Practice Exam D) are freestyle: questions are mixed up to better simulate the real exam. Each exam is followed by in-depth explanations. Be sure to read them carefully. Don't move on to another exam until you have mastered the first one by scoring 90% or higher. Be positive that you understand the concepts before moving on to another exam. This will make you an efficient test-taker and allow you to benefit the most from this book.

Consider timing yourself. Give yourself 90 minutes to complete each exam. Write down your answers on a piece of paper. When you are finished, if there is still time left, review your answers for accuracy.

Each exam gets progressively more difficult. Don't get overconfident if you do well on the first exam because your skills will be tested more thoroughly as you progress. And don't get too concerned if you don't score 90% on the first try. That just means you need to study more and try the test again later. Keep studying and practicing!

After each exam is an answer key, followed by the in-depth answers/explanations. Don't skip the explanations, even if you think you know the concept. I often add my two cents, which can add insight to the nature of the question, as well as help you to answer other similar questions correctly.

Ready yourself: prepare the mind, and then go ahead and begin the first 220-802 exam!

CHAPTER 7

220-802 Practice Exam A

Welcome to the first 220-802 practice exam. This practice exam is categorized in order of the domains. You will see 33 questions on Operating Systems, 22 questions on Security, 9 questions on Mobile Devices, and 36 questions on Troubleshooting, for a total of 100 questions. This is the easiest of the four 220-802 exams. The other three will get progressively harder.

Take this first exam slowly. The goal is to make sure you understand all of the concepts before moving on to the next test.

Write down your answers and check them against the answer key, which immediately follows the exam. After the answer key you will find the explanations for all of the answers. Good luck!

Practice Questions

Domain 1.0: Operating Systems

1. Which of the following are Microsoft operating systems? (Select all correct answers.)

   ○ **A.** Windows XP

   ○ **B.** iOS

   ○ **C.** Vista

   ○ **D.** Android

   ○ **E.** Linux

   ○ **F.** Windows 7

   Quick Answer: **150**
   Detailed Answer: **152**

2. Of the following, which is *not* a method of installing Windows 7?

   ○ **A.** Over the network

   ○ **B.** CD-ROM

   ○ **C.** DVD-ROM

   ○ **D.** USB flash drive

   ○ **E.** Image

   Quick Answer: **150**
   Detailed Answer: **152**

3. What is the default file system used by Windows 7?

   ○ **A.** FAT32

   ○ **B.** CDFS

   ○ **C.** NTFS

   ○ **D.** FAT

   Quick Answer: **150**
   Detailed Answer: **152**

4. Where is the Notification Area located in Windows 7?

   ○ **A.** In the System Properties dialog box

   ○ **B.** In the System32 folder

   ○ **C.** On the Taskbar

   ○ **D.** Within the Start menu

   Quick Answer: **150**
   Detailed Answer: **152**

5. Windows service packs are _____.

   ○ **A.** A new version of the operating system

   ○ **B.** Resource Kit utilities

   ○ **C.** Compilations of software updates and patches

   ○ **D.** Driver updates

   Quick Answer: **150**
   Detailed Answer: **152**

6. What is the minimum amount of RAM needed to install Windows Vista?

Quick Answer: **150**
Detailed Answer: **152**

- ○ **A.** 128 MB
- ○ **B.** 256 MB
- ○ **C.** 512 MB
- ○ **D.** 1 GB

7. What is the minimum amount of RAM needed to install Windows 7? (Select the two best answers.)

Quick Answer: **150**
Detailed Answer: **152**

- ○ **A.** 256 MB
- ○ **B.** 512 MB
- ○ **C.** 1 GB
- ○ **D.** 2 GB

8. In Windows 7/Vista, an MMC is blank by default. What would you add to the MMC to populate it with programs?

Quick Answer: **150**
Detailed Answer: **152**

- ○ **A.** Applets
- ○ **B.** Files
- ○ **C.** Directories
- ○ **D.** Snap-ins

9. Which file is the boot loader in Windows XP?

Quick Answer: **150**
Detailed Answer: **153**

- ○ **A.** Ntdetect.com
- ○ **B.** Boot.ini
- ○ **C.** ntldr
- ○ **D.** Ntoskrnl.exe

10. Which file is the boot loader in Windows 7/Vista?

Quick Answer: **150**
Detailed Answer: **153**

- ○ **A.** Winload.exe
- ○ **B.** BCD
- ○ **C.** Setup.exe
- ○ **D.** Ntoskrnl.exe

11. What tool enables you to create a partition in Windows?

Quick Answer: **150**
Detailed Answer: **153**

- ○ **A.** Disk Administrator
- ○ **B.** Disk Management
- ○ **C.** Computer Management
- ○ **D.** Disk Cleanup

12. Which type of partition should an operating system be installed to?

Quick Answer: **150**
Detailed Answer: **153**

- ○ **A.** Primary
- ○ **B.** Extended
- ○ **C.** Volume
- ○ **D.** Logical drive

13. What is the minimum requirement of RAM for Windows XP Professional?

Quick Answer: **150**
Detailed Answer: **153**

- ○ **A.** 64 MB
- ○ **B.** 128 MB
- ○ **C.** 256 MB
- ○ **D.** 32 MB

14. Which tool enables you to find out how much memory a particular application is using?

Quick Answer: **150**
Detailed Answer: **153**

- ○ **A.** Msconfig
- ○ **B.** Task Manager
- ○ **C.** Chkdsk
- ○ **D.** System Information

15. Where would you go to start, stop, or restart services?

Quick Answer: **150**
Detailed Answer: **153**

- ○ **A.** Computer Management
- ○ **B.** Task Manager
- ○ **C.** Performance Monitor
- ○ **D.** MMC

16. Where is the Windows Update feature located in Windows?

Quick Answer: **150**
Detailed Answer: **154**

- ○ **A.** Start > All Programs > Accessories
- ○ **B.** Start > All Programs
- ○ **C.** Start > All Programs > Control Panel
- ○ **D.** Start > All Programs > Administrative Tools

17. Which user account permissions are needed to install device drivers on Windows Vista?

Quick Answer: **150**
Detailed Answer: **154**

- ○ **A.** User
- ○ **B.** Guest
- ○ **C.** Administrator
- ○ **D.** Power user

18. Which of the following commands creates a new directory in the Windows Command Prompt?

- ○ **A.** CD
- ○ **B.** MD
- ○ **C.** RD
- ○ **D.** SD

19. To learn more about the DIR command, what would you enter at the command line? (Select the two best answers.)

- ○ **A.** DIR HELP
- ○ **B.** HELP DIR
- ○ **C.** DIR /?
- ○ **D.** DIR ?

20. Which interface should you use to launch the command IPCONFIG?

- ○ **A.** Command Prompt
- ○ **B.** Control Panel
- ○ **C.** MMC
- ○ **D.** Task Manager

21. A customer's computer is using FAT32. Which file system can you upgrade it to when using the convert command?

- ○ **A.** NTFS
- ○ **B.** HPFS
- ○ **C.** exFAT
- ○ **D.** NFS

22. Which of the following answers can be used to keep disk drives free of errors and ensure that Windows runs efficiently? (Select the two best answers.)

- ○ **A.** Disk Management
- ○ **B.** Disk Defragmenter
- ○ **C.** Check Disk
- ○ **D.** System Restore
- ○ **E.** Task Scheduler

23. What is Windows 7's recovery environment known as? (Select the two best answers.)

Quick Answer: **150**
Detailed Answer: **154**

- ○ **A.** WinRE
- ○ **B.** Recovery Console
- ○ **C.** Advanced Boot Options
- ○ **D.** System Recovery Options

24. Which log file contains information about Windows 7/Vista setup errors?

Quick Answer: **150**
Detailed Answer: **155**

- ○ **A.** setupact.log
- ○ **B.** setuperr.log
- ○ **C.** unattend.xml
- ○ **D.** setuplog.txt

25. What is the RAM limitation of Windows Vista?

Quick Answer: **150**
Detailed Answer: **155**

- ○ **A.** 32 GB
- ○ **B.** 64 GB
- ○ **C.** 128 GB
- ○ **D.** 192 GB

26. A customer's Device Manager shows an arrow pointing down over one of the devices. What does this tell you?

Quick Answer: **150**
Detailed Answer: **155**

- ○ **A.** The device's driver has not been installed.
- ○ **B.** The device is not recognized.
- ○ **C.** The device is disabled.
- ○ **D.** The device is in queue to be deleted.

27. Which of the following is not an advantage of NTFS over FAT32?

Quick Answer: **150**
Detailed Answer: **155**

- ○ **A.** NTFS supports file encryption.
- ○ **B.** NTFS supports larger file sizes.
- ○ **C.** NTFS supports larger volumes.
- ○ **D.** NTFS supports more file formats.

28. Which of the following switches (options) copy all files, folders, and subfolders, including empty subfolders in the TEST folder?

Quick Answer: **150**
Detailed Answer: **155**

- ○ **A.** xcopy *.* c:\test /T /S
- ○ **B.** xcopy *.* c:\test /S
- ○ **C.** xcopy *.* c:\test /E
- ○ **D.** xcopy *.* c:\test /S /T

29. A co-worker just installed a second hard disk in his Windows 7 computer. However, he does not see the disk in Windows Explorer. What did he forget to do? (Select the three best answers.)

- ○ **A.** Format the drive
- ○ **B.** Partition the drive
- ○ **C.** Run FDISK
- ○ **D.** Initialize the drive
- ○ **E.** Set up the drive in the BIOS

Quick Answer: **150**
Detailed Answer: **155**

30. Which of the following Windows editions do *not* include Aero? (Select the two best answers.)

- ○ **A.** Windows 7 Starter
- ○ **B.** Windows 7 Ultimate
- ○ **C.** Windows XP Professional
- ○ **D.** Windows Vista Business
- ○ **E.** Windows Vista Home

Quick Answer: **150**
Detailed Answer: **155**

31. To create a restore point in Windows 7, what must you do?

- ○ **A.** Run Disk Defragmenter from the MMC ✗
- ○ **B.** Run NTBackup from the Control Panel
- ○ **C.** Run the System Restore program from the System Tools menu
- ○ **D.** Run the Disk Cleanup program from the System Tools menu

Quick Answer: **150**
Detailed Answer: **155**

32. Which of the following can you *not* do from the Printer Properties screen?

- ○ **A.** Modify spool settings
- ○ **B.** Add ports
- ○ **C.** Pause printing
- ○ **D.** Enable sharing

Quick Answer: **150**
Detailed Answer: **155**

33. You are setting up auditing on a Windows Vista Business computer. If it's set up properly, which log should have entries?

- ○ **A.** Application log
- ○ **B.** System log
- ○ **C.** Security log
- ○ **D.** Maintenance log

Quick Answer: **150**
Detailed Answer: **155**

Domain 2.0: Security

34. Which type of virus propagates itself by tunneling through the Internet and networks?

- ○ **A.** Macro
- ○ **B.** Phishing
- ○ **C.** Trojan
- ○ **D.** Worm

Quick Answer: **150**
Detailed Answer: **156**

35. Which component of Windows 7/Vista enables users to perform common tasks as non-administrators and, when necessary, as administrators without having to switch users, log off, or use Run As?

- ○ **A.** USMT
- ○ **B.** UAC
- ○ **C.** USB
- ○ **D.** VNC

Quick Answer: **150**
Detailed Answer: **156**

36. What can you do to secure your WAP/router? (Select all that apply.)

- ○ **A.** Change the default SSID name
- ○ **B.** Turn off SSID broadcasting
- ○ **C.** Enable DHCP
- ○ **D.** Disable DHCP

Quick Answer: **150**
Detailed Answer: **156**

37. When you connect to a website to make a purchase by credit card, you want to make sure the website is secure. What are two ways you can tell whether a site is secured? (Select the two best answers.)

- ○ **A.** Look for the padlock (in the locked position) toward the top or bottom of the screen
- ○ **B.** Look for the padlock (in the unlocked position) toward the top or bottom of the screen
- ○ **C.** Look for the protocol HTTP in the address or URL bar
- ○ **D.** Look for the protocol HTTPS in the address or URL bar

Quick Answer: **150**
Detailed Answer: **156**

38. Which type of software helps protect against viruses that are attached to e-mail?

- ○ **A.** Firewall software
- ○ **B.** Antivirus software
- ○ **C.** Windows Defender
- ○ **D.** Hardware firewall

39. Which of these is an example of social engineering?

- ○ **A.** Asking for a username and password over the phone
- ○ **B.** Using someone else's unsecured wireless network
- ○ **C.** Hacking into a router
- ○ **D.** A virus

40. Where are software-based firewalls usually located?

- ○ **A.** On routers
- ○ **B.** On servers
- ○ **C.** On clients
- ○ **D.** On every computer

41. Making data appear as if it is coming from somewhere other than its original source is known as what?

- ○ **A.** Hacking
- ○ **B.** Phishing
- ○ **C.** Cracking
- ○ **D.** Spoofing

42. A fingerprint reader is which type of security technology?

- ○ **A.** Biometrics
- ○ **B.** Smart card
- ○ **C.** Barcode reader
- ○ **D.** SSID

43. Which of these is the most secure password?

- ○ **A.** marquisdesod
- ○ **B.** Marqu1sDeS0d
- ○ **C.** MarquisDeSod
- ○ **D.** Marqu1s_DeS0d

44. Which shortcut key combination immediately locks Windows?

   ○ **A.** Ctrl+Alt+Del

   ○ **B.** Windows+R

   ○ **C.** Windows+M

   ○ **D.** Windows+L

Quick Answer: **150**
Detailed Answer: **157**

45. You are required to set up a secure connection between two offices over the Internet. Which technology should you select?

   ○ **A.** VPN

   ○ **B.** FTP

   ○ **C.** VLAN

   ○ **D.** HTTP

Quick Answer: **150**
Detailed Answer: **157**

46. Which is the most secure file system in Windows?

   ○ **A.** FAT

   ○ **B.** FAT16

   ○ **C.** NTFS

   ○ **D.** FAT32

Quick Answer: **150**
Detailed Answer: **157**

47. Which of the following is the most secure for your wireless network?

   ○ **A.** WEP

   ○ **B.** WPA2

   ○ **C.** TKIP

   ○ **D.** WPA

Quick Answer: **150**
Detailed Answer: **158**

48. Which term refers to when people are manipulated into giving access to network resources?

   ○ **A.** Hacking

   ○ **B.** Social engineering

   ○ **C.** Phishing

   ○ **D.** Cracking

Quick Answer: **150**
Detailed Answer: **158**

49. A customer's Windows Vista computer needs a new larger, faster hard drive. Another technician in your company installs the new drive and then formats the old drive before delivering it to you for disposal. How secure is the customer's data?

Quick Answer: **150**
Detailed Answer: **158**

○ **A.** Completely unsecure

○ **B.** Very unsecure

○ **C.** Secure

○ **D.** Completely secured

50. Which type of malicious software types will create multiple pop-ups on a computer?

Quick Answer: **150**
Detailed Answer: **158**

○ **A.** Grayware

○ **B.** Spyware

○ **C.** Worms

○ **D.** Adware

51. Which of the following offers hardware authentication?

Quick Answer: **150**
Detailed Answer: **158**

○ **A.** NTFS

○ **B.** Smart card

○ **C.** Strong passwords

○ **D.** Encrypted passwords

52. Which protocol encrypts transactions through a website?

Quick Answer: **150**
Detailed Answer: **158**

○ **A.** HTTP

○ **B.** SSL

○ **C.** Putty

○ **D.** Kerberos

53. Which of the following is a common local security policy?

Quick Answer: **150**
Detailed Answer: **158**

○ **A.** Use of RAID

○ **B.** Password length

○ **C.** Router passwords

○ **D.** Use of a password to log in

54. Which of the following can a limited account *not* perform?

Quick Answer: **150**
Detailed Answer: **158**

○ **A.** Connect to the Internet with a browser

○ **B.** Send e-mail with Outlook

○ **C.** Log on to Instant Messenger

○ **D.** Install programs

55. A co-worker downloads a game that ends up stealing information from the computer system. What is this?

Quick Answer: **150**
Detailed Answer: **158**

- ○ **A.** Worm
- ○ **B.** Spam
- ○ **C.** Trojan
- ○ **D.** Spyware

Domain 3.0: Mobile Devices

56. Which of the following is an open-source operating system?

Quick Answer: **150**
Detailed Answer: **159**

- ○ **A.** Android
- ○ **B.** iOS
- ○ **C.** Windows CE
- ○ **D.** Windows Mobile

57. What is a common CPU for a tablet computer?

Quick Answer: **150**
Detailed Answer: **159**

- ○ **A.** Core i5
- ○ **B.** Phenom II
- ○ **C.** ARM
- ○ **D.** FX

58. Which of the following is a common charging port on an Android smartphone?

Quick Answer: **150**
Detailed Answer: **159**

- ○ **A.** Standard A USB
- ○ **B.** Mini-A USB
- ○ **C.** Standard B USB
- ○ **D.** Micro-B USB

59. Which of the following does a laptop have, yet a tablet does not?

Quick Answer: **150**
Detailed Answer: **159**

- ○ **A.** Mouse
- ○ **B.** Display
- ○ **C.** Keyboard
- ○ **D.** Wireless network adapter

60. Where can you obtain applications for mobile devices? (Select all that apply.)

Quick Answer: **150**
Detailed Answer: **159**

- ○ **A.** Android Market
- ○ **B.** App Store
- ○ **C.** Google Play
- ○ **D.** iTunes

61. Which of the following makes use of the X, Y, and Z axes?

Quick Answer: **150**
Detailed Answer: **159**

- ○ **A.** Gyroscope
- ○ **B.** Lock Rotation
- ○ **C.** Accelerometers
- ○ **D.** Geotracking

62. You need to locate a mobile device that was stolen. Which technology can aid in this?

Quick Answer: **150**
Detailed Answer: **159**

- ○ **A.** GPS
- ○ **B.** Screen orientation
- ○ **C.** Passcode locks
- ○ **D.** Gmail

63. Which kinds of data would you synchronize on a smartphone? (Select the two best answers.)

Quick Answer: **150**
Detailed Answer: **159**

- ○ **A.** Contacts
- ○ **B.** Word docs
- ○ **C.** E-mail
- ○ **D.** Databases

64. Which of the following are wireless connections to the Internet that you would commonly make use of on a smartphone? (Select the two best answers.)

Quick Answer: **150**
Detailed Answer: **159**

- ○ **A.** GSM
- ○ **B.** Bluetooth
- ○ **C.** Wi-Fi
- ○ **D.** Fiber optic

Domain 4.0: Troubleshooting

65. At the beginning of the workday, a user informs you that the computer is not working. When you examine the computer, you notice that nothing is on the display. What should you check first?

- ○ **A.** Check whether the monitor is connected to the computer
- ○ **B.** Check whether the monitor is on
- ○ **C.** Check whether the computer is plugged in
- ○ **D.** Reinstall the video driver

66. What is the second step of the A+ troubleshooting methodology?

- ○ **A.** Identify the problem
- ○ **B.** Establish a probable cause
- ○ **C.** Test the theory
- ○ **D.** Document

67. Bob is having an issue with his display. He guesses that a problem exists with the video driver. How should he boot his Windows XP system to bypass the video driver?

- ○ **A.** Press F8, and then select Safe Mode
- ○ **B.** Press F6
- ○ **C.** Press Ctrl, and then select Safe Mode
- ○ **D.** Press F1

68. A user hands you her laptop in the hopes that you can repair it. What should you do first before making any changes?

- ○ **A.** Back up the important data
- ○ **B.** Reinstall the operating system
- ○ **C.** Open the laptop and analyze the components inside
- ○ **D.** Modify the Registry

69. You successfully modified the Registry on a customer's PC. Now the customer's system gets onto the Internet normally. What should you do next?

- ○ **A.** Bill the customer
- ○ **B.** Move on to the next computer
- ○ **C.** Document your solution
- ○ **D.** Run Disk Defrag

70. A customer reports that when his computer is turned on the screen is blank except for some text and a flashing cursor. The customer also tells you that there are numbers counting upward when the computer beeps and then freezes. Which of the following is the most likely cause of this problem?

- ○ **A.** Computer has faulty memory.
- ○ **B.** There is a corrupt MBR.
- ○ **C.** The OS is corrupted.
- ○ **D.** The computer is attempting to boot off of the network.

71. Which of these is part of step five of the CompTIA A+ troubleshooting process?

- ○ **A.** Identify the problem
- ○ **B.** Document findings
- ○ **C.** Establish a new theory
- ○ **D.** Implement preventative measures

72. You start a new computer and nothing seems to happen. Upon closer inspection, you can hear the hard drive spinning; however, nothing is coming up on the monitor. Which of the following would *not* be a reason for this?

- ○ **A.** The monitor is not on.
- ○ **B.** The video card is not properly seated.
- ○ **C.** The monitor is not connected to the PC.
- ○ **D.** The PC is not connected to the AC outlet.

73. Jake's Windows Vista computer has several programs running in the system tray that take up a lot of memory and processing power. He would like you to turn them off permanently. Which tool should you use to do this?

- ○ **A.** MSCONFIG.EXE
- ○ **B.** SYSEDIT.EXE
- ○ **C.** IPCONFIG /RELEASE
- ○ **D.** Task Manager

74. Buzz gets an error that says "Error log full." Where should you go to clear his Error log?

- ○ **A.** Device Manager
- ○ **B.** System Information
- ○ **C.** Recovery Console
- ○ **D.** Event Viewer

75. What would you need to access to boot the computer into Safe Mode?

- ○ **A.** WinRE
- ○ **B.** Recovery Console
- ○ **C.** Advanced Boot Options
- ○ **D.** System Restore

76. A customer is trying to use a laptop with a video projector and cannot get the projector to display the computer screen. Which of the following should you attempt first?

- ○ **A.** Replace the video cable to the projector
- ○ **B.** Toggle the function key for the display
- ○ **C.** Put a new bulb in the projector
- ○ **D.** Check the power to the projector

77. Which tool checks protected system files?

- ○ **A.** Chkdsk
- ○ **B.** Xcopy
- ○ **C.** Scandisk
- ○ **D.** SFC

78. Joey's computer was working fine for weeks, and suddenly it cannot connect to the Internet. Joey runs the command `ipconfig` and sees that the IP address his computer is using is 169.254.50.68. What can he conclude from this?

- ○ **A.** The computer cannot access the DHCP server.
- ○ **B.** The computer cannot access the POP3 server.
- ○ **C.** The computer cannot access the DNS server.
- ○ **D.** The computer cannot access the WINS server.

79. Which of the following commands pings the loopback address?

- ○ **A.** `PING 127.0.0.1`
- ○ **B.** `PING 10.0.0.1`
- ○ **C.** `PING 1.0.0.127`
- ○ **D.** `PING \\localhost`

80. A laptop with an external USB hard drive and an external monitor is not booting from the internal drive. Power has been verified and the battery is fully charged. However, the laptop appears to be stopping after the POST. Which of the following will aid you while troubleshooting?

- ○ **A.** Turn off the external monitor
- ○ **B.** Disconnect the external monitor
- ○ **C.** Remove the laptop battery
- ○ **D.** Format the external USB hard drive

Quick Answer: **150**
Detailed Answer: **161**

81. After installing a new hard drive on a Windows computer, Len tries to format the drive. Windows does not show the format option in Disk Management. What did Len forget to do first?

- ○ **A.** Run CHKDSK
- ○ **B.** Partition the drive
- ○ **C.** Defragment the drive
- ○ **D.** Copy system files

Quick Answer: **150**
Detailed Answer: **161**

82. How can a paper jam be resolved? (Select all that apply.)

- ○ **A.** Clear the paper path.
- ○ **B.** Use the right type of paper.
- ○ **C.** Check for damaged rollers.
- ○ **D.** Check for a damaged primary corona wire.

Quick Answer: **150**
Detailed Answer: **161**

83. What could cause a ghosted image on the paper outputted by a laser printer?

- ○ **A.** Transfer corona wire
- ○ **B.** Primary corona wire
- ○ **C.** Pickup rollers
- ○ **D.** Photosensitive drum

Quick Answer: **150**
Detailed Answer: **162**

84. Mary installed a new sound card and speakers; however, she cannot get any sound from the speakers. What could the problem be? (Select all that apply.)

- ○ **A.** Speaker power is not plugged in.
- ○ **B.** Sound card driver is not installed.
- ○ **C.** Sound card is plugged into the wrong slot.
- ○ **D.** Speaker connector is in the wrong jack.

Quick Answer: **150**
Detailed Answer: **162**

85. A laptop with an integrated 802.11 n/g card is unable to connect to any wireless networks. Just yesterday the laptop was able to connect to wireless networks. What is the most likely the cause?

Quick Answer: **150**
Detailed Answer: **162**

   ○ **A.** The wireless card drivers are not installed.

   ○ **B.** The wireless card is disabled in bios.

   ○ **C.** The wireless card firmware requires an update.

   ○ **D.** The wireless hardware switch is turned off.

86. When you reboot a computer, you get a message stating "No OS present, press any key to reboot." What is the most likely problem?

Quick Answer: **150**
Detailed Answer: **162**

   ○ **A.** The hard drive is not jumpered properly.

   ○ **B.** The hard drive is not getting power.

   ○ **C.** There is no active partition.

   ○ **D.** The hard drive driver is not installed.

87. After you install Windows, the computer you are working on displays a blue screen of death (BSOD) when rebooting. Which of the following are possible causes? (Select the two best answers.)

Quick Answer: **150**
Detailed Answer: **162**

   ○ **A.** BIOS needs to be flashed to the latest version.

   ○ **B.** IRQ conflict.

   ○ **C.** Virus in the MBR.

   ○ **D.** Incompatible hardware device.

88. Ray's computer is running Windows. In the Device Manager, you notice that the NIC has a black exclamation point. What does this tell you?

Quick Answer: **151**
Detailed Answer: **162**

   ○ **A.** The device is disabled.

   ○ **B.** The device isn't on the hardware compatibility list.

   ○ **C.** The device is malfunctioning.

   ○ **D.** The device is infected with malware.

89. The IP address of Davidprowse.com is 63.25.148.73. You can ping the IP address 63.25.148.73 but cannot ping Davidprowse.com. What is the most likely cause?

Quick Answer: **151**
Detailed Answer: **163**

   ○ **A.** Davidprowse.com is down.

   ○ **B.** The DHCP server is down.

   ○ **C.** The DNS server is down.

   ○ **D.** THE ADDS server is down.

90. In which troubleshooting step should you perform backups?

   ○ **A.** Identify the problem

   ○ **B.** Test the theory to determine cause

   ○ **C.** Verify a full system functionality

   ○ **D.** Document findings actions and outcomes

91. Which Windows Vista System Recovery Option attempts to automatically fix problems?

   ○ **A.** System Restore

   ○ **B.** Startup repair

   ○ **C.** Complete PC Restore

   ○ **D.** Recovery Console

92. What is the fourth step of the CompTIA 6-step troubleshooting process?

   ○ **A.** Identify the problem

   ○ **B.** Establish a theory of probable cause

   ○ **C.** Establish a plan of action

   ○ **D.** Document findings

93. A newly built computer runs through the POST, but it doesn't recognize the specific CPU that was just installed. Instead, it recognizes it as a generic CPU. What is the first thing to check?

   ○ **A.** Whether the CPU is seated properly

   ○ **B.** The version of the firmware for the motherboard

   ○ **C.** Whether it is the correct CPU for the motherboard

   ○ **D.** The version of Windows installed

94. Which command displays a network interface card's MAC address?

   ○ **A.** `Ping`

   ○ **B.** `Ipconfig/all`

   ○ **C.** `Ipconfig`

   ○ **D.** `Ipconfig/release`

95. A customer reports that print jobs sent to a local printer are printing as blank pieces of paper. What can help you to determine the cause?

Quick Answer: **151**
Detailed Answer: **163**

- ○ **A.** Reload the printer drivers
- ○ **B.** Stop and restart the print spooler
- ○ **C.** Replace the printer cable
- ○ **D.** Print and internal test page

96. Signal strength for a laptop's wireless connection is low (yellow in color and only one bar). The laptop is on the first floor of a house. The wireless access point (WAP) is in the basement. How can the signal strength be improved? (Select the two best answers.)

Quick Answer: **151**
Detailed Answer: **163**

- ○ **A.** Use a WAP signal booster
- ○ **B.** Move the WAP from the basement to the first floor
- ○ **C.** Download the latest driver for the NIC
- ○ **D.** Download the latest BIOS for the laptop

97. A computer cannot get on the Internet; what is the first thing you should check?

Quick Answer: **151**
Detailed Answer: **163**

- ○ **A.** NIC driver
- ○ **B.** Disk defrag
- ○ **C.** Patch cable
- ○ **D.** Firewall settings

98. Which utility enables you to troubleshoot an error with a file such as NTOSKRNL.EXE?

Quick Answer: **151**
Detailed Answer: **163**

- ○ **A.** Registry
- ○ **B.** Event Viewer
- ○ **C.** Windows Update
- ○ **D.** Recovery Console

99. A blue screen is most often caused by _____.

Quick Answer: **151**
Detailed Answer: **164**

- ○ **A.** Driver failure
- ○ **B.** Memory failure
- ○ **C.** Hard drive failure
- ○ **D.** CD-ROM failure

Quick Check

Quick Answer: **151**
Detailed Answer: **164**

100. A technician is installing a program on a Windows 7 computer and the installation fails. Which of the following is the next step?

- ○ **A.** Run the installer as an administrator
- ○ **B.** Contact the program's manufacturer
- ○ **C.** Reinstall Windows XP on the computer
- ○ **D.** Upgrade to Windows 7

Quick-Check Answer Key

1. A, C, and F	30. A and C	59. A
2. B	31. C	60. A, B, C, and D
3. C	32. C	61. C
4. C	33. C	62. A
5. C	34. D	63. A and C
6. C	35. B	64. A and C
7. C and D	36. A, B, and D	65. B
8. D	37. A and D	66. B
9. C	38. B	67. A
10. A	39. A	68. A
11. B	40. C	69. C
12. A	41. D	70. A
13. A	42. A	71. D
14. B	43. D	72. D
15. A	44. D	73. A
16. B	45. A	74. D
17. C	46. C	75. C
18. B	47. B	76. B
19. B and C	48. B	77. D
20. A	49. B	78. A
21. A	50. D	79. A
22. B and C	51. B	80. B
23. A and D	52. B	81. B
24. B	53. B	82. A, B, and C
25. C	54. D	83. D
26. C	55. C	84. A, B, and D
27. D	56. A	85. D
28. C	57. C	86. C
29. A, B, and D	58. D	87. A and D

88. C

89. C

90. A

91. B

92. C

93. B

94. B

95. D

96. A and B

97. C

98. B

99. A

100. A

Answers and Explanations

Domain 1.0: Operating Systems

1. **Answers: A, C and F.** Windows XP, Windows Vista, and Windows 7 are all Microsoft operating systems that you should know for the exam. iOS is the operating system Apple uses on its mobile devices. Android is the competitor of iOS and is an open-source operating system used on many other manufacturers' mobile devices. Android is developed from Linux. The original Linux was made for PCs with the goal of being a freely accessible, open-source platform. Okay, that was an easy one...moving on!

2. **Answer: B.** The only answer listed that is not an option for installing Windows 7 is CD-ROM. If you wish to install Windows 7 by disc, it would be by DVD-ROM. Windows 7 can be installed over the network, deployed as an image, and installed from USB flash drive if you really want to!

3. **Answer: C.** The New Technology File System (NTFS) is the default file system used by Windows 7. FAT and FAT32 are older, less desirable file systems that offer less functionality and less security and access smaller partition sizes. CDFS is the file system used by an optical disc.

4. **Answer: C.** The Notification Area (also known as the system tray) is the area toward the bottom-right of your screen within the taskbar. It contains the time and any applications (shown as icons) currently running in memory. The System Properties dialog box contains configuration tabs for the computer name and network, hardware, system restore, and more. You can access any of the tabs in that dialog box quickly by going to Start > Run and typing systempropertiescomputername.exe, systempropertiesadvanced.exe, and so on. The System32 folder resides within the Windows folder; it contains the critical Windows system files such as ntoskrnl.exe as well as applications such as cmd.exe. The Start menu gives access to most programs and configurations in Windows.

5. **Answer: C.** Microsoft releases many patches for its operating systems and normally bundles these bug fixes and security patches together as service packs. New versions of operating systems are just that: Windows Vista, Windows 7, and Windows 8 are different "versions". And they cost money. Service packs are updates, which are free. Windows Resource Kits are usually a combination of a book and disc that offer advanced technical guidance for the operating system. Service packs might include driver updates, but that is only a small portion of what they do.

6. **Answer: C.** Windows Vista requires a minimum of 512 MB of RAM for installation. Microsoft recommends 1 GB of RAM.

7. **Answers: C and D.** Windows 7 32-bit requires 1 GB of RAM. Windows 7 64-bit requires 2 GB of RAM. The 32-bit version can run on a 32-bit or 64-bit CPU. The 64-bit version runs on a 64-bit CPU only.

8. **Answer: D.** The MMC (Microsoft Management Console) is a blank shell until you add snap-ins (such as Computer Management or the Performance Monitor) for functionality. Some people refer to each program in the Control Panel as an *applet*; the term was made famous by Apple. You don't add actual files or directories (folders) to

the MMC; you add other programs within Windows. The MMC acts as an index for your programs and remembers the last place you were working (if you save it).

9. **Answer: C.** In Windows XP, ntldr is the first file to be loaded from the hard drive when the computer is started and is known as the boot loader. NTdetect.com detects hardware installed on the system. Boot.ini contains a menu of operating systems that can be selected and booted to. Ntoskrln.exe is the core operating system file of Windows XP, Vista, and 7.

10. **Answer: A**. Winload.exe is the Windows boot loader program for Windows 7 and Vista. It works in conjunction with the Bootmgr file (Windows Boot Manager) to take the place of ntldr. Bootmgr is the first file to load in Windows 7/Vista. It reads the BCD and displays an OS menu (if there is more than one OS). The BCD is the Boot Configuration Data store; it is the successor to boot.ini. Setup.exe is the default name of the file that starts installations of Windows and many other programs. Ntoskrnl.exe is the main system file of Windows—without it, the system would crash and the file would have to be replaced or repaired.

11. **Answer: B**. Disk Management is a tool found in Computer Management and allows for the creation, deletion, and formatting of partitions and logical drives. To view this application, right-click Computer and select Manage. Then click the Disk Management icon. Disk Administrator is a much older version of this program used in older, unsupported versions of Windows. Disk Cleanup is a built-in Windows program that can remove temporary files and other data that you probably won't use.

12. **Answer: A**. Primary partitions are the first partitions created on a disk. An OS should always be installed to a primary partition, but before installing the OS, the primary partition should be set to active. If you are installing to a new hard disk, Windows will automatically set the partition to active for you. A hard disk can have four primary partitions maximum, each with its own drive letter. If you need to subdivide the hard drive further, you can also use an extended partition, which is then broken up into logical drives. Any drive that you click on in Windows that has a drive letter is known as a volume.

13. **Answer: A**. Windows XP Home and Professional versions need only 64 MB to be installed. Microsoft recommends more, but 64 is the bare minimum needed to run the system. Windows XP Media Center, however, requires 256 MB of RAM.

14. **Answer: B**. The Task Manager enables you, via a click of the Processes tab, to view all current processes that are running and see how much memory each of them uses. The Task Manager can be opened by right-clicking the Taskbar and selecting Start Task Manager, going to Run and typing taskmgr, pressing Ctrl + Shift + Esc, or pressing Ctrl + Alt + Del and selecting Task Manager. Msconfig is a utility in Windows that allows you to enable and disable applications and services and boot Windows in different modes. Chkdsk is a Command Prompt utility that will search for errors and fix them (with the /F or /R switches). The System Information tool gives a summary of hardware resources, components, and the software environment; it can be opened by going to Run and typing msinfo32.

15. **Answer: A.** You can start, stop, and restart services within Computer Management > Services and Applications > Services. From there, right-click the service in question and configure it as you wish. You can also open Services from Start > All Programs > Administrative Tools or by going to the Run prompt and typing services.msc. The Task

Manager is a tool that allows you to see which applications and processes are running and analyze the performance of the CPU, RAM, and the networking connection. Performance Monitor analyzes the computer in much more depth than the Task Manager. The MMC is the Microsoft Management Console, which is the index that can store other console windows such as Computer Management.

16. **Answer: B.** Windows Update is simply located in Start > All Programs. Depending on the version of Windows, it might be in a slightly different location within All Programs, but that is the default for Windows 7, Vista, and XP. You can also access it from the Control Panel if you have the Control Panel configured as Large icons, Small icons, or Classic view. By the way, that is what the CompTIA A+ objectives calls for you to know: each of the individual programs in the icons view of Control Panel.

17. **Answer: C.** The administrator is the only account level that can install device drivers. Standard user, and especially guest, accounts cannot install drivers or programs. The Power User group is an older group from the Windows XP days that was carried over to Windows 7/Vista, but it has no real power in those operating systems.

18. **Answer: B.** MD is short for make directory and is the command to use when creating directories in the Command Prompt. CD is change directory. RD is remove directory, and SD deals with memory cards and is not a valid command in the Command Prompt.

19. **Answers: B and C.** To learn more about any command, type the command and then /?, or type HELP DIR. DIR HELP would attempt to find the file 'HELP' within the current directory. DIR ? would attempt to find information about ?.

20. **Answer: A.** Use the Command Prompt to launch the command IPCONFIG. IPCONFIG is a networking command that will display the configuration of your network adapter. You can open the Command Prompt in a variety of ways. However, many commands require you to open the Command Prompt as an administrator. You can open the default Command Prompt by going to Run and typing cmd.exe or by going to Start > All Programs > Accessories. At this point, to run it as an administrator, right-click it and select Run as Administrator. Or, you could type CMD in the search field and then press Ctrl + Shift + Enter.

21. **Answer: A.** Convert is used to upgrade FAT and FAT32 volumes to NTFS without loss of data. HPFS is the High Performance File System developed by IBM and is not used by Windows. exFAT (FAT64) is especially designed for flash drives. NFS is the Network File System, something you might see in a storage area network.

22. **Answers: B and C.** Disk Defragmenter keeps Windows running more efficiently by making the files contiguous, lowering the amount of physical work the hard drive has to do. Check Disk checks the hard drive for errors. Both tools can be found in Start > All Programs > Accessories > System Tools. Disk Management is used to partition and format drives. System Restore allows you to take a snapshot of the OS, enabling you to revert to older settings if something goes wrong. The Task Scheduler (previously Scheduled Tasks), as the name implies, enables you to set what time you want particular tasks to run.

23. **Answers: A and D.** The Windows 7 (and Vista) recovery environment (WinRE) is also known as System Recovery Options. From here you can restore the system, fix file

errors, and work in an unprotected Command Prompt. The Recovery Console is the predecessor of WinRE, available in Windows XP. Advanced Boot Options is the menu that can be accessed by pressing F8, which is available in 7/Vista/XP. It is also referred to as ABOM.

24. **Answer: B.** Setuperr.log contains information about setup errors during the installation of Windows 7/Vista. Start with this log file when troubleshooting. A file size of 0 bytes indicates no errors during installation. Setupact.log contains the events that occurred during the installation. Unattend.xml is the answer file used by Windows 7/Vista during unattended installations. Setuplog.txt records events that occurred during the text portion installation of Windows XP. Windows 7/Vista does not have a text portion during installation.

25. **Answer: C.** 128 GB is the limit of RAM that Windows Vista can access. This is a software limitation, not a hardware limitation. Even though 64-bit CPUs can address a realistic maximum of 256 terabytes (TB), software is always far more limited. There are some versions of Windows 7 that can access a maximum of 192 GB of RAM.

26. **Answer: C.** The arrow pointing down tells you that the device is disabled in Windows 7 and Vista. In Windows XP it is indicated with a red *X*. In many cases, it can easily be enabled by right-clicking it and selecting Enable. If the driver had not been installed, the device would most likely be sitting in a category called Unknown Devices. If the device is not even recognized by Windows, it will not show up on the list or will show up under Unknown Devices. There is no queue to be deleted.

27. **Answer: D.** NTFS and FAT32 support the same number of file formats. This is the only listed similarity between the two. Otherwise, NTFS has the advantage: it supports file encryption in the form of EFS and BitLocker, supports larger file sizes, and supports much larger volumes.

28. **Answer: C.** /E is needed to copy the files, directories, subdirectories, *including* empty subdirectories. /S will copy files, directories, and subdirectories, but *not* empty subdirectories. If you add /T on to the end, you get the directory structure but no files are copied. Be sure to check out the xcopy help file for more on its switches. And remember that *.* means all the files within a particular directory.

29. **Answers: A, B, and D.** For secondary drives, you must go to Disk Management and initialize, partition, and format them. FDISK is an older DOS command. Today's computers' BIOS should see the drive automatically with no configuration needed. In special cases a hard disk might require special drivers.

30. **Answers: A and C.** Windows 7 Starter and Windows XP Professional. Windows 7 Starter is a very basic, and 32-bit only, OS. Aero was released with Windows Vista, so no version of Windows XP had it. All the rest of the listed answers include Aero.

31. **Answer: C.** System Restore is the tool used to create restore points. In Windows 7 it can be found in Start > All Programs > Accessories > System Tools. The disk defragmenter is used to fix hard drives that have become slow with fragmentation. NTBackup is the backup program included with Windows XP. Disk Cleanup removes unwanted junk from the system such as temporary files.

32. **Answer: C.** Pausing printing in general and pausing individual documents is done by double-clicking on the printer in question and making the modifications from the ensuing window. All the others can be modified from the Printer Properties screen.

33. **Answer: C.** After Auditing is turned on and specific resources are configured for auditing, you need to check the Event Viewer's Security log for the entries. These could be successful logons or misfired attempts at deleting files; there are literally hundreds of options. The Application log contains errors, warnings, and informational entries about applications. The System log deals with drivers and system files and so on. A system maintenance log can be used to record routine maintenance procedures; it is not something that is included in Windows.

Domain 2.0: Security

34. **Answer: D.** Worms travel through the Internet and through local area networks (LANs). They are similar to viruses but differ in that they self-replicate. Macros are viruses that attach to programs like Microsoft Word and Word files. Trojans are viruses that look like programs and often seek to gain backdoor access to a system. Phishing is an attempt to fraudulently acquire information, often by e-mail or phone.

35. **Answer: B.** With User Account Control (UAC) enabled, users perform common tasks as nonadministrators and, when necessary, as administrators without having to switch users, log off, or use Run As. If the user is logged in as an administrator, a pop-up window will appear verifying that the user has administrative privileges before action is taken; the user need only click Yes. If the user is not logged on as an administrator, clicking Yes will cause Windows to prompt the user for an administrative username and password. USMT stands for User State Migration Tool, which is used to move files and user settings from one system (or systems) to another. USB is the Universal Serial Bus and has little to do with this question except to serve to confuse the unwary with another acronym. VNC stands for Virtual Network Computing; it's a type of program that allows a person at a computer to remotely take control of another computer or device. Examples include RealVNC and TightVNC.

36. **Answers: A, B, and D.** A multifunction network device that acts as both a wireless access point (WAP) and router comes with a standard, default SSID name (that everyone knows). It is a good idea to change it. After PCs and laptops have been associated with the wireless network, turn off SSID broadcasting so that no one else can find your WAP (with normal means). Disabling DHCP and instead using static IP addresses removes one of the types of packets that are broadcast from the WAP, making it more difficult to hack, but of course less functional and useful! Other ways to secure the wireless access point include changing the password; incorporating strong encryption such as Wi-Fi Protected Access version 2 (WPA2) with Advanced Encryption Standard (AES); and initiating MAC filtering, which only allows the computers with the MAC addresses you specify access to the wireless network.

37. **Answers: A and D.** The padlock in the locked position tells you that the website is using a secure certificate to protect your session. This padlock could be in different locations depending on the web browser used. Hypertext Transfer Protocol Secure (HTTPS) also defines that the session is using either the Secure Sockets Layer (SSL) protocol or the Transport Layer Security (TLS) protocol. HTTP by itself is enough for regular web sessions when you read documents and so on, but HTTPS is required when you log in to a site, purchase items, or do online banking. HTTPS opens a secure channel on port 443 as opposed to the default, insecure HTTP port 80.

38. **Answer: B.** Antivirus software (such as McAfee or Norton) updates automatically so as to protect you against the latest viruses, whether they are attached to e-mails or are lying in wait on removable media. Firewalls protect against intrusion but not viruses. They could be hardware-based, such as the ones found in most SOHO multifunction network devices, or software-based, such as the Windows Firewall. Windows Defender is free Microsoft software that protects against spyware/malware.

39. **Answer: A.** Social engineering is the practice of obtaining confidential information by manipulating people. Using someone else's network is just plain theft. Hacking into a router is just that, hacking. And a virus is a program that spreads through computers and networks (if executed by the user) that might or might not cause damage to files and applications.

40. **Answer: C.** Software-based firewalls, such as the Windows Firewall, normally run on client computers. It is possible that they will run on servers, especially if the server is acting as a network firewall, but otherwise the servers will usually rely on a hardware-based network firewall and/or an IDS/IPS solution. Hardware-based firewalls are also found in multifunction network devices. Some people might refer to these devices as *routers*, but the router functionality is really just one of the roles of the multifunction network device—separate from the firewall role. Plus, higher-end routers for larger networks are usually not combined with firewall functionality.

41. **Answer: D.** Spoofing is when a malicious user makes web pages, data, or e-mail appear to be coming from somewhere else. Hacking is a general term that describes an attacker trying to break into a system. Phishing is when a person fraudulently attempts to gain confidential information from unsuspecting users. Cracking is a term that is used to describe breaking passwords.

42. **Answer: A.** Biometrics is the study of recognizing humans. A fingerprint reader falls into this category as a biometric device. Smart cards are often the size of credit cards and store information that is transmitted to a reader. A barcode reader is a device that scans codes made up of different-width parallel lines, and SSID is a form of device identification that is broadcast from a wireless access point.

43. **Answer: D.** A password gets more secure as you increase its length and then add capital letters, numbers, and finally special characters. Note that Marqu1s_DeS0d has a capital *M*, a 1 in the place of an *I*, an underscore, a capital *D*, a capital *S*, and a zero. The only thing that this password lacks to make it a super password is the length. Fifteen characters or more is an industry standard for highly secure passwords.

44. **Answer: D.** Windows+L automatically and immediately locks the computer. Only the person who locked it or an administrator can unlock it. (Unless, of course, another user knows your password.) Ctrl+Alt+Del brings up the Windows Security dialog box. From there, you can lock the computer, too, but with an extra step. Windows+M minimizes all open applications, and Windows+R brings up the Run prompt.

45. **Answer: A.** You should install a virtual private network (VPN). This enables a secure connection between two offices using the Internet. It utilizes one of two tunneling protocols to make the secure connection: Point-to-Point Tunneling Protocol (PPTP) or Layer Two Tunneling Protocol (L2TP). FTP is the File Transfer Protocol; by default it is not secure. VLAN stands for virtual local area network; a VLAN is confined within a single office but does offer some security in the form of compartmentalization.

Hypertext Transfer Protocol (HTTP) is used to make connections to websites but is not secure by itself; that would require HTTPS.

46. **Answer: C.** NTFS is Windows' New Technology File System. It secures files and folders (and in fact, the whole partition) much better than any FAT system does. EFS, BitLocker, and NTFS permissions are just a few of the advantages of an NTFS partition. FAT is just another name for FAT16, which you will rarely see. FAT32 is also uncommon, though you might see removable media formatted to this file system.

47. **Answer: B.** WPA2 is superior to WPA, and WEP and takes much longer to crack (if crackable at all). It works best with AES. Wired Equivalent Privacy (WEP) is deprecated (outdated) and is considered insecure. It should be avoided unless it is the only encryption option you have; even then, you should consider new hardware and software. TKIP stands for Temporal Key Integrity Protocol; it is a deprecated encryption protocol used with WEP and WPA. The replacement is CCMP.

48. **Answer: B.** Social engineering is when fraudulent individuals try to get information from users through manipulation. Compare this to hacking, which is attempting to break into a system with technology, and cracking, which is breaking passwords with software. Phishing is a type of social engineering; it is implemented via e-mail or over the phone (vishing).

49. **Answer: B.** Many tools can recover data from a drive after it is formatted. Many companies will low-level format the drive and keep it in storage indefinitely.

50. **Answer: D.** Adware creates those pesky pop-up windows. All of the listed answers are types of malicious software (malware). Grayware is a classification of malware that behaves in an annoying manner but is not necessarily detrimental to the computer system. Spyware is software that tracks a user's actions on the Internet, without the user's knowledge. A worm is a piece of code that infects files and systems; it self-replicates and spreads throughout networks on its own.

51. **Answer: B.** Smart cards are actual physical cards that you use as authentication tools. They are sometimes referred to as *tokens* and have built-in processors. Examples of smart cards include the Personal Identity Verification (PIV) card used by U.S. government employees and the Common Access Card (CAC) used by Department of Defense personnel. All of the other answers are software related and are logical in their implementations.

52. **Answer: B.** Secure Sockets Layer (SSL) and the newer Transport Layer Security (TLS) encrypt the transactions through the website. These SSL certificates are often accompanied by the protocol HTTPS. HTTP by itself is not secure. Putty is a tool used for secure text-based connections to hosts and does not involve the website. Kerberos is the protocol used on a domain to encrypt passwords.

53. **Answer: B.** Common local security policies include password length, duration, and complexity. Just the use of a password doesn't constitute a password policy. An example of a password policy would be when an organization mandates that passwords be 15 characters in length with at least 1 capital letter, 1 number, and 1 special character.

54. **Answer: D.** Part of the point of the limited account is to limit it to doing everyday tasks only and not installing (possibly malicious) programs. Limited accounts are used in Windows XP. The equivalent of this in any Windows system is the standard user account.

55. **Answer: C.** A Trojan is a disguised program that is used to gain access to a computer and either steal information or take control of the computer. A worm is code that infects a system and self-replicates to other systems. Spam is the abuse of e-mail and the bane of mankind. Spyware is software unwittingly downloaded from the Internet that tracks a user's actions while surfing the Web.

Domain 3.0: Mobile Devices

56. **Answer: A.** Android is an open-source OS. It is freely downloadable and can be modified by manufacturers of mobile devices to suit their specific hardware. Apple's iOS and Microsoft's two mobile OSes—Windows CE and Windows Mobile—are closed-source; a company would have to pay a fee for every license of the OS.

57. **Answer: C.** Tablets and other mobile devices will often use Advanced RISC Machine (ARM) CPUs. These are designed for simplicity and low-power usage compared to desktop computer CPUs such as the Intel Core i5 and AMD Phenom II and FX CPUs.

58. **Answer: D.** The micro-B USB port is a common charging/data port for Android devices. Some manufacturers modify the design to create a proprietary micro-B USB port. Mobile devices do not use the standard size USB ports that desktop computers do, and it is uncommon for them to use mini-USB ports.

59. **Answer: A.** Tablets do not have a mouse; instead you use your finger(s) or a stylus to tap on the display (known as a *touchscreen*). Tablets have displays and wireless network adapters. They also have an onscreen keyboard. The question did not specify physical or virtual keyboard. Be ready for vagaries such as those on the real exam.

60. **Answers: A, B, C, and D.** Android users download applications (apps) from the Android Market (now known as Google Play). Apple users download apps from the App Store or from within iTunes.

61. **Answer: C.** Accelerometers are combinations of hardware and software that measure velocity on the X axis (left to right), the Y axis (up and down), and the Z axis (back to front). This aids in screen orientation on mobile devices. The gyroscope adds the measurements of pitch, roll, and yaw, which are necessary for today's mobile games and other apps. Lock Rotation is a setting (and a switch) on Apple iPad devices that stops the screen from reorienting as you rotate it. Geotracking is the practice of tracking and recording the location of a mobile device.

62. **Answer: A.** The Global Positioning System (GPS) technology can be instrumental in locating lost or stolen mobile devices. Many devices have this installed; others rely on geotracking or Wi-Fi hotspot locating techniques. (You are being watched!) Screen orientation is how the screen is displayed depending on how you hold the device: vertical or horizontal (or upside down). It can be calibrated on Android devices with the G-Sensor calibration tool. Passcode locks are sets of numbers that are required to be entered when a mobile device is turned on or taken out of sleep mode. Gmail is a web-based e-mail service by Google. It is incorporated into the Android operating system.

63. **Answers: A and C.** Some of the things you might synchronize on a smartphone include contacts, e-mail, programs, pictures, music, and videos. However, mobile devices (as of the writing of this book) do not run Microsoft Office, so you would have no need to back up Word documents. Databases are not often backed up; they are often not even run on mobile devices, but the mobile device might make connections to databases.

64. **Answers: A and C.** The Global System for Mobile Communications (GSM) and the general packet radio service (GPRS) are used to connect to the Internet at 2G, 3G, and 4G speeds. Wi-Fi connections also allow connections to the Internet given there is a hotspot available. They work the same way Wi-Fi does with PCs and laptops. Bluetooth is used to connect wireless devices to the mobile device—for example, headsets. Fiber optic is not wireless, and mobile devices do not make use of it.

Domain 4.0: Troubleshooting

65. **Answer: B.** When troubleshooting a computer system, always look for the most likely and simplest solutions first. The fact that the user might not have turned her monitor on when she first came in is a likely scenario. Afterward, you could check whether the computer is on, if the computer and monitor are plugged into the AC outlet, and whether the monitor is plugged into the computer. Reinstalling the video driver is much further down the list.

66. **Answer: B.** The second step is to establish a theory of probable cause. You are looking for the obvious or most probable cause for the problem. This comes after identifying the problem and before testing your theory. Documentation is last.

67. **Answer: A.** When Windows XP is first starting, pressing F8 brings up the Windows Advanced Boot Options Menu (ABOM), which includes several options for Safe mode (among other options). This is similar to the ABOM in Windows 7/Vista. Ctrl brings up a special menu that contains only the Safe mode options (not available in Windows 7/Vista/XP). When you enter Safe mode, the video driver is bypassed and only a simple VGA driver is loaded, allowing Bob to troubleshoot his video driver. (F5 also brings up the Windows Advanced Boot Options menu on some systems.)

68. **Answer: A.** Back up data before making any changes to the computer. This way, if your changes affect the functionality of the system, you can always restore the data later. You should do this before making any changes to the software or OS and before opening the computer.

69. **Answer: C.** Documentation is the final step in the troubleshooting process. This helps you to better understand and articulate exactly what the problem (and solution) was. If you see this problem in the future, you can consult your documentation for the solution. Plus, others on your team can do the same. In addition, it is common company policy to document all findings as part of a trouble ticket.

70. **Answer: A.** Chances are that the computer has faulty memory or memory that needs to be reseated properly. The flashing cursor on the screen tells you that the system is not posting properly. The numbers counting up are the system checking the RAM. If the system beeps and freezes during this count-up, then the RAM has an issue. It could also be incompatible with the motherboard. A corrupt MBR would either give a

message stating "missing OS" or "the MBR is corrupt". If the OS was corrupted, you would get a message to that effect. If the computer attempts to boot off of the network, you will see gray text and a spinning pipe sign as it attempts to find a DHCP server.

71. **Answer: D.** Implement preventative measures as part of step 5 to ensure that the problem will not happen again. The entire step is "Verify full system functionality and if applicable implement preventive measures." It comes just after establishing a plan of action and just before documenting findings.

72. **Answer: D.** If the PC is not connected to the AC outlet, the hard drive will not spin, so it isn't a possible reason for why nothing is coming up on the monitor, given the question's scenario. All other answers are possible reasons for why nothing is showing up on the display. Also, the monitor might not be plugged in.

73. **Answer: A.** MSCONFIG can turn programs on and off in the Startup tab. By modifying this, you effectively create a selective startup. Task Manager can turn off programs, but only temporarily; when the system restarts, those programs will run again.

74. **Answer: D.** The Event Viewer contains the error logs; they are finite in size. You could either clear the log or increase the size of the log. The other three do not contain error logs.

75. **Answer: C.** The Advanced Boot Options menu has many options, including Safe Mode. This menu can be accessed by pressing F8 when the computer first boots up. *Know those ABOM options!*

76. **Answer: B.** Try pressing the video toggle button or combination key on the laptop's keyboard first. If that doesn't work, check all cables and power. Finally, you might try changing the bulb in the projector, though you can usually tell if the bulb is working by accessing the menu buttons on the projector.

77. **Answer: D.** System File Checker (SFC) checks protected system files and replaces incorrect versions. None of the other options check system files. Chkdsk can check for and repair errors, but just regular files. Xcopy is used to copy entire directories of information. Scandisk is an older command-line scanning tool that today's versions of Windows don't use. It is replaced by Chkdsk.

78. **Answer: A.** If you get any address that starts with 169.254, it means the computer has self-assigned that address. It is known as an APIPA address (Automatic Private IP Addressing). Normally, DHCP servers will not use this network number. A simple `ipconfig/release` and `ipconfig/renew` might fix the problem, if a DHCP server is actually available. The POP3 server is for incoming mail, the DNS server is for resolving domain names to IP addresses, and the WINS server is for resolving NETBIOS names to IP addresses.

79. **Answer: A.** 127.0.0.1 is the built-in loopback IP address for every computer with TCP/IP installed. Alternatively, you could ping any number on the 127 network or ping localhost without the double backslash. This helps you determine if TCP/IP works on the local computer's network adapter, but it doesn't indicate if you have a working network connection.

80. **Answer: B.** Disconnect the external monitor. You might also choose to disconnect the USB hard drive. External devices and peripherals could cause conflicts in a computer

system that stops it from posting properly and booting. Turning off the monitor does-n't change the fact that it is connected to the laptop's port. Removing the battery will only tell you if the system will still work on AC power only. Formatting the external USB drive will wipe out all data stored on it and probably won't fix the problem, unless the laptop's BIOS was incorrectly set to boot from the external drive instead of the internal drive, *and* if the external drive had an OS installed to it.

81. **Answer: B.** You must partition the drive before formatting. Copying files can be done only after formatting is complete. CHKDSK has little value on an unformatted drive as it checks files for errors and integrity. Something else not mentioned here is that a second drive would have to be initialized in Windows before use.

82. **Answers: A, B, and C.** There are several possible reasons a paper jam might occur. The paper could be stuck somewhere in the paper path, the paper could be too thick, or the rollers could be damaged. However, the primary corona wire doesn't cause paper jams; instead, a damaged primary corona wire might cause lines or smearing.

83. **Answer: D.** Ghosted images or blurry marks could be a sign that the drum has some kind of imperfection or is dirty, especially if the image reappears at equal intervals. Replace the drum (or toner cartridge). Another possibility is that the fuser assembly has been damaged and needs to be replaced.

84. **Answers: A, B, and D.** Always make sure that the speaker power (if any) is plugged into an AC outlet and that the speakers are on (if they have a power button). When a sound card is first installed, Windows should recognize it and either install a driver through plug-and-play or ask for a driver CD. For best results, use the manufacturer's driver, the latest of which can be found on its website. Make sure that you plug the speakers into the correct 1/8" RCA jack. The speaker out is the one with concentric cir-cles and an arrow pointing out. Or you might have 5.1 surround sound; in which case, you would use the standard front speaker jack, which is often a green jack. Finally, it's quite hard to plug a sound card into a wrong slot. For example, if you have a PCI 32-bit sound card (a common standard), you can then plug that sound card into any of the available PCI slots on your motherboard and it will be recognized. (Word to the wise, if you ever remove the sound card when upgrading, make sure you put it back in the same slot.) PCI cards will not fit in ISA, AGP, or PCIe slots.

85. **Answer: D.** The wireless hardware switch (or button) is turned off. Always check that Wi-Fi switch. If it is enabled, then make sure that the wireless adapter is enabled in Windows. Check if the laptop is within range of the wireless access point. The drivers and the firmware should not be an issue because the laptop was able to connect yes-terday. However, you never know what might have happened, so check those later on in your troubleshooting process.

86. **Answer: C.** The primary partition must be set to active to boot to the operating sys-tem. If there is only one drive, the jumper setting probably won't matter, and if it is wrong, the drive simply won't be seen by the BIOS. The same holds true for power; if the drive does not get power, the BIOS will not recognize it. Finally, hard drives do not need drivers to simply be recognized.

87. **Answers: A and D.** Older PCs might need the BIOS to be upgraded before an installa-tion. Always flash the latest BIOS before performing an upgrade or a fresh install. Always check the hardware on the HCL before performing an install or upgrade. If the

220-802 Practice Exam A

CPU or RAM is not compatible or if you have a corrupt driver file, a blue screen could occur. The blue screen is technically referred to as a Stop Error. IRQ conflicts will not cause BSODs, but they will render the affected devices inoperable. Viruses in the MBR could cause the computer to simply not boot.

88. **Answer: C.** A black exclamation point on a yellow field tells you that the device is in a problem state and is probably malfunctioning. The device might need to be replaced or reseated, or the firmware might need to be upgraded. (This can be displayed as a yellow exclamation point in Windows XP.) If the device was disabled, it would show an arrow pointing down (Windows 7/Vista) or a red *X* (Windows XP). The device might not be on the HCL, but the Device Manager doesn't have an icon to tell you that specifically. Also, the Device Manager won't tell you if a system is infected with malware. Individual devices generally don't get infected with malware anyway; normally the operating system does.

89. **Answer: C.** The purpose of a DNS server is to resolve (convert) hostnames and domain names to the IP address. Computers normally communicate via IP address, but it is easier for humans to type in names. If Davidprowse.com is down, you cannot ping the corresponding IP address at all. As to the incorrect answers: If the DHCP server is down, your workstation will probably not have an IP on the network and again will not ping the corresponding IP address. ADDS is Active Directory Directory Services, meaning a domain controller, which doesn't have much to do with this, except that in many smaller companies, the domain controller and DNS server are one and the same.

90. **Answer: A.** You should perform backups during the first step: Identify the problem. The idea is that you back up the data before you actually *do* anything to the computer. Testing theories is step 3. Verifying full functionality is step 5. Documenting findings is step 6.

91. **Answer: B.** Startup repair attempts to fix issues automatically. This is available in Windows 7/Vista's WinRE System Recovery Options.

92. **Answer: C.** The fourth step of the CompTIA six-step troubleshooting process is: Establish a plan of action to resolve the problem and implement the solution. Identify the problem is step 1. Establish a theory of probable cause is step 2. Document findings is step 6.

93. **Answer: B.** You must have the correct firmware to recognize the latest CPUs. If the CPU is not seated properly or if you have an incorrect CPU, the system simply won't boot. Windows does not affect the POST at all. In some cases, you might purchase a motherboard that says it can support a specific new processor. However, the firmware might not have been written yet to actually work with that processor!

94. **Answer: B.** IPCONFIG/ALL shows a lot of information, including the MAC address. Plain old IPCONFIG shows only the IP address, subnet mask, and gateway address. Ping tests whether other computers are alive on the network. Ipconfig/release is used to troubleshoot DHCP-obtained IP addresses. It is often used in conjunction with ipconfig/renew.

95. **Answer: D.** First try printing an internal test page, meaning from the printer's onscreen display. If that doesn't work, you need to start troubleshooting the printer; perhaps the

toner cartridge is empty, or maybe a corona wire is malfunctioning. If the test page prints fine, you can check the printer drivers and other settings at the computer that uses the printer. Restarting the spooler should not help in this situation. If the spooler stalled, then no paper should come out of the printer. Likewise, the printer cable should not have to be replaced.

96. **Answers: A and B.** The easiest and (probably) cheapest way is to move the WAP. Basements are usually the worst place for an access point because of concrete foundations and walls, electrical interference, and so on. Signal boosters might also work, but often the cost of a signal booster is the same as buying a newer, more powerful WAP! Unfortunately, new drivers and firmware usually will not help the situation.

97. **Answer: C.** The simplest solution is often the most common. Check cables and see whether the power is on for your devices and computers.

98. **Answer: B.** The Event Viewer logs all errors that occur on a system. Particularly, the System log would contain the information useful in troubleshooting this error.

99. **Answer: A.** The most common reason for a BSOD (blue screen of death, otherwise known as a stop error) is driver failure. Second on the list is memory/processor-related errors. Hard drives and CD-ROMs themselves should not cause stop errors, but their drivers might.

100. **Answer: A.** Run the installer as an administrator. Programs cannot be installed by standard users or guests. You must have administrative rights to do so.

CHAPTER EIGHT

220-802 Practice Exam B

The previous 220-802 exam was the introduction. This next test will take it to the next level and could be considered an intermediate practice test. I'll be blending in some more difficult questions this time. Unlike the first exam, this one is freestyle, meaning the questions are randomized. You can expect questions from any of the four domains, in any order.

The main goal of this practice exam is to make sure you understand all of the concepts before moving on to the next test. If you didn't already, I suggest taking a break between exams. If you just completed the first exam, give yourself a half-hour or so before you begin this one. If you didn't score 90% or higher on exam A, go back and study; then retake exam A until you pass with 90% or higher.

Write down your answers and check them against the answer key, which immediately follows the exam. After the answer key you will find the explanations for all of the answers. Good luck!

Practice Questions

1. In which step of the CompTIA A+ troubleshooting process would you question the user?

   - ◉ **A.** Identify the problem
   - ○ **B.** Establish a theory
   - ○ **C.** Establish a plan of action
   - ○ **D.** Document findings

2. Which tool would you be using if you were setting the computer to boot with the Selective Startup feature?

   - ○ **A.** Task Manager
   - ○ **B.** Recovery Console
   - ○ **C.** Safe Mode
   - ◉ **D.** Msconfig

3. You have been given the task of installing a new hard drive on a server for a customer. The customer will be supervising your work. What should you ask the customer first?

   - ○ **A.** What is the administrator password?
   - ◉ **B.** Are there any current backups?
   - ○ **C.** Do you want me to shut down the server?
   - ○ **D.** Which version of Windows Server is this?

4. You just upgraded the president's computer's video driver. Now, the Windows XP system will not boot. Which of the following should you try first?

   - ○ **A.** Access the Recovery Console
   - ◉ **B.** Boot into Safe mode and roll back the driver
   - ○ **C.** Reinstall the operating system
   - ○ **D.** Boot into Directory Services Restore mode

5. Which tool is used to analyze and diagnose a video card?

   - ○ **A.** Device Manager
   - ○ **B.** DxDiag
   - ○ **C.** Services.msc
   - ○ **D.** USMT

6. Which of the following is a feature of Windows 7 but not Windows Vista?

- ○ **A.** UAC
- ○ **B.** Aero
- ○ **C.** Application dock
- ○ **D.** Sidebar

7. Where is registry hive data stored?

- ○ **A.** \%systemroot%\Windows
- ○ **B.** \%systemroot%\Windows\System32\Config
- ○ **C.** \%systemroot%\System32
- ○ **D.** \%systemroot%\System32\Config

8. You just built a PC, and when it first boots you hear some beep codes. If you don't have the codes memorized, what are the best devices to examine first? (Select all that apply.)

- ◉ **A.** RAM
- ○ **B.** CD-ROM
- ○ **C.** Video card
- ○ **D.** CPU

9. What is the default initial size of virtual memory in Windows?

- ○ **A.** 1.5 times RAM
- ○ **B.** 3 times RAM
- ○ **C.** 6 times RAM
- ○ **D.** The same as the amount of RAM on the system

10. A co-worker needs to print to a printer from a laptop running Windows 7. The printer has a USB and an Ethernet connector. What is the easiest way to connect the printer to the laptop?

- ○ **A.** Use the parallel port
- ○ **B.** Use the network connection
- ◉ **C.** Use the USB connector
- ○ **D.** Use the Ethernet connector

11. How can you restart the Print Spooler service? (Select the two best answers.)

- ○ **A.** Enter `net stop spooler` and then `net start spooler` in the command line
- ○ **B.** Enter `net stop print spooler` and then `net start print spooler` in the command line
- ○ **C.** Go to Computer Management > Services and restart the Print Spooler service
- ○ **D.** Go to Computer Management > Services and Applications > Services and restart the Print Spooler service

12. Clinton needs a more secure partition on his hard drive. Currently, the only partition on the drive (C:) is formatted as FAT32. He cannot lose the data on the drive but must have a higher level of security, so he is asking you to change the drive to NTFS. What is the proper syntax for this procedure?

- ○ **A.** Change C: /FS:NTFS
- ○ **B.** Change C: NTFS /FS
- ○ **C.** Convert C: /FS:NTFS
- ○ **D.** Convert C: NTFS /FS

13. You work in an Internet cafe that has publicly used desktop computers. The computers need to be accessible by anyone. Which type of password should you set in the BIOS?

- ○ **A.** User
- ○ **B.** Administrator
- ● **C.** Supervisor
- ○ **D.** Guest

14. What is a common risk when installing Windows drivers that are unsigned?

- ● **A.** System stability may be compromised.
- ○ **B.** Files might be cross-linked.
- ○ **C.** The drive might become fragmented.
- ○ **D.** Physical damage to devices might occur.

15. Which of the following utilities can be used to view the startup programs?

- ○ **A.** Ipconfig
- ○ **B.** Ping
- ○ **C.** Regedit
- ○ **D.** DxDiag

16. Tom has a 30 GB hard disk partition (known as C:) on a Windows Vista computer. He has 1.5 GB free space on the partition. How can he defrag the partition?

- ● **A.** He can run the Disk Defragmenter in Computer Management.
- ○ **B.** He can run DEFRAG.EXE -f in the command line.
- ○ **C.** He can run DEFRAG.EXE -v in the command line.
- ○ **D.** He can run DEFRAG.EXE -A in the command line.

17. If you get a Code 1 message about a particular device in the Device Manager, what should you do?

- ○ **A.** Close applications and install RAM
- ○ **B.** Disable the device
- ○ **C.** Update the driver
- ○ **D.** Reinstall the driver

18. Which of the following settings must be established if you want to make a secure wireless connection? (Select all that apply.)

- ○ **A.** The brand of access point
- ○ **B.** The wireless standard used
- ○ **C.** The encryption standard used
- ○ **D.** The SSID of the access point

19. Which Windows utility is used to prepare a disk image for duplication across the network?

- ○ **A.** XCOPY
- ○ **B.** SYSPREP
- ○ **C.** Ghost
- ○ **D.** Image Clone

20. You have had several support requests for one PC located in a school cafeteria kitchen. You have already reseated the PCIe and PCI cards and replaced the hard drive in the PC. Computers located in the business office or the classrooms have not had this issue. What most likely causing the issue?

- ● **A.** Excessive heat
- ○ **B.** Faulty RAM
- ○ **C.** 240 V outlets
- ○ **D.** Power brownouts

21. In Windows Vista, when will a computer dump the physical memory?

- ○ **A.** When the wrong processor is installed
- ○ **B.** When a device is missing drivers
- ○ **C.** When the computer was shut down improperly
- ● **D.** When the computer detects a condition from which it cannot recover

22. If a person takes control of a session between a server and a client, it is known as which type of attack?

- ○ **A.** DDoS
- ○ **B.** Smurf
- ● **C.** Session hijacking
- ○ **D.** Malicious software

23. The message "The Windows Boot Configuration Data File Is Missing Required Information" appears on the screen. Which command would you type to repair this issue?

- ○ **A.** `bootrec /fixboot`
- ○ **B.** `bootrec /fixmbr`
- ○ **C.** `bootrec /rebuildbcd`
- ○ **D.** `boot\bcd`

24. What can be described as a mobile device sharing its Internet connection with other Wi-Fi capable devices?

- ○ **A.** USB tethering
- ○ **B.** Wi-Fi sharing
- ○ **C.** Internet pass-through
- ○ **D.** Wi-Fi tethering

25. Which of the following should be performed during a hard drive replacement to best maintain data privacy?

- ⬤ **A.** Completely erase the old drive prior to disposal
- ○ **B.** Format the new hard drive twice prior to installation
- ○ **C.** Only use FAT32 file systems when formatting the new drives
- ○ **D.** Install antivirus software on the computer before removing the old hard drive

26. You are utilizing WSUS and are testing new updates on PCs. What is this an example of?

- ○ **A.** Host-based firewall
- ○ **B.** Application baselining
- ○ **C.** Patch management
- ○ **D.** Virtualization

27. In Windows XP, how do you fix the "NTLDR is missing or corrupt" error?

- ○ **A.** Run the System Restore utility
- ○ **B.** Restore the registry
- ○ **C.** Restart in Safe Mode
- ⬤ **D.** Run the Recovery Console utility

28. Which of the following troubleshooting steps is next after determining the cause?

- ○ **A.** Document findings, actions, and outcomes
- ○ **B.** Verify full system functionality and, if applicable, implement preventative measures
- ⬤ **C.** Establish a plan of action to resolve the problem and implement the solution
- ○ **D.** Question the user and identify user changes

29. Which tool would you use to back up data on the C: drive in Windows Vista?

- ○ **A.** NTBackup
- ○ **B.** Backup Status and Configuration
- ○ **C.** Task Manager
- ○ **D.** ASR

30. What is the minimum processor requirement for Windows Vista?

- ○ **A.** 133 MHz
- ○ **B.** 233 MHz
- ● **C.** 800 MHz
- ○ **D.** 1 GHz

31. What is the minimum processor requirement for Windows 7?

- ○ **A.** 800 MHz
- ● **B.** 1 GHz
- ○ **C.** 2 GHz
- ○ **D.** 2 GB

32. Where would you go to find out if the hardware in your system is compatible with Windows 7?

- ○ **A.** System Tools
- ○ **B.** System Properties
- ○ **C.** Windows Compatibility Center
- ○ **D.** Resource Monitor

33. You create an answer file to aid in installing Windows 7. Which type of installation are you performing? (Select the best answer.)

- ○ **A.** Disk image installation
- ○ **B.** USB installation
- ○ **C.** Multiboot installation
- ● **D.** Unattended installation

34. How much free disk space is required to install Windows Vista?

- ○ **A.** 20 GB
- ○ **B.** 2 GB
- ○ **C.** 4 GB
- ○ **D.** 15 GB

35. How much free disk space is required to install Windows 7? (Select the two best answers.)

- ○ **A.** 8 GB
- ○ **B.** 10 GB
- ● **C.** 16 GB
- ● **D.** 20 GB

36. A user with a laptop frequently goes into the office to work. However, the laptop only has two USB ports and the user is unable to connect the keyboard, mouse, monitor, and scanner at the same time. What would resolve this problem?

- ○ **A.** KVM switch
- ○ **B.** IEEE 1394 connection
- ◉ **C.** Docking station
- ○ **D.** Bluetooth adapter

Quick Answer: **187**
Detailed Answer: **194**

37. Which component of the Windows GUI includes the clock and other programs that run in the background?

- ○ **A.** Quick Launch
- ○ **B.** Task bar
- ○ **C.** Notification Area
- ○ **D.** Desktop

Quick Answer: **187**
Detailed Answer: **194**

38. How can the Command Prompt be opened as an administrator (known as elevated mode) in Windows 7/Vista? (Select all that apply.)

- ○ **A.** Click Start > All Programs > Accessories; then right-click Command Prompt and select Run as Administrator.
- ○ **B.** Click Start > All Programs >Accessories; then right-click Command Prompt and select Run in elevated mode.
- ○ **C.** Click Start and type **cmd** in the search field, and instead of pressing Enter, press Ctrl+Shift+Enter.
- ○ **D.** Click Start and type **cmd** in Run prompt, and instead of pressing Enter, press Ctrl+Shift+Enter.

Quick Answer: **187**
Detailed Answer: **194**

39. Which version of Windows 7 does *not* include Windows XP Mode?

- ○ **A.** Home Premium
- ○ **B.** Professional
- ○ **C.** Ultimate
- ○ **D.** Enterprise

Quick Answer: **187**
Detailed Answer: **195**

40. Which version of Windows Vista does *not* include remote desktop connection functionality?

Quick Answer: **187**
Detailed Answer: **195**

- ● **A.** Home Premium
- ○ **B.** Business
- ○ **C.** Ultimate
- ○ **D.** Enterprise

41. What should you do first if a printer fails to print very large documents but still prints smaller documents without a problem?

Quick Answer: **187**
Detailed Answer: **195**

- ○ **A.** Check if the correct type of paper is being used
- ○ **B.** Replace the communications cable
- ○ **C.** Change the toner cartridges
- ○ **D.** Add memory to the printer

42. You print an image to your printer, but the page shows a ghosted image. What could be the problem?

Quick Answer: **187**
Detailed Answer: **195**

- ● **A.** The drum needs replacing.
- ○ **B.** The printer is offline.
- ○ **C.** There's an incorrect driver.
- ○ **D.** There's a dirty primary corona wire.

43. A co-worker notices that the battery light on a laptop is flashing when the laptop is in a docking station. Which of the following should you try first to fix the problem?

Quick Answer: **187**
Detailed Answer: **195**

- ○ **A.** Replace the laptop battery
- ○ **B.** Reinstall the operating system
- ● **C.** Reseat in the docking station
- ○ **D.** Remove and reseat the battery

44. One of your customers reports that there is a large amount of spam in her e-mail inbox. What should you recommend the user do?

Quick Answer: **187**
Detailed Answer: **195**

- ○ **A.** Tell the user to create a new e-mail account
- ● **B.** Tell the user to add the senders to the junk e-mail sender list
- ○ **C.** Tell the user to find a new ISP
- ○ **D.** Tell the user to reply to all spam and opt out of future e-mails

45. In Windows Vista, where can devices like the display and hard drives be configured to turn off after a certain amount of time?

- ⦿ **A.** Power plans
- ◯ **B.** Display Properties
- ◯ **C.** Computer Management
- ◯ **D.** Power Options Properties window

46. How can you find out which type of connection the printer is using?

- ◯ **A.** Right-click the printer, select Properties, and click the Sharing tab
- ◯ **B.** Right-click the printer, select Properties, and click the Advanced tab
- ◯ **C.** Right-click the printer, select Properties, and click the Separator Page button
- ⦿ **D.** Right-click the printer, select Properties, and click the Ports tab

47. Your customer is having problems printing from an application. You attempt to send a test page to the printer. Why should a test page be used to troubleshoot the issue?

- ◯ **A.** It allows you to see the quality of the printer output.
- ◯ **B.** The output of the test page allows you to initiate diagnostic routines on the printer.
- ◯ **C.** It verifies the connectivity and illuminates possible application problems.
- ◯ **D.** It clears the print queue and resets the printer memory.

48. A computer's CPU overheats and shuts down the system intermittently. What should you check to fix the problem? (Select the two best answers.)

- ⦿ **A.** Check if the heat sink is secure.
- ◯ **B.** Check the BIOS temperature threshold.
- ⦿ **C.** Check if the fan is connected.
- ◯ **D.** Check if the RAM needs to be reseated.

49. Which programs can you use to test your RAM? (Select the two best answers.)

- ◯ **A.** Task Manager
- ◯ **B.** System Information
- ◯ **C.** Chkdsk
- ◯ **D.** CPU-Z

50. A user's hard drive seems very slow in its reaction time when opening applications. What could be causing this?

Quick Answer: **187**
Detailed Answer: **196**

- ○ **A.** The drive needs to be initialized.
- ○ **B.** The temporary files need to be deleted.
- ◉ **C.** The drive is fragmented.
- ○ **D.** The drive's SATA data connector is loose.

51. A tablet device is having trouble accessing the wireless network. What should you do to troubleshoot the problem? (Select the three best answers.)

Quick Answer: **187**
Detailed Answer: **196**

- ◉ **A.** Power cycle the device
- ○ **B.** Use GPRS instead
- ◉ **C.** Check if the SSID was correct
- ○ **D.** Set up a static IP
- ○ **E.** Forget the network and reconnect to it

52. Which of the following will *not* secure a functioning computer workstation?

Quick Answer: **187**
Detailed Answer: **197**

- ○ **A.** Setting a strong password
- ○ **B.** Changing default usernames
- ○ **C.** Disabling the guest account
- ◉ **D.** Sanitizing the hard drive

53. A user recently purchased a new wireless 802.11n router. After connecting a laptop to the wireless network, he notices that the signal strength on the laptop is poor and only connects at 11 Mbps. The user moved the laptop next to the WAP and is still experiencing the same issue. Which of the following is most likely the cause?

Quick Answer: **187**
Detailed Answer: **197**

- ○ **A.** The cable modem is faulty.
- ◉ **B.** The laptop is connecting to the incorrect wireless network.
- ○ **C.** The router's wireless card drivers are faulty.
- ○ **D.** The wireless antennas on the router need to be replaced.

54. Which utility enables you to implement auditing on a single Windows computer?

Quick Answer: **187**
Detailed Answer: **197**

- ○ **A.** Local Security Policy
- ○ **B.** Group Policy Editor

  ○ **C.** ADDS

  ○ **D.** Services.msc

55. Which file contains ARC paths like the one shown here:
default=multi(0)disk(0)rdisk(0)partition(1)\WINDOWS?

  ○ **A.** NTLDR

  ⊚ **B.** Boot.ini

  ○ **C.** Ntdetect.com

  ○ **D.** Ntbootdd.sys

Quick Answer: **187**
Detailed Answer: **197**

56. What does a device driver do?

  ○ **A.** Modifies applications

  ○ **B.** Works with memory more efficiently

  ○ **C.** Improves device performance

  ⊚ **D.** Allows the OS to talk to the device

Quick Answer: **187**
Detailed Answer: **197**

57. After installing Windows 7 successfully, what should you do next?
(Select the two best answers.)

  ○ **A.** Create policies

  ○ **B.** Connect to WLANs

  ⊚ **C.** Enable the Windows Firewall

  ⊚ **D.** Run Windows Update

Quick Answer: **187**
Detailed Answer: **197**

58. Where are restore points stored after they are created?

  ○ **A.** The Recycler folder

  ○ **B.** The System32 folder

  ○ **C.** The %systemroot% folder

  ○ **D.** The System Volume Information folder

Quick Answer: **187**
Detailed Answer: **198**

59. Which of the following are types of social engineering? (Select the
two best answers.)

  ○ **A.** Malware

  ⊚ **B.** Shoulder surfing

  ⊚ **C.** Tailgating

  ○ **D.** Rootkits

Quick Answer: **187**
Detailed Answer: **198**

60. This is the service that controls the printing of documents in a Windows computer.

Quick Answer: **187**
Detailed Answer: **198**

- ○ **A.** Printer
- ○ **B.** Print server
- ○ **C.** Print pooling
- ◉ **D.** Print spooler

61. Which of the following is the best way to ensure that a hard drive is secure for disposal?

Quick Answer: **187**
Detailed Answer: **198**

- ◉ **A.** Magnetically erase the drive
- ○ **B.** Format the drive
- ○ **C.** FDISK the drive multiple times
- ○ **D.** Convert the drive to NTFS

62. Which user group permission level has the highest amount of access on a Windows computer?

Quick Answer: **187**
Detailed Answer: **198**

- ○ **A.** Supervisor
- ◉ **B.** Administrator
- ○ **C.** Power User
- ○ **D.** Backup operator

63. A burning smell comes from the computer. What is the most likely source?

Quick Answer: **187**
Detailed Answer: **198**

- ○ **A.** Thermal compound
- ○ **B.** Keyboard
- ◉ **C.** Power supply
- ○ **D.** AC outlet

64. A month ago, you set up a wireless access point/router for a small business that is a customer of yours. Now, the customer calls and complains that Internet access is getting slower and slower. As you look at the WAP/router, you notice that it was reset at some point and is now set for open access. You then guess that neighboring companies are using the service connection. How can you restrict their access to your customer's wireless connection? (Select the two best answers.)

Quick Answer: **187**
Detailed Answer: **198**

- ◉ **A.** Configure the wireless access point to use WPA
- ○ **B.** Configure MS-CHAP on the WAP/router
- ◉ **C.** Disable SSID broadcasting
- ○ **D.** Move the WAP/router to another corner of the office

65. A first-level help desk support technician receives a call from a customer and works with the customer to resolve the call for several minutes unsuccessfully. Which of the following should the technician do next?

- ○ **A.** Explain to the customer that he will receive a callback when someone more qualified is available
- ◉ **B.** Escalate the call to another technician
- ○ **C.** Explain to the customer that the problem cannot be resolved and end the call
- ○ **D.** Continue working with the customer until the problem is resolved

66. A customer complains that there is nothing showing on the display of his laptop. What should you attempt first on the computer?

- ○ **A.** Replace the inverter
- ○ **B.** Reinstall the video drivers
- ○ **C.** Boot into Safe mode
- ◉ **D.** Check whether the laptop is in Standby or Hibernate mode

67. Which of the two following components can affect the POST from completing successfully? (Select the two best answers.)

- ○ **A.** Hard drive
- ○ **B.** USB hub
- ◉ **C.** CPU
- ◉ **D.** RAM
- ○ **E.** CD-ROM

68. You just installed a new floppy drive into a computer you use for testing. When the computer boots, you notice that the light for the floppy stays on. What does this mean?

- ○ **A.** The BIOS needs to be reconfigured.
- ○ **B.** The cable is connected backward.
- ○ **C.** The floppy drive has failed.
- ○ **D.** There is too much voltage to the floppy.

69. During an installation of Windows 7, you are given an opportunity to load alternative third-party drivers. Which device are you most likely loading drivers for?

Quick Answer: **187**
Detailed Answer: **199**

- ○ **A.** CD-ROM
- ⊗ **B.** SCSI drive
- ○ **C.** USB mouse
- ○ **D.** BIOS

70. A computer in a Windows workgroup can have how many concurrent connections?

Quick Answer: **187**
Detailed Answer: **200**

- ○ **A.** 10 or fewer
- ○ **B.** 15 or fewer
- ○ **C.** 20 or fewer
- ○ **D.** 25 or fewer

71. You get a message upon booting the system that says "No Hard Disk." What should you check? (Select the two best answers.)

Quick Answer: **187**
Detailed Answer: **200**

- ◉ **A.** That there is power to the hard drive
- ◉ **B.** That there is no controller cable connected to the drive
- ○ **C.** That the CD-ROM is jumpered correctly
- ○ **D.** That the hard drive driver is installed

72. Which of the following disk arrays provides for fault tolerance? (Select the two best answers.)

Quick Answer: **187**
Detailed Answer: **200**

- ○ **A.** Spanned volume
- ○ **B.** RAID 0
- ⊗ **C.** RAID 1
- ⊗ **D.** RAID 5

73. Megan's laptop runs perfectly when at work, but when she takes it on the road, it cannot get on the Internet. Internally, the company uses static IP addresses for all computers. What should you do to fix the problem?

Quick Answer: **187**
Detailed Answer: **200**

- ○ **A.** Tell Megan to get a wireless cellular card and service
- ○ **B.** Tell Megan to use DHCP
- ○ **C.** Tell Megan to configure the alternate configuration tab of TCP/IP properties
- ○ **D.** Configure a static IP address in the Alternate Configuration tab of the user's TCP/IP properties and enable DHCP in the General tab

74. Which command will show you the current network sessions from a PC to the Internet?

- ○ **A.** Ipconfig
- ◉ **C.** Netstat
- ○ **B.** Ping
- ○ **D.** Nbtstat

75. Before implementing a solution to a problem, which of the following should be done?

- ○ **A.** Determine what has changed
- ◉ **B.** Perform a system backup
- ○ **C.** Test the solution
- ○ **D.** Document the solution

76. Which power-saving mode enables for the best power savings, while still allowing the session to be reactivated later?

- ○ **A.** Standby
- ○ **B.** Suspend
- ○ **C.** Hibernate
- ○ **D.** Shutdown

77. John's computer has two hard drives, each 300 GB. The first is the system drive and is formatted as NTFS. The second is the data drive and is formatted as FAT32. Which two of the following statements are true? (Select the two best answers.)

- ◉ **A.** Files on the system drive can be secured.
- ○ **B.** Larger logical drives can be made on the data drive.
- ○ **C.** The cluster size is larger, and storage is more efficient on the system drive.
- ○ **D.** The cluster size is smaller, and storage is more efficient on the system drive.

78. When using the command-line, a switch _____.

- ○ **A.** Enables the command to work across any operating system
- ○ **B.** Is used in application icons
- ○ **C.** Changes the core behavior of a command, forcing the command to perform unrelated actions
- ○ **D.** Alters the actions of a command, such as widening or narrowing the function of the command

79. To connect a Bluetooth headset to a smartphone, what do you need to do? (Select the two best answers.)

- ○ **A.** Pair the device to the phone
- ○ **B.** Install Bluetooth drivers
- ○ **C.** Enter a passcode
- ○ **D.** Disable Wi-Fi

80. A co-worker was installing a new program when the computer suddenly restarted. Now, when the computer starts, it gets partially through the boot process and then reboots. Which of the following is the quickest method to get the computer running without losing any of the user's data?

- ○ **A.** Reinstall the OS
- ○ **B.** Boot using Last Known Good configuration
- ○ **C.** Boot into Safe Mode and perform a Windows System Restore
- ○ **D.** Perform a factory restore

81. In the Recovery Console, what will the command `fixmbr` do?

- ○ **A.** Delete all viruses from the floppy disk
- ○ **B.** Delete all viruses from the hard drive
- ○ **C.** Delete all viruses from the boot sector
- ○ **D.** Delete all viruses from the CD-ROM

82. You need to view any application errors that have occurred today. Which tool should you use?

- ○ **A.** Event Viewer
- ○ **B.** Local Security Policy
- ○ **C.** Msconfig
- ○ **D.** SFC /SCANNOW

83. Which of the following commands can help you modify the start-up environment?

- ○ **A.** Msconfig
- ○ **B.** Ipconfig
- ○ **C.** Boot Config Editor
- ○ **D.** Registry Editor

84. You need to find out which router within the nine steps between you and another computer has failed. Which tool should you use?

Quick Answer: **187**
Detailed Answer: **201**

    ○ **A.** Ping

    ◉ **B.** Tracert

    ○ **C.** Ipconfig

    ○ **D.** Net

85. Which of the following log files would reference third-party software error messages?

Quick Answer: **187**
Detailed Answer: **202**

    ○ **A.** Security log

    ○ **B.** System log

    ◉ **C.** Application log

    ○ **D.** Setuperr.log

86. Mary's printer is printing hundreds of pages, and she can't get it to stop. She has tried to delete the job by double-clicking the printer and deleting the print job. What is the best way to stop the printer?

Quick Answer: **187**
Detailed Answer: **202**

    ○ **A.** Clear the print spooler

    ○ **B.** Unplug the printer

    ○ **C.** Reset the printer

    ○ **D.** Turn off the printer

87. Which troubleshooting command enables you to determine connectivity problems on a Windows XP computer that cannot connect to the Internet?

Quick Answer: **187**
Detailed Answer: **202**

    ○ **A.** `ipconfig /release`

    ○ **B.** `ipconfig /flushdns`

    ◉ **C.** `ipconfig /all`

    ○ **D.** `ipconfig /renew`

88. You are troubleshooting a co-worker's computer. When you ping the loopback address, you receive no response. What does this most likely indicate?

Quick Answer: **188**
Detailed Answer: **202**

    ○ **A.** The LAN is unresponsive.

    ○ **B.** The DHCP server is down.

    ○ **C.** The Ethernet cable needs to be replaced.

    ○ **D.** The TCP/IP protocol is not functioning.

Quick Check

89. You have connected several Bluetooth devices together in an ad-hoc network. Which type of network have you created?

Quick Answer: **188**
Detailed Answer: **202**

○　**A.** LAN

○　**B.** WAN

◉　**C.** PAN

○　**D.** MAN

90. Which of the following provides the lowest level of wireless security protection?

Quick Answer: **188**
Detailed Answer: **202**

○　**A.** Disable the SSID broadcast

○　**B.** Use RADIUS

○　**C.** Use WPA2

○　**D.** Enable WEP on the wireless access point

91. A customer uses an unencrypted wireless network. One of the users has shared a folder for access by any computer. The customer complains that files sometimes appear and disappear from the shared folder. What can you do to fix the problem? (Select the two best answers.)

Quick Answer: **188**
Detailed Answer: **202**

○　**A.** Enable encryption on the router and the clients

○　**B.** Encrypt the disk that has the share using EFS (Encrypting File System)

○　**C.** Increase the level of security on the NTFS folder by changing the permissions

○　**D.** Change the share-level permissions on the shared folder

92. A customer is having difficulties with his hard drive, and the system won't boot. You discover that the operating system has to be reloaded. What is the best way to explain this to the customer?

Quick Answer: **188**
Detailed Answer: **203**

○　**A.** "I need to rebuild the computer."

○　**B.** "I need to format the hard drive and reload the software."

○　**C.** "I need to FDISK the computer."

◉　**D.** "I need to restore the system; data loss might occur."

93. Which of these commands makes a duplicate of a file?

Quick Answer: **188**
Detailed Answer: **203**

○　**A.** Move

⊗　**B.** Copy

○　**C.** Dir

○　**D.** Edit

94. You are troubleshooting a Bluetooth connection that is malfunctioning. What should you attempt? (Select the two best answers.)

Quick Answer: **188**
Detailed Answer: **203**

- ○ **A.** Verify that WLAN is enabled
- ○ **B.** Check if you are in range
- ○ **C.** Unpair the devices
- ○ **D.** Turn Bluetooth off and on

95. Which of the following is the correct sequence to install a keyboard layout in Windows 7?

Quick Answer: **188**
Detailed Answer: **203**

- ○ **A.** Start > Control Panel> Display
- ○ **B.** Start > Control Panel > Region and Language > Keyboards and Languages > Change Keyboard
- ○ **C.** Start > Control Panel> Languages and Region> Personalization
- ○ **D.** Start > Control Panel> Region and Language> Change Keyboard

96. The Windows Vista sidebar contains _____.

Quick Answer: **188**
Detailed Answer: **203**

- ◉ **A.** Gadgets
- ○ **B.** Widgets
- ○ **C.** Bracelets
- ○ **D.** Icons

97. Which tool in Windows enables a user to easily see how much memory a particular process uses?

Quick Answer: **188**
Detailed Answer: **203**

- ○ **A.** System Information Tool
- ○ **B.** Registry
- ◉ **C.** Task Manager
- ○ **D.** Performance Console

98. Windows 7 was installed on a computer with two hard drives: a C: drive and a D: drive. Windows is installed to C:, and it works normally. The user of this computer complains that his applications are disk intensive and that they slow down the computer. How can you resolve the problem?

Quick Answer: **188**
Detailed Answer: **203**

- ◉ **A.** Move the paging file to the D: drive
- ○ **B.** Reinstall Windows on the D: drive rather than on the C: drive
- ○ **C.** Defrag the D: drive
- ○ **D.** Decrease the paging file size

99. You have installed a new maintenance kit for a laser printer with multiple trays that were having paper jam issues. What should you do to ensure that the problem has been resolved?

Quick Answer: **188**
Detailed Answer: **203**

- ◉ **A.** Print a test page from all paper trays
- ○ **B.** Reset the printer's configuration settings
- ○ **C.** Fill the trays with paper
- ○ **D.** Print a calibration page

100. You are troubleshooting a computer that is having trouble connecting to the network. Another technician supposedly just connected it to the LAN with a patch cable. Upon inspection of the patch cable, you find that each plug is wired differently. What should you do?

Quick Answer: **188**
Detailed Answer: **204**

- ◉ **A.** Replace the cable with a straight-through cable
- ○ **B.** Replace the cable with a cross-over cable
- ○ **C.** Replace the cable with a rolled cable
- ○ **D.** Replace the cable with a 568B to 568A cable

Quick-Check Answer Key

1. A	**30.** C	**59.** B and C
2. D	**31.** B	**60.** D
3. B	**32.** C	**61.** A
4. B	**33.** D	**62.** B
5. B	**34.** D	**63.** C
6. C	**35.** C and D	**64.** A and C
7. D	**36.** C	**65.** B
8. A and C	**37.** C	**66.** D
9. A	**38.** A and C	**67.** C and D
10. C	**39.** A	**68.** B
11. A and D	**40.** A	**69.** B
12. C	**41.** D	**70.** A
13. C	**42.** A	**71.** A and B
14. A	**43.** C	**72.** C and D
15. C	**44.** B	**73.** D
16. B	**45.** A	**74.** C
17. C	**46.** D	**75.** B
18. C and D	**47.** C	**76.** C
19. B	**48.** A and C	**77.** A and D
20. A	**49.** A and D	**78.** D
21. D	**50.** C	**79.** A and C
22. C	**51.** A, C and E	**80.** B
23. C	**52.** D	**81.** C
24. D	**53.** B	**82.** A
25. A	**54.** A	**83.** A
26. C	**55.** B	**84.** B
27. D	**56.** D	**85.** C
28. C	**57.** C and D	**86.** A
29. B	**58.** D	**87.** C

88. D

89. C

90. A

91. A and C

92. D

93. B

94. B and D

95. B

96. A

97. C

98. A

99. A

100. A

Answers and Explanations

1. **Answer: A.** You would question the user during step 1 of the CompTIA A+ troubleshooting process: Identify the problem. Also during that step you would identify user changes and perform backups. Afterward, you move on to step 2: Establish a theory of probable cause. Next, it's step 3: Test the theory to determine cause. And after that is step 4: Establish a plan of action to resolve the problem and implement the solution. Next is step 5: Verify full system functionality and, if applicable, implement preventive measures. Finally, step 6: Document findings, actions, and outcomes.

2. **Answer: D.** Msconfig enables you to modify the startup selection. You can boot the computer in different modes with Msconfig. You can also enable and disable services and applications. The Task Manager gives you a snapshot of your system's performance and allows you to shut down applications (tasks) or processes, even if the application is hanging or frozen. The Recovery Console is the command-line repair environment in Windows XP. From here, you can fix system file issues and repair the MBR and boot sector. Safe Mode is one of the options in the Advanced Boot Options Menu (ABOM). It starts the computer with a basic set of drivers, so that you can troubleshoot why devices have failed. It is also instrumental when dealing with viruses.

3. **Answer: B.** Always check whether there are backups and physically inspect and verify the backup before changing out any drives. Making sure that a backup is available is the first order of business. Once the backup has been taken care of, you can have the customer give you the password to log in (or let the customer log in) and find out which version of Windows Server is running.

4. **Answer: B.** By rolling back the driver (which is done in the Device Manager) while in Safe Mode, you can go back in time to the old working video driver. The Recovery Console will not help you with drivers. Reinstalling the OS would wipe the partition of the president's data (and probably wipe you of your job). Directory Services Restore mode (although listed in the Advanced Startup Options) is only for Windows Server domain controllers. Note that Last Known Good configuration would probably be able to help you, but not in all cases.

5. **Answer: B.** The DxDiag utility is used to analyze a video card and check if drivers are digitally signed. It can be accessed by going to Run and typing dxdiag. The Device Manager is used to install drivers for devices. Services.msc is the console window where you can start and stop and enable/disable services such as the Print Spooler. USMT stands for User State Migration Tool, a command-line tool used to migrate user files and settings from one or more computers.

6.. **Answer: C.** The application dock in Windows 7 is not available in Vista. The application dock is an enhanced version of the taskbar. With this, you can hover over applications that are running in the taskbar and view their current statuses (for example, if you have a video running in IE or are downloading something). You can also click and drag applications to and from the dock and close apps if you wish. Docking applications is fairly standard practice nowadays, and several other operating system manufacturers have similar functionality. User Account Control (UAC) and Aero have been available since Windows Vista. The sidebar is available only in Vista; it houses gadgets. However, you can still use gadgets in Windows 7—no sidebar is necessary.

7. **Answer: D.** Remember that %systemroot% is a variable. It takes the place of whatever folder contains the operating system. This will usually be Windows (for Windows 7/Vista/XP). For example, if you were to run a default installation of Windows 7, the path to the Registry hives would be C:\Windows\System32\Config. The main hives are SAM, SECURITY, SOFTWARE, SYSTEM, and DEFAULT. These are accessed and configured by opening the Registry Editor (Run > regedit.exe) and opening the HKEY_LOCAL_MACHINE subtree. Other hive information is stored in the user profile folders.

8. **Answers: A and C.** It is common to have an unseated RAM stick or video card. These are the most common culprits of beep codes during the POST. If the CPU is not installed properly, you might not even get any beep codes at all. And the CD-ROM's functionality has little bearing on the POST.

9. **Answer: A.** By default, Windows (when first installed) analyzes the amount of RAM in the computer and sets the hard drive's initial virtual memory size to 1.5 times that amount. Maximum size is set to 3 times RAM. So, for example, if a user has 1 GB of RAM (1024 MB), the initial virtual memory file (pagefile.sys) is 1.5 GB (1536 MB) and the maximum file size is 3 GB (3072 MB). You can also configure Windows to automatically manage the paging file size.

10. **Answer: C.** Use the USB connector. By far this is the easiest method. Windows will sense the USB connection and attempt to install the print driver automatically (though you should still install the latest proper driver from the printer manufacturer's website). Yes, the printer has an Ethernet connection as well (that *is* the network connection), but that will require you to connect it to the network. What if there is no network? And even if there is, the printer would have to be configured for the network, and then the laptop would have to connect to the printer over the network. If the laptop is the only system that will use the printer, USB becomes much easier. The parallel port (such as LPT1) is the older way of connecting to printers; virtually no PCs or laptops have these anymore. That standard's connection name is IEEE 1284.

11. **Answer: A and D.** In the command line, this service is simply known as Spooler. Type `net stop spooler` and `net start spooler` to restart the service. In Computer Management, the Print Spooler service is found in Services and Applications > Services. Or you could open the Run prompt and type `services.msc`. From there you can start, stop, enable, and disable services.

12. **Answer: C.** The convert command turns a FAT32 drive into a NTFS drive without data loss, allowing for a higher level of data security. The proper syntax is `convert volume /FS:NTFS`.

13. **Answer: C.** The BIOS has several password types, including user and supervisor. The supervisor password is the password needed to actually access the BIOS. The user password is what acts as a safeguard from anyone getting into the operating system. Because these computers can be used by anyone, the user password is not necessary. However, the supervisor password is important to thwart end users from accessing the BIOS (and possibly changing important settings such as the boot sequence). Administrator is an account type in the operating system, as is guest. The computers' operating systems should be configured for guests. This means enabling the guest account and setting that one as the default login. This way, users won't have the ability to install programs or make changes on the computer. However, you should still set a complex password on those computers and change it every month or sooner.

14. **Answer: A.** By installing a driver that is not signed by Microsoft, you are risking insta-bility of the operating system. The driver has no effect on files or drive fragmentation. It is extremely uncommon for a driver to cause physical damage to a device.

15. **Answer: C.** Regedit can be used to view startup programs. This is the executable that opens the Registry Editor. A common place to find some of the startup programs is the path HKEY_LOCAL_MACHINE\SOFTWARE\Microsoft\Windows\CurrentVersion\Run. There are several other subkeys, mostly within the CurrentVersion, that also house startup program information. On another, simpler note, you can also find out programs that run from Startup by going to Start > All Programs > Startup. Ipconfig shows the network configuration of all network adapters. Ping is used to test if other computers on the network can respond to TCP/IP packets of information, thus proving they are functional. DxDiag is used to analyze video cards and the version of DirectX that is running.

16. **Answer: B.** Use defrag.exe –f. You need to have 15 percent free space on your partition to defrag it in the Disk Defragmenter GUI-based utility. However, you can force a defrag on a partition even if you don't have enough free space by using the –f switch in the command line. (-f is not necessary in Windows 7.) The –v switch gives you verbose (or wordy) output. The –a switch gives analysis only and does not perform any defragmentation.

17. **Answer: C.** A Code 1 message means that a device is not configured correctly. Usually this means that the driver should be updated. Another common code, Code 10, means the device cannot start; again, the solution is usually to update the driver. More information on Device Manager codes can be found at the following link: http://support.microsoft.com/kb/943104. Closing an application won't affect the conditions of a device in the Device Manager. Disabling the device is a neat way of sweeping the problem under the rug. One of the keys to a properly running computer is a clean Device Manger, free of all exclamation points, question marks, and down arrows. Reinstalling the same driver will not fix the problem; it will just maintain the status quo, and you'll be left to troubleshoot further.

18. **Answer: C and D.** To make a secure connection, you first need to know the service set identifier (SSID) of the AP and then the encryption being used (for example, WEP or WPA). The SSID takes care of the "connection" portion, and the encryption takes care of the "secure" portion. After all computers are connected, consider disabling the SSID for increased security. Knowing the wireless standard being used can help you verify whether your computer is compatible (802.11n or g), but the brand of access point isn't really helpful.

19. **Answer: B.** SYSPREP is one of the utilities built in to Windows for image deployment over the network. Ghost and Image Clone are third-party offerings. XCOPY copies entire directories (in the same physical order, too) but not from one system to another. SYSPREP preps the system to be moved as an image file.

20. **Answer: A.** Excessive heat is the most likely cause of the problem. This could be an unfortunate result of ovens and other equipment. Computers in environments such as these are often prone to dirt collecting inside the CPU fans and other devices inside the case. Faulty RAM wouldn't cause hard drives to fail or un-seat expansion cards.

The cards probably moved around due to thermal expansion and contraction. 240 V outlets are most likely going to be found in this environment, but the computer shouldn't use those; in the United States the computer should be connected to a 120 V outlet. The computer should be changed to 240 V only if it is brought to another country—for example, in Europe. Power brownouts could cause failures of the power supply, and maybe even the hard drive, but would not cause the adapter cards to be un-seated.

21. **Answer: D.** If the computer fails and cannot recover, you usually see some type of critical or stop error. At this point, you must restart the computer to get back into the operating system (unless it is configured to do so automatically, which is the default setting in Windows 7/Vista). The reason for the physical dump of memory is for later debugging. The physical dump writes the contents of memory (when the computer failed) to a file on the hard disk. Missing drivers will not cause this error, but a failed driver might. If the wrong processor is installed, you can probably not get the system to boot at all. Shutting down the computer improperly just means that the computer recognizes this upon the next reboot and asks whether you want to go into Safe Mode.

22. **Answer: C.** Session hijacking is when an unwanted mediator takes control of the session between a client and a server (for example, an FTP or HTTP session). DDoS is a distributed denial-of-service attack, an attack perpetuated by hundreds or thousands of computers in an effort to take down a single server; the computers are often unknowingly part of a botnet. A Smurf attack is a type of denial-of-service attack that relies on the use of many ping echoes. Malicious software is any compromising code or software that can damage a computer's files; examples include viruses, spyware, and Trojans.

23. **Answer: C.** Bootrec /rebuildbcd attempts to rebuild the boot configuration store. Bootrec /fixboot is one of the methods you can try to repair bootmgr.exe in Windows 7/Vista. Bootrec /fixmbr rewrites the master boot record in 7/Vista. Boot\bcd is where the boot configuration store is located.

24. **Answer: D.** Wi-Fi tethering is when a mobile device shares its Internet connection (effectively becoming its own hotspot) with other Wi-Fi capable devices. USB tethering is when a mobile device shares its Internet connection with a PC or laptop via USB. *Wi-Fi sharing* is not a typically used term. Internet pass-through is when a mobile device connects to a PC via USB, making use of the PC's Internet connection—basically the reverse of USB tethering.

25. **Answer: A.** The drive should be completely erased with bit-level erasure software. Formatting is not enough, as data remanence (residue) is left on the drive from which files can be reconstructed by smart people with some smart software. It is a waste of time to install AV software on a drive *before* removing it. However, AV software should be loaded up when the new drive is installed.

26. **Answer: C.** Patch management is the patching of many systems from a central location. It includes the planning, testing, implementing, and auditing stages. There are various software packages you can use to perform patch management. Windows Server Update Services (WSUS) is an example of Microsoft patch management software. Other Microsoft examples include the System Center Configuration Manager (SSCM) and its predecessor Systems Management Center (SMS), but there are plenty

of third-party offerings as well. A host-based firewall is a software firewall that is loaded on a computer to stop attackers from intruding on a network. Application baselining is the performance measurements of an application over time. Virtualization is when an operating system is installed to a single file on a computer. Often, it runs virtually on top of another OS.

27. **Answer: D.** The Recovery Console is a special recovery tool that is run by booting off of the Windows XP CD. When it is running, you can copy the NTLDR file (from the CD x:\I386) to the root of the hard drive. The recovery console can also be installed to the Windows XP computer's hard drive by accessing the CD and typing x:\i386\winnt32.exe /cmdcons where x is the CD-ROM drive. System Restore is used in Windows 7/Vista/XP to create restore points, snapshots in time that allow you to revert the system back to an earlier configuration. If the NTLDR is missing or corrupt, you won't be able to get to the System Restore utility in Windows XP. You also won't be able to restore the registry, but that doesn't matter because the registry does not have a copy of NTLDR. Finally, restarting in Safe Mode won't work; again, we are dependent on the NTLDR file to get into the OS.

28. **Answer: C.** Establish a plan of action to resolve the problem and implement the solution is the next step after determining the cause, or more specifically: Test the theory to determine cause. It is step four of the six-step CompTIA A+ troubleshooting process. Document findings, actions, and outcomes is the sixth and last step. Verify full system functionality and, if applicable, implement preventative measures is the fifth step. Question the user and identify user changes is part of the first step: Identify the problem.

29. **Answer: B.** Windows Vista's Backup Status and Configuration utility enables a user to back up files or the entire PC. It takes the place of Windows XP's NTBackup. The Windows 7 successor to this is Backup and Restore. The Task Manager is a tool that gives real-time performance statistics of the CPU, RAM, and network card, it allows you to stop services, processes, and applications. ASR stands for Automated System Recovery, an option in Windows XP's NTBackup that enables you to back up and restore the system state (user accounts, settings, boot files, and so forth). It requires a floppy disk for the ASR information in addition to the backup media.

30. **Answer: C.** Windows Vista requires a *minimum* processor frequency of 800 MHz, whereas Windows XP requires 233 MHz, and the unsupported Windows 2000 requires only 133 MHz. 1 GHz is the *recommended* minimum for Windows Vista but not the bare minimum required.

31. **Answer: B.** Windows 7 requires a *minimum* processor frequency of 1 GHz. Windows Vista requires 800 MHz. 2 GHz is not a valid answer for Windows as of the writing of this book. 2 GB is the minimum RAM requirement for 64-bit versions of Windows 7.

32. **Answer: C.** The Windows Compatibility Center is a website (http://www.microsoft.com/windows/compatibility/) that has a hardware section which can tell you if your hardware is compatible. It is the successor to the Hardware Compatibility List (HCL). Other ways to see if your system meets the hardware compatibility requirements are to use the System Information tool in Windows or third-party downloadable analysis tools. As for the incorrect answers: System Tools

is a folder within Start > Accessories that has components such as the Control Panel, Disk Cleanup, and the Resource Monitor, a utility that charts the performance of the computer's components.

33. **Answer: D.** An unattended installation of Windows 7 requires an answer file. This file (normally named unattend.xml) can be created by using the Windows System Image Manager (SIM) program. Unattended installations can be done locally or as part of a network installation using Windows Deployment Services (Server 2008) or Remote Installation Services (Server 2003). Disk image installations use third-party programs such as Ghost or work with a System Restore image created within Windows. Local installation from USB is possible if you copy the Windows 7 .iso file to the USB flash drive (if the drive is big enough) and obtain the USB/DVD download tool from the Microsoft website. A multiboot installation means that more than one operating system are being installed to the same drive. One or both of these could possibly be unattended installations. Remember that with multiboot installs, each OS should inhabit its own primary partition.

34. **Answer: D.** Windows Vista installations require a minimum of 15 GB free space on a 20 GB partition. The important amount to remember for the exam is the free space necessary.

35. **Answers: C and D.** Windows 7 32-bit installations require a minimum of 16 GB free space. 64-bit installations require 20 GB free space. It could get a little confusing, but try to remember: Windows 7 32-bit installs require 16 GB free space, but Windows *Vista* installs require 15 GB free space.

36. **Answer: C.** The docking station will allow the user to connect more USB devices. If the keyboard, mouse, and scanner all use USB, then the laptop doesn't have enough USB ports and the docking station will resolve the problem. Another solution would be a USB hub (perhaps a cheaper one at that, and mobile). The monitor will connect to either a VGA or DVI port, which isn't mentioned in the scenario, though most laptops *and* docking stations will have a secondary video port. KVM switches are used to control two or more computers from a single group of devices: keyboard, mouse, and display. IEEE 1394 connections are great solutions for external hard drives and audio/video devices, but not for scanners. Bluetooth adapters can be used for keyboards and mice, but it's the scanner that is causing the need for extra ports. Scanners often connect via USB and not Bluetooth.

37. **Answer: C.** The Notification Area (also known as the System Tray or systray) includes the clock and programs that run behind the scenes without user intervention. The Quick Launch area houses shortcuts to files and applications. The Taskbar consists of programs that are currently running (and the Windows 7 application dock), the Start button, the Quick Launch, and the Notification Area. The desktop is the area of the GUI that has a wallpaper or background, although some users refer to the entire display as the desktop.

38. **Answers: A and C.** Programs can be run in elevated mode (as an administrator) in Windows 7/Vista by right-clicking the program and selecting Run as Administrator or by using the search field to run the program and pressing Ctrl+Shift+Enter instead of just Enter.

39. Answer: A. Windows 7 Home Premium is the only answer listed that does not include Windows XP Mode. This mode, if installed by downloading additional components from the Microsoft website, allows a person to work in a replica of the Windows XP environment.

40. Answer: A. Windows Vista Home Premium is the only answer listed that does not include Remote Desktop. This tool allows you to take control of remote Windows systems on the network.

41. Answer: D. Add memory to the printer. Large documents, especially ones with graphics, require more memory to print. A printer's memory can be upgraded in a similar manner to a PC's. The paper won't have an effect on large documents, but it could be an issue if the entry rollers are grabbing more than one piece of paper at a time; that would indicate that the pound size of the paper is too thin. If the communications cable was faulty, no pages would print at all; you would probably get a message on the printer's display warning of a bad connection. If a toner cartridge begins to fail, you will see white lines, smearing, or faded ink.

42. Answer: A. A ghosted image or one that seems to repeat usually means the drum (or the entire toner cartridge including the drum) needs to be replaced. If the printer is offline, you won't be able to print to the printer. An incorrect driver will often result in a garbage printout (garbled characters) that is quite unreadable (unless you know garbage printout language). A dirty primary corona wire will often result in lines or smearing.

43. Answer: C. You should first attempt reseating the laptop in the docking station; the laptop probably doesn't have a sturdy connection, resulting in a blinking battery light telling you the laptop is not charging properly (or at all). Do this before you attempt to reseat or replace the battery. This is a hardware issue; the operating system does not have an effect on the blinking battery light.

44. Answer: B. You should recommend that the user add the senders to the junk e-mail sender list. This will block that sender's e-mail address (or the entire domain can be blocked). However, this could take a lot of time; another option is to increase the level of security on the spam filter within the e-mail program. Any further spam can then be sent to the junk e-mail sender list. Users need their e-mail accounts, and creating a new one can result in a lot of work for the user. Finding a new ISP is overreacting a bit; plus the user has no idea if one ISP will be better at stopping spam than another. Never tell a user to reply to spam. Spam e-mails should be sent to the spam folder and never replied to—unless you want ten times the amount of spam.

45. Answer: A. To turn off devices after a specified period of time in Windows 7/Vista, access Control Panel > Power Options. Then click Change Plan Settings for the appropriate power plan. This can be done in Windows XP from the Power Options Properties window in the Power Schemes tab. Display Properties allows you to modify things such as screen resolution. Computer Management is the most used console window in Windows 7/Vista; it includes the Event Viewer, Disk Management, and Services.

46. **Answer: D.** The Ports tab is where you can find how the printer is connected to the computer. This can be an LTP, USB, COM, or TCP/IP port. The Sharing tab allows you to share a locally connected (or remotely controlled) printer on the network. The Advanced tab has options such as print spooling and printer pooling. The Separator page button allows you to configure a page that is inserted after every print job.

47. **Answer: C.** The test page will verify connectivity and give you insight as to possible application problems at the computer that is attempting to print. In this case you aren't worried about the quality of the printer output; it's the computer and the application that you are troubleshooting. Test pages are used to make sure the computer can print properly to the printer, not to initiate diagnostic routines. Those would be initiated from the built-in display and menu on the printer. Printing a test page does not clear the print queue or reset printer memory. This would have to be done at the printer and/or at the computer controlling the printer.

48. **Answers: A and C.** You should make sure that the heat sink is secure and that the fan is connected. Either of these could cause the CPU to overheat. Also make sure that thermal compound was applied to the heat sink. If you didn't log that you did this in writing somewhere, then you will have to take the heat sink off and inspect it. It's a good idea to log when you apply thermal compound because if you remove the heat sink, you will need to reapply thermal compound before reinstalling it. The BIOS temperature threshold is what tripped, causing the system to shut down. Now, you could increase the threshold, which would fix the problem temporarily but could cause permanent damage to the CPU. The threshold is there to protect the CPU; therefore, "BIOS temperature threshold" is not the best answer. If the RAM needed to be reseated, you might get one of several errors or beeps, but the system should not automatically shut down.

49. **Answers: A and D.** Use the Task Manager or CPU-Z to test RAM. CPU-Z is an excellent third-party tool that can be used to test RAM, but there are other third-party tools available as well. In Windows you could also use the Performance Monitor to test how well RAM responds to things such as opening applications and working with media files. System Information will give you information about RAM—for example, how much and what kind—but it is a static utility and has no testing ability. Chkdsk tests the hard drive, not the RAM.

50. **Answer: C.** The drive is fragmented. This is why it is very slow in its reaction time. It's also possible that the OS is infected with a virus. You should analyze and defragment the drive and run an AV sweep of the system. If a drive is not seen by Windows, it might have to be initialized; this can happen when you add a second drive to a system that already has Windows installed. Surplus temporary files might slow down the login process but shouldn't slow the hard drive when opening applications. They can be removed with the Disk Cleanup program or with third-party applications. If the hard drive's SATA data connector were loose, the drive should not be able to access applications. In fact, you would probably get a message that says "Missing OS" or something to that effect.

51. **Answers: A, C, and E.** You can try power cycling the device, checking if the SSID was correct, and forgetting the network and then reconnecting to it. You should also check if the device is within range of the wireless access point, if the device supports the

necessary encryption, and if Internet pass-through or other Internet sharing technologies aren't conflicting. Furthermore, you can power cycle the Wi-Fi program, check if any Wi-Fi sleep is enabled, and try enabling best Wi-Fi performance if the device offers it. As to the incorrect answers: Using the cellular GPRS connection is not a valid option when troubleshooting the Wi-Fi connection. Setting up a static IP on a mobile device is usually not a good idea and not necessary—in fact, this is one of the things you should check in the Advanced settings of the device. If a static IP is applied to the Wi-Fi adapter, it could prevent the device from connecting to all wireless networks except the one that uses that IP network number.

52. Answer: D. Sanitizing the hard drive will not secure a computer workstation. It will, however, prevent anyone from accessing data on the drive, but the computer workstation won't be functional anymore. Setting strong passwords, changing default usernames, and disabling the guest account are all ways of securing a computer workstation.

53. Answer: B. The laptop is probably connecting to a different wireless network either in the home next door or an adjacent business—one without encryption it would seem. Verify the SSID name of the 802.11n router, forget the current wireless network, and connect to the new network. The cable modem isn't a part of the equation in this scenario. We are only interested in connecting to the wireless network to start. A router (wireless access point) won't have a wireless card such as the ones in a PC or laptop. Also, we don't know if the device is faulty yet because the laptop never connected to it. The same goes for the wireless antennae.

54. Answer: A. Because there is only one computer, you can implement auditing only locally. This is done with the *Local* Security Policy. The Group Policy Editor and ADDS are used by Windows Servers in a domain environment. Some versions of Windows have the *Local* Group Policy editor, where auditing can also be turned on. If typed in the Run prompt, services.msc will open the Services console window; services can be turned on and off and enabled and disabled from here.

55. Answer: B. In Windows XP, Boot.ini contains all the ARC paths, which contain the path to the operating system through the hardware and the software. NTLDR is the boot loader file in Windows XP. Ntdetect.com searches for basic hardware on the system. Ntbootdd.sys is necessary if Windows XP is to boot off of a SCSI drive.

56. Answer: D. Device drivers are the connection between the operating system and the device itself. It is a program that makes the interaction between the two run efficiently. It simplifies programming by using high-level application code. The best device drivers come from the manufacturer of the device. They are the ones who developed the device, so it stands to reason that their code would be the most thoroughly tested and debugged.

57. Answers: C and D. To protect the computer, it is important to enable the Windows Firewall or make sure that a third-party firewall is installed and running properly. Windows Update will download the latest security patches for Windows. After a routine installation of Windows, this first Windows update could be time-consuming. It is not recommended to connect to WLANs (wireless networks) before running Windows Update and enabling the firewall.

58. **Answer: D.** After a restore point is made, it is stored in the System Volume Information folder. To view this folder, you must log on as an administrator, show hidden files and folders, and then assign permissions to the account that wants to view that folder.

59. **Answers: B and C.** Shoulder surfing and tailgating are both types of social engineering. A shoulder surfer is someone who attempts to view information on a person's desk or display without the person's knowledge. Tailgating is when a person attempts to gain access to a secure area by following closely on the heels of another employee, usually without his knowledge. A rootkit is a program that is designed to gain administrator level access to a computer. It is a type of malicious software abbreviated as malware.

60. **Answer: D.** The print spooler controls the queue and the printing of documents. The printer is the physical printing device; Microsoft also refers to the print driver software as the printer. A print server is a device that controls one or more printers; it is usually connected to the network. Print pooling is when two or more printers are grouped together so that a user's document will print faster: if one printer is occupied, the other takes over.

61. **Answer: A.** Magnetically erase the drive. Degaussing the drive is an excellent way to remove all traces of data, but only if the drive is electromagnetic! Formatting the drive is not enough due to the data residue that is left behind. FDISK is an older DOS-based command that is used to remove or create partitions on a disk. This will not remove all data either; in fact, it only rewrites data in the master boot record and partition table. The data remains. Converting the drive from FAT to NTFS (with the convert command) keeps the data intact.

62. **Answer: B.** Administrators can have access to everything. Supervisor is something you would see in the BIOS or in other operating systems besides Microsoft Windows. Power users can install software but do not have access to all data by default in Windows XP; however, they are considered a legacy group in Windows 7/Vista and are treated the same as standard users. Backup operators have access to tape backups and backup programs.

63. **Answer: C.** The power supply is the most likely source of a burning smell: When the power supply is brand new, it has a "burn-in" period of 24–48 working hours; when the power supply is about to fail, or does fail, it could burn up the motor that drives the fan. It is possible but unlikely that the thermal compound will cause a burning smell; however, if this does occur, it will be much less noticeable and more chemical in nature. The keyboard should not present a burning smell no matter how fast you type on it. The AC outlet could possibly be the cause of a burning smell and that would be bad news—turn off the circuit breaker immediately. However, the AC outlet is not part of the computer.

64. **Answers: A and C.** If the WAP/router was reset, any security settings that you originally set up are most likely gone. If you backed up the settings previously, you could restore them. Either way, some type of encryption protocol is necessary. The passphrase or network key generated by the WAP/router needs to be installed on each client before it can be recognized on the network. This passphrase/key should be kept

secret, of course. After all the clients have been associated with the WAP/router, disable SSID broadcasting so that no one else can "see" the router (without more advanced software).

65. **Answer: B.** The tech should escalate the call to another technician. This is exactly why help desks are configured in groups: Level 1, Level 2, and the masters (Level 3) and possibly beyond! Don't try to be a superhuman. In technology there is always someone who knows more than you about a specific subject. Route the call to the next level tech and wish the customer good luck. Good help desks are set up in such a way so someone is always available. Every problem can be resolved! It's just a matter of knowledge and persistence. (Remember that when you take the real exams.) Don't try to fix the problem regardless of the time necessary. Your time, and the customer's time, is very valuable. Escalate, so that you, your organization, and the customer can approach and solve the problem efficiently.

66. **Answer: D.** The computer might need a special keystroke, a press of the power button, or just a little more time to come out of Hibernation mode. Remember, check the simple, quick solutions first because they are usually the culprits. Booting into Safe Mode, reinstalling video drivers, and replacing the inverter are all quite time-consuming, but, if necessary, should be attempted in that order—after checking the power state.

67. **Answers: C and D.** The following items can cause the POST to fail: CPU, RAM, motherboard, and video card. Those are considered the big four (to check) when it comes to troubleshooting POST issues. Hard drive failure might be recorded by the BIOS and POST but won't stop the BIOS from attempting to boot, which it won't be able to do and will promptly display a message stating "Missing OS" or something similar. A USB hub is a peripheral device that doesn't affect the POST. CD-ROM drives will not affect the POST either. They won't affect the boot process unless there is a disk in the drive and the CD-ROM drive was first in the BIOS boot order.

68. **Answer: B.** If the controller cable to the floppy is connected backward, the light will stay on and the drive will not function. If a floppy disk were in the drive, it has probably been rendered useless. The BIOS need be reconfigured only if the floppy drive was not recognized or was disabled. If the floppy drive failed, the light probably wouldn't turn on at all, or at the least would not read disks properly. Too much voltage could cause the floppy drive to fail, but the real problem to investigate would be why the drive received too much power. The power supply would have to be troubleshot carefully. Floppy drives are older devices that you don't find on a typical computer anymore, but you might find them in testing environments, scenarios where older programs on floppy disks are used, and older computers in general. Plus, they are still on the CompTIA objectives, so know your floppy technology.

69. **Answer: B.** The SCSI hard drive is the most likely answer. SCSI hard drives and RAID controllers will need special drivers during the installation process of Windows if they are not recognized automatically. In Windows XP you have to press F6 during the text portion of the installation, but in Windows 7/Vista you just click the option for loading third-party drivers. Optical drives and USB devices do not require third-party drivers. The BIOS doesn't use a driver; it is firmware.

70. Answer: A. Any Windows computer in a Windows workgroup can have 10 maximum concurrent connections to it over the network. If you need more, you will want to consider a Microsoft Domain. There are versions of Microsoft's Small Business Server that allow maximums of 25 concurrent connections and 75 connections. If you need more than that, then you require the full version of Windows Server.

71. Answers: A and B. If you get a message stating that there is no hard disk, chances are that one of the connections is missing or loose. In the uncommon case, the hard drive might be bad (although it does happen). The CD-ROM should not have any bearing on this; plus, only IDE CD-ROM drives require jumpers, and those are less common than SATA drives.

72. Answer: C and D. RAID 1 (mirroring) provides fault tolerance by copying information to two drives. RAID 5 (striping with parity) provides fault tolerance by keeping a compressed copy of the data (in the form of parity) on each of the disks other than where the original data is stored. RAID 0 is striping only, and a spanned volume is one that stores data on two or more drives, but as whole files, not as stripes of data.

73. Answer: D. Megan shouldn't do anything. As a technician, you should fix the problem. The issue is that she needs to obtain an IP address through DHCP when on the road. But setting the network adapter to obtain an IP address automatically is not enough. In order to connect to the internal company network, the Alternate Configuration tab will need to be configured as a "User Configured" static IP address. This solution enables Megan to connect to networks while on the road by obtaining IP addresses automatically and allows her to connect to the internal company network with the static IP address.

74. Answer: C. Netstat shows the network statistics of a computer. It displays the network connections by name, IP address, and port of the local and remote computers. Ipconfig shows the network card's configuration. Ping tests if a computer is alive on the network. Nbtstat stands for NetBIOS over TCP/IP statistics. This displays protocol statistics and name tables.

75. Answer: B. Most of the time you should perform a backup of data before making changes to a system or implementing a solution. It's not always necessary—for example, if a network cable was unplugged or a disc is stuck in the DVD-ROM drive. But if you need to make changes to the OS, you should perform a backup. It is part of step 1 of the six-step troubleshooting process: Identify the problem. Determining what has changed is also part of step 1. Testing the solution is part of step 5: Verify full system functionality. Documenting the solution is part of step 6: Document findings.

76. Answer: C. Hibernate mode saves all the contents of RAM (as hiberfil.sys in the root of C:) and then shuts the system down so that it is using virtually no power. To reactivate the system, you must press the power button. At that point, the entire session is loaded from RAM and you can continue on with the session. Standby and suspend modes turn off the hard drive and display and throttle down the CPU and RAM, but they still use power, and although these power modes use less power than the computer being powered on, altogether they end up using much more power than Hibernate mode does. Shutdown is great for power savings, but the session is lost when the computer is shut down.

77. **Answers: A and D.** NTFS can use NTFS file-level security, whereas FAT32 cannot. NTFS cluster sizes are smaller than FAT32 clusters. NTFS partitions are therefore more efficient (when installed correctly) than FAT32 partitions. NTFS can create larger partitions (or logical drives) than FAT32 in general.

78. **Answer: D.** A switch (aka option) alters the action of the command but *not* by forcing it to perform unrelated actions. The switch will work only at the current time within the operating system you are currently using, so "work across any operating system" wouldn't make sense in this scenario. Switches are not used in application icons. They are used within commands—for example, dir /p, which would display directory contents by the page.

79. **Answers: A and C.** To connect a Bluetooth headset to a smartphone, you must pair the device to the phone; then, if necessary, you enter a passcode into the phone to use the device. Most mobile devices have Bluetooth installed and will usually recognize devices automatically. If not, you might have to update Bluetooth on the device or update the device's OS. Disabling Wi-Fi is not necessary; however, Wi-Fi and Bluetooth have been known to have conflicts, and sometimes one must be disabled to use the other.

80. **Answer: B.** You should boot the system to the Advanced Boot Options Menu (ABOM) and select Last Known Good Configuration. This will revert the system back to the last known good as long as someone has not logged in successfully to the computer. If, however, that didn't work, you could try booting into Safe Mode (also in the ABOM) and perform a System Restore (or restore from the DVD WinRE). After you have exhausted all possibilities, try a factory restore or reinstall the OS.

81. **Answer: C.** Fixmbr in Windows XP rewrites a new Master Boot Record (MBR) to the primary hard disk, killing all boot sector viruses. In the old days (although still usable today with a DOS boot disk), the DOS equivalent of this was fdisk /mbr. To delete viruses from any disk or disc, you would need to use antivirus scanning software.

82. **Answer: A.** The Event Viewer contains the log files of all the errors that occur on the machine. In this case, you would go to the Application log. Another common log is the System log, which will show errors concerning the OS and drivers. On Windows XP, Dr. Watson also shows many of the application errors that occur. Local Security Policy is where you can set up auditing and create password policies for the computer. Msconfig enables you to boot the computer in different modes and enable/disable services and applications. SFC /SCANNOW is a command run in the Command Prompt (as an administrator only) that scans the integrity of the protected system files and repairs them if possible.

83. **Answer: A.** The MSCONFIG.EXE utility enables you to modify the startup environment via the General and Startup tabs. Ipconfig displays all network adapters' settings. The Boot Config Editor is BCDEdit; it is used to modify the Boot Configuration Data (BCD) store. You might need to modify this if you are trying to dual-boot a computer. The Registry Editor allows you to make changes to Windows by accessing various hives of information and individual entries.

84. **Answer: B.** Use the tracert (traceroute) command. This will identify all the routers along the way between you and the final destination. You will know if one has failed because the trace will either stop working or you will see asterisks instead of

ping times. A similar option to this is the command `pathping`. `Ping` by itself only tests the final destination; it doesn't show anything in-between. `ipconfig` displays the configurations for each network adapter. The `net` command has many uses—for example, `net stop spooler`, which stops the print spooler service.

85. **Answer: C.** The application log in the Event Viewer will display errors concerning Windows applications as well as third-party applications. The security log shows auditing events. The system log shows events concerning system files, drivers, and operating system functionality. Setuperr.log is a log file that is created during the installation of Windows. If it is created, it is stored in %windir%\Panther and is not within the Event Viewer.

86. **Answer: A.** Try not to turn off the printer unless absolutely necessary. Instead, clear the printer spooler. You would do this by stopping the Print Spooler service in Computer Management (or in the command prompt by entering `net stop spooler`) and then deleting the files in the path C:\Windows\System32\Spool\ Printers.

87. **Answer: C.** `ipconfig /all` gives the most information about the network connection. Many networking issues can be analyzed and troubleshot from this command. `ipconfig /release` and `ipconfig /renew` are for releasing and renewing DHCP addresses. `ipconfig /flushdns` purges the DNS resolver cache.

88. **Answer: D.** Pinging the loopback address should return results even if you are not physically connected to the network. It deals with the computer internally and doesn't even need a LAN. You can ping the local computer with the commands `ping loopback` and `ping localhost`; however, the best option is to ping the actual loopback IP address by typing `ping 127.0.0.1`. This removes any possible name resolution that might try to occur in Windows. Pinging the loopback address doesn't make use of the network, so the LAN, DHCP servers, and the Ethernet cable do not play into the scenario.

89. **Answer: C.** A personal area network (PAN) is a network of small computers, smartphones, and other similar devices. Using Wi-Fi or Bluetooth is very common when creating a cable-free type of PAN known as a wireless PAN or WPAN. Ad-hoc means that there is no wireless access point controlling the network. A local area network (LAN) is a network that is inhabited by PCs, laptops, and mobile devices; everything connects to a central connecting device such as a switch (or a SOHO router). A wide area network (WAN) connects two or more LANs over a large geographic area. A metropolitan area network (MAN) connects two or more LANs in a smaller geographic area—for example, two buildings.

90. **Answer: A.** Disabling the SSID broadcast is a security precaution, but it only keeps out the average user. Any attacker with two bits of knowledge can scan for other things the wireless access point broadcasts. Interestingly, using WEP is considered more secure than not using it and disabling the SSID. RADIUS is an external method of authenticating users; it often requires a Windows Server. WPA2 is very secure; if you had one security option you could enable, make it WPA2.

91. **Answers: A and C.** Use WPA or WPA2 on the router (and clients) to deny wardrivers and other stragglers access to the customer's network. Increase the level of NTFS security by changing the permissions in the Security tab of the shared folder. EFS isn't

necessary if you set up WPA2 on the wireless access point, but if you are dealing in seriously confidential information, you might consider it as well. Here's the deal: Share-level permissions are rarely modified. NTFS permissions take precedence and are more configurable, so that is where the bulk of your time configuring permissions will go.

92. Answer: D. Always explain specifically and exactly what you must do and what the ramifications are. Do not use acronyms or jargon, and make sure the customer is fully aware of the situation.

93. Answer: B. Copy is used to make a duplicate of the file in another location. Move enables you to take a file and shift it to another location. Dir gives you the contents of a specific folder. Edit enables you to create and edit text files.

94. Answers: B and D. Check if you are within range; the range of Bluetooth devices is limited—for example, Class 2 devices are limited to 10 meters. Also try power cycling the Bluetooth program. In addition to those correct answers, you can try charging the device, restarting the device, working with a known good Bluetooth device, attempting to forget the device, and reconnecting it.

95. Answer: B. Start > Control Panel > Region and Language > Keyboards and Languages > Change Keyboard is the correct sequence. The Display option has no settings for keyboards. It is called Region and Language, not Languages and Region. You click the Change Keyboard button after accessing the Keyboards and Languages tab, a key step.

96. Answer: A. The sidebar in Windows Vista contains gadgets that offer specialized information like weather and traffic. Windows 7 doesn't use the Sidebar, but you can still make use of Gadgets. Widgets are the same types of small applications but are usually web-based. Icons are files or programs on the desktop. Bracelets belong on people, not on computer screens.

97. Answer: C. The Task Manager enables a user to see the amount of memory and % of processing power a particular process uses in real-time. This can be done on the Processes tab. System Information gives you information about the hardware and software of the computer, but it is static (text only) and doesn't change in real-time. The registry stores all of the settings of Windows and is modified with the Registry Editor. Performance Console can graph the performance of the different components in the computer and, if configured properly, can do the same thing as the Task Manager in this scenario, but not as easily.

98. Answer: A. By moving the paging file (or swap file, aka virtual memory) to the D: drive, you are freeing up C: to deal with those disk-intensive programs. Reinstalling Windows is a huge process that you should avoid at all costs, especially when unnecessary, such as in this example. Defragging the C: drive would help if that is where the OS and applications are, but defragging the D: drive will not speed up the applications. Decreasing the page file size never helps. However, increasing the size, moving it, and adding RAM are all ways to make applications run faster.

99. Answer: A. Always test after a job is "finished." The job actually isn't complete until you have tested the solution. In this case, print a test page from each of the paper trays. Resetting configuration settings might cause the printer to print in a way that is undesirable to customers. Don't change settings unless you are asked to do so by the customer or if something fails; remember, in this scenario you are maintaining the printer. Filling the trays with paper won't really prove anything, but it is a nice thing to do. Printing a calibration page is standard practice whenever installing or performing maintenance to a printer, but that also does not resolve any problems—unless the problem was printer calibration!

100. Answer: A. The patch cable should be wired the same on both ends. Normally, a computer will connect to a switch (or to an RJ45 jack) with a straight-through cable. This cable is wired the same way on each end, usually adhering to the 568B standard. Always carry an extra straight-through cable with you! A cross-over cable is wired differently on each end—568B on one end and 568A on the other. It is used to connect a computer to another computer or a switch to another switch. This could be what the other technician mistakenly installed. You can see this if you look carefully at the plugs on each end, but it would be easier to use a patch cable tester. A rolled cable is one that allows connectivity from a computer's serial port to the console port of a router. Each of these cables uses RJ45 plugs so they can be somewhat difficult to differentiate between.

CHAPTER NINE

220-802 Practice Exam C

Let's turn up the heat a bit more. The previous 220-802 exam was the intermediate test. This next test could be considered an advanced practice test. A large percentage of the questions will have a higher difficult rating. Be ready for questions with longer, more in-depth scenarios and more complex answers. This exam is freestyle, meaning the questions are randomized. You can expect questions from any of the four domains, in any order.

If you didn't already, I suggest taking a break between exams. If you just completed the second exam, give yourself a half-hour or so before you begin this one. If you didn't score 90% or higher on exam B, go back and study; then retake exam B until you pass with 90% or higher.

Write down your answers and check them against the answer key, which immediately follows the exam. After the answer key you will find the explanations for all of the answers. Good luck!

Practice Questions

1. A customer brings in a computer that doesn't display anything when it is turned on. You verify that the computer and monitor are receiving power and that the monitor is securely connected to the computer's only video port. Which of the following could possibly cause this problem? (Select all that apply.)

   - **A.** Motherboard
   - **B.** RAM
   - **C.** Hard drive
   - **D.** DVD-ROM
   - **E.** CPU
   - **F.** Power supply
   - **G.** Video card
   - **H.** SATA data cable

Quick Answer: **228**
Detailed Answer: **230**

2. What protects confidential information from being disclosed publicly?

   - **A.** Classification
   - **B.** Social engineering
   - **C.** RAS
   - **D.** Hard drive wipe

Quick Answer: **228**
Detailed Answer: **230**

3. Your co-worker just installed a new printer, replacing his older one. However, when he tries to print from Microsoft Word, the old printer comes up in the print window. What should you tell him?

   - **A.** Save the print job by printing to file, and then print the file with the new printer selected
   - **B.** Select the new printer from the list every time a document is printed
   - **C.** Open the Printers folder, right-click the new printer, and then select Properties > Security Tab > Make This the Default Printer
   - **D.** Open the Printers folder, right-click the new printer, and then click Set as Default Printer

Quick Answer: **228**
Detailed Answer: **230**

4. Programs that run when Windows starts are stored in which of the following registry hives?

   ◯ **A.** HKEY_CURRENT_CONFIG

   ◯ **B.** HKEY_USERS

   ◯ **C.** HKEY_LOCAL_MACHINE

   ◯ **D.** HKEY_CLASSES_ROOT

Quick Answer: **228**
Detailed Answer: **230**

5. Typically, which Windows tool enables you to configure a SOHO router?

   ◯ **A.** Internet Explorer

   ◯ **B.** Device Manager

   ◯ **C.** Msconfig

   ◯ **D.** Windows Explorer

Quick Answer: **228**
Detailed Answer: **231**

6. Which of the following steps is performed first when running a clean install of Windows 7 Professional on a new hard drive?

   ◯ **A.** Format the partition

   ◯ **B.** Partition the drive

   ◯ **C.** Configure Windows settings

   ◯ **D.** Load RAID drivers

Quick Answer: **228**
Detailed Answer: **231**

7. A co-worker maps a network drive for a user, but after rebooting, the drive is not seen within Windows Explorer. Which of the following steps should be taken to ensure that the drive remains mapped?

   ◉ **A.** Check Reconnect at Logon when mapping the drive

   ◯ **B.** Select the drive letter needed to connect each time the co-worker logs on

   ◯ **C.** Check the Folder connection when mapping the drive

   ◯ **D.** Use the net use command instead

Quick Answer: **228**
Detailed Answer: **231**

8. Based on the physical hardware address of the client's network device, which of the following is commonly used to restrict access to a network?

   ◯ **A.** WPA key

   ◯ **B.** DHCP settings

   ◯ **C.** MAC filtering

   ◯ **D.** SSID broadcast

Quick Answer: **228**
Detailed Answer: **231**

9. While troubleshooting a network problem, you discover that one set of LED lights on a switch is blinking rapidly even when all other nodes are disconnected. Which of the following is most likely the cause? (Select the two best answers.)

   ○ **A.** A switch that is not plugged into a server
   ○ **B.** A defective hard drive in the computer
   ○ **C.** A defective network card in the computer
   ○ **D.** An unplugged server
   ○ **E.** A defective port on the network switch

10. A user with an Android phone is attempting to get e-mail to work properly. The user can send e-mail but cannot receive it. The user is required to connect to an IMAP server, as well as an SMTP server that uses SSL. Which port is configured incorrectly?

    ○ **A.** 25
    ○ **B.** 110
    ○ **C.** 143
    ○ **D.** 443

11. You are called to a school lab to fix a computer. The computer supposedly worked fine the day before, but now it does not power on. The computer is plugged into a power strip with another computer. The other computer works fine. Which of the following could be the problem? (Select the two best answers.)

    ○ **A.** The power cable is unplugged from the computer.
    ○ **B.** The power strip is overloaded.
    ○ **C.** The monitor is unplugged.
    ○ **D.** The voltage switch on the computer is set incorrectly.
    ○ **E.** The power strip is unplugged.

12. Tracy cannot connect to the network. She asks you to help. What should you do first?

    ○ **A.** Replace the NIC
    ○ **B.** Reconfigure TCP/IP
    ○ **C.** Check for a link light on the NIC
    ○ **D.** Install the latest NIC drivers

13. A print job fails to leave the print queue. Which of the following services may need to be restarted?

Quick Answer: **228**
Detailed Answer: **232**

- ○ **A.** Print driver
- ◉ **B.** Print spooler
- ○ **C.** Network adapter
- ○ **D.** Printer

14. After installing a network application on a computer running Windows, the application does not communicate with the server. Which of the following actions should be taken first?

Quick Answer: **228**
Detailed Answer: **232**

- ○ **A.** Uninstall the service pack
- ○ **B.** Reinstall the latest service pack
- ◉ **C.** Add the port number and name of the service to the Exceptions list of Windows Firewall
- ○ **D.** Add the port number to the network firewall

15. A customer reports a problem with a PC located in the same room as cement testing equipment. The room appears to have adequate cooling. The PC will boot up but locks up after 5–10 minutes of use. After a lockup it will not reboot immediately. Which the following is the most likely problem?

Quick Answer: **228**
Detailed Answer: **232**

- ○ **A.** The PC has a virus.
- ◉ **B.** The PC air intakes are clogged with cement dust.
- ○ **C.** The CPU heat sink is underrated for the CPU.
- ○ **D.** The power supply is underrated for the electrical load of the PC.

16. Which of the following commands facilitates viewing the entire path from you to a server on the other side of the country?

Quick Answer: **228**
Detailed Answer: **233**

- ○ **A.** Ipconfig
- ○ **B.** Ping
- ○ **C.** Nslookup
- ◉ **D.** Tracert

17. Which of the following hardware cards enables the full functionality of the Windows 7 Media Center Live TV option?

Quick Answer: **228**
Detailed Answer: **233**

- ◉ **A.** TV tuner
- ○ **B.** Modem
- ○ **C.** Video card
- ○ **D.** Network adapter

18. When accessing an NTFS shared resource, which of the following is required? (Select the two best answers.)

○ **A.** An active certificate

◉ **B.** Correct user permissions

○ **C.** Local user access

◉ **D.** Correct share permissions

19. A friend of yours is experiencing unusual problems with a printer due to voltage fluctuations in the wall outlet. Which of the following should be used to eliminate the fluctuations?

◉ **A.** UPS

○ **B.** Multimeter

○ **C.** Surge protector

○ **D.** Gas generator

20. Your co-worker's iPad is having trouble connecting to e-mail. How should you troubleshoot this? (Select the three best answers.)

◉ **A.** Verify Internet access

○ **B.** Check for Bluetooth connectivity

◉ **C.** Check port numbers

○ **D.** Make sure that GPS is enabled

◉ **E.** Verify username/password

21. Which of the following protocols should you set up for the most secure wireless connection?

○ **A.** WEP

○ **B.** WPA

◉ **C.** WPA2

○ **D.** WAP

22. You observe that the lights in a customer's building flicker periodically during the course of the day. Which of the following should you recommend to protect the customer's computer equipment?

○ **A.** Power supply

◉ **B.** UPS

○ **C.** Generator

○ **D.** Heavy-duty electrical cord

23. You are contracted to recover data from a laptop. In which two locations might you find irreplaceable, valuable data? (Select the two best answers.)

- ○ **A.** Ntoskrnl.exe
- ○ **B.** Windows folder
- ◉ **C.** Pictures
- ◉ **D.** E-mail
- ○ **E.** System32 folder   1 - OS 2 - profiles

24. You just installed Microsoft Windows to a computer with three internal SATA hard drives and one external USB hard drive. SATA hard drive 1 contains the operating system. SATA hard drive 2 contains the user profiles. SATA hard drive 3 and the external USB hard drive are empty. Where should you place the page file for maximize performance?

- ○ **A.** External USB hard drive
- ○ **B.** Internal SATA hard drive 1
- ○ **C.** Internal SATA hard drive 2
- ◉ **D.** Internal SATA hard drive 3

Quick Answer: **228**
Detailed Answer: **234**

25. Which utility enables auditing at the local level?

- ○ **A.** Group Policy
- ◉ **B.** Local Security Policy
- ○ **C.** Active Directory Policy
- ○ **D.** Site Policy

Quick Answer: **228**
Detailed Answer: **234**

26. Which of the following can you do to optimize an infrared connection between a laptop and a printer? (Select the two best answers.)

- ◉ **A.** Shorten the distance
- ○ **B.** Install a repeater device
- ○ **C.** Boost the power
- ◉ **D.** Maintain a clear line of sight
- ○ **E.** Change the transmission channel

Quick Answer: **228**
Detailed Answer: **234**

27. How does NAT provide additional security for users who are behind a gateway?

- ○ **A.** It sets the hours that users can access the Internet.
- ○ **B.** It blocks computers on the Internet from accessing computers on the LAN.
- ○ **C.** It limits users from accessing particular websites.
- ○ **D.** It blocks computers on the LAN from accessing computers on the Internet.

Quick Answer: **228**
Detailed Answer: **234**

28. A customer plugs in a new USB barcode reader and the computer recognizes it, but the reader is unable to work properly. What is the most likely reason?

- ○ **A.** Faulty USB cable.
- ○ **B.** The operating system needs to be updated.
- ◉ **C.** Software drivers need to be updated.
- ○ **D.** Too many USB devices are plugged in.

29. A customer has forgotten his password. He can no longer access his company e-mail address. What should you tell him?

- ○ **A.** That he should remember his password ✗
- ◉ **B.** That you need information confirming his identity
- ○ **C.** That the password will be reset in several minutes
- ○ **D.** That he shouldn't do that ✗

30. What can help locate a lost or stolen mobile device?

- ○ **A.** Passcode
- ○ **B.** Auto-erase
- ◉ **C.** GPS
- ○ **D.** Encryption

31. One of your customers is having difficulty with two network connections in the accounting office. The accounting office is adjacent to the building's mechanical room. Network cables run from the accounting office, through the drop ceiling of the mechanical room, and into the server room next door. What should you recommend to the customer?

- ○ **A.** UTP ✗
- ○ **B.** Plenum-rated cable ✗
- ○ **C.** 568B ✗
- ◉ **D.** Fiber optic

32. Which the following can be disabled to help prevent access to a wireless network?

- ○ **A.** MAC filtering
- ◉ **B.** SSID broadcast
- ○ **C.** WPA2 passphrase
- ○ **D.** WPA key

33. John can't get any sound out of his laptop's speakers. What are two possible issues that could cause this? (Select the two best answers.)

- ⊘ **A.** The sound driver needs to be installed.
- ○ **B.** The laptop is on battery power.
- ○ **C.** He's using the wrong version of Windows Media Player.
- ◉ **D.** The volume is turned down.

34. A customer reports that a computer is very loud and occasionally turns itself off. The computer is located under a desk directly on top of the carpet. How would you remedy the situation? (Select the two best answers.)

- ◉ **A.** Remove the computer from the floor
- ○ **B.** Install a new hard drive
- ○ **C.** Replace the power cord
- ○ **D.** Wipe the computer down with a cloth
- ◉ **E.** Clean the inside of the computer

35. After booting his laptop, Jason complains that instead of just letters, he is getting numbers and letters when he types in his username. Because of this, he cannot log on to Windows. What could be the issue?

- ○ **A.** The Caps Lock is on.
- ○ **B.** Bad keyboard.
- ○ **C.** Numlock is on.
- ○ **D.** Wrong keyboard driver.

36. Which of the following commands would be used to set the time on a workstation?

- ⊘ **A.** Time
- ○ **B.** Net time
- ○ **C.** Net timer
- ○ **D.** Net time set

37. Michelle's laptop powers on only when the AC adapter is connected to it. What is wrong with the laptop?

- ○ **A.** Bad transformer
- ○ **B.** Bad AC port on the laptop
- ◉ **C.** Bad battery
- ○ **D.** Bad CMOS battery

38. Which of the following commands would result in the following output?

```
192.168.1.100  00-1C-C0-09-08-07
```

- ○ **A.** Arp -a
- ○ **B.** Ping
- ○ **C.** Nbtstat -a
- ○ **D.** Arp

Quick Answer: **228**
Detailed Answer: **236**

39. In Windows Vista, which utility enables you to select and copy characters from any font?

- ○ **A.** Language bar
- ○ **B.** Sticky keys
- ○ **C.** Control Panel > Fonts
- ◉ **D.** Character map

Quick Answer: **228**
Detailed Answer: **236**

40. Which of the following can be described as removing the limitations of Apple iOS?

- ○ **A.** Rooting
- ○ **B.** Jailbreaking
- ○ **C.** VirusBarrier
- ○ **D.** Super-admin powers

Quick Answer: **228**
Detailed Answer: **236**

41. Which of the following built-in applets should a technician use to configure offline files and folders in Windows 7?

- ○ **A.** Microsoft PowerToys
- ○ **B.** USMT
- ○ **C.** Robust file copy
- ◉ **D.** Sync Center

Quick Answer: **228**
Detailed Answer: **236**

42. Which language support for representing characters is built in to Windows?

- ○ **A.** Unicode
- ○ **B.** EBCDIC
- ○ **C.** ASCII
- ○ **D.** ITU-T

Quick Answer: **228**
Detailed Answer: **237**

43. A user has just moved to a new office and is unable to access the network. You suspect the user's network settings need to be changed. Which of the following commands should you issue on the Windows XP computer to view the network settings?

- ○ **A.** Tracert
- ◉ **B.** Ipconfig
- ○ **C.** Netdiag
- ○ **D.** Pathping

44. Tony's printer is printing all blank pages. What is the cause of this?

- ○ **A.** No power to the transfer corona.
- ○ **B.** Dirty primary corona.
- ○ **C.** Toner cartridge needs to be replaced.
- ○ **D.** Printer is not plugged into the USB port.

45. Which of the following is the best source of information about malicious software detected on a computer?

- ○ **A.** Operating system documentation
- ◉ **B.** Anti-spyware software website
- ○ **C.** Readme.txt file included with the anti-spyware software installation
- ○ **D.** The user of a previously infected computer

46. Your company's network printer is no longer printing. All cables and settings are correct. You can ping the gateway but not the printer's IP. Which is most likely the problem?

- ○ **A.** The printer memory is full.
- ○ **B.** The printer needs a new maintenance kit.
- ○ **C.** The printer is not running in full duplex.
- ◉ **D.** The printer NIC is faulty.

47. Viruses have been detected and removed on a customer's computer several times during the course of several weeks. Which of the following will best help prevent future occurrences?

- ○ **A.** Delete temporary files, cookies, and browser history
- ○ **B.** Defragment the hard drive
- ○ **C.** Install antivirus software that uses manual updates
- ◉ **D.** Discuss safer web browsing habits with the customer

48. Which of the following sends an invitation by e-mail asking for help?

- ○ **A.** Remote Desktop
- ○ **B.** Service call
- ○ **C.** VNC
- ○ **D.** Remote Assistance

49. When performing a clean installation, which of the following is the default location for the system files of Windows 7?

- ○ **A.** C:\Windows
- ○ **B.** C:\Windows\System32\Config
- ○ **C.** C:\System Files
- ○ **D.** C:\Windows\System32

50. You are required to set up a remote backup solution for an Android tablet. The files cannot be stored at any company location. Which technology should you select?

- ○ **A.** iCloud
- ◉ **B.** Android Cloud backup
- ○ **C.** Microsoft Cloud
- ○ **D.** Local NAS device

51. You need to copy and paste information from a web page, but you want to remove all formatting so that it can be pasted cleanly into Word. Which program should you use as an intermediary?

- ○ **A.** CMD
- ○ **B.** Excel
- ◉ **C.** Notepad
- ○ **D.** MMC

52. A computer is responding slowly and the Windows Task Manager shows that spoolsv.exe is using 95% of system resources. Which of the following is most likely the cause of this problem?

- ○ **A.** Windows update is running.
- ○ **B.** A virus infection has occurred.
- ○ **C.** Hyperthreading has been disabled.
- ○ **D.** The printing subsystem.

53. Which of the following descriptions classifies the protocol IMAP?

- ○ **A.** A protocol that allows real-time messaging
- ○ **B.** An e-mail protocol that allows users to selectively download messages
- ○ **C.** An e-mail protocol that allows users to send but not to receive messages
- ○ **D.** A protocol that authenticates users who are sending e-mail

54. A user reports that a laser printer is printing poorly. You observe that the pages have wrinkles and random patterns of missing print. What is the most likely problem?

- ◉ **A.** The fuser needs to be replaced.
- ○ **B.** The toner cartridge is defective. ✗
- ○ **C.** The corona wire is frayed. ✗
- ○ **D.** There is high humidity in the room. ✗

55. Which of the following is a user-defined collection of folders that acts as logical representations of the user's content?

- ○ **A.** Metadata
- ○ **B.** My Documents
- ◉ **C.** Libraries
- ○ **D.** Public Documents

56. From which of the following locations could you disable a hardware component on a laptop in Windows?

- ◉ **A.** Device Manager
- ○ **B.** Task Manager
- ○ **C.** Computer
- ○ **D.** Services console

57. A user asks you to explain a message that comes up on the computer display before the operating system boots. The message states that the BIOS logged a chassis intrusion. What would be your explanation to the user?

- ○ **A.** The CD drive tray is open. ✗
- ○ **B.** The CPU is loose. ✗
- ○ **C.** A malicious individual has hacked the system. ✗
- ◉ **D.** The computer case has been opened.

58. A school classroom is set up with removable drives to train students in Windows 7 and Windows Vista. One student tells you that one of the computers will not boot up and receives an error: no operating system found. All of the cables are plugged in securely to the computer. Which of the following is the most likely cause?

Quick Answer: **228**
Detailed Answer: **239**

- ○ **A.** The monitor is not functioning.
- ◉ **B.** The removable drive is not locked.
- ○ **C.** The lab network is down.
- ○ **D.** The memory is not seated properly.

59. You are experiencing intermittent connectivity to the website www.davidlprowse.com and want to check the status of the connectivity to that web server over a span of half an hour. Which of the following commands should you use?

Quick Answer: **228**
Detailed Answer: **240**

- ○ **A.** `ping -t`
- ○ **B.** `ipconfig /all`
- ○ **C.** `nslookup`
- ○ **D.** `ping -l`

60. A customer's Android smartphone was running a third-party VNC application that froze. What should you do? (Select the two best answers.)

Quick Answer: **228**
Detailed Answer: **240**

- ○ **A.** Initiate a soft reset
- ○ **B.** Initiate a hard reset
- ○ **C.** Pull the battery
- ○ **D.** Remove the memory card

61. Which command-line tool in Windows XP will find all of the unsigned drivers in the computer?

Quick Answer: **228**
Detailed Answer: **240**

- ◉ **A.** sigverif
- ○ **B.** dxdiag
- ○ **C.** ping
- ○ **D.** msconfig

62. Users are reporting to you that a Windows 7 feature asks them for confirmation before running certain applications or when making system changes. What is the name of this Windows feature, and where should you direct users to turn the functionality off?

Quick Answer: **228**
Detailed Answer: **240**

- ◉ **A.** Security Center; it can be turned off in the services MMC snap in.
- ○ **B.** User Account Control; it can be turned off under Security in the Control Panel.

○ **C.** Windows Firewall; it can be turned off under System Properties.

○ **D.** User Account Control; it can be turned off under User Accounts in the Control Panel.

63. James is a LAN administrator in charge of printers. Which of the following should he check first if a Windows user is trying to print a document and gets the error message "Print sub-system not available"?

○ **A.** Correct printer driver is installed.

○ **B.** Printer has been added.

○ **C.** Spooler service is running.

○ **D.** Printer has power from the jack.

Quick Answer: 228
Detailed Answer: 240

64. A customer installed a new hard disk on a computer and now cannot boot the machine. You notice that the hard drive LED stays on. What should you do to troubleshoot this problem? (Select the two best answers.)

○ **A.** Check the power cable to the hard disk

○ **B.** Check the power supply for proper voltages

○ **C.** Check the BIOS settings for the drive controller

○ **D.** Check the drive cable to make sure it is oriented correctly on both the drive and the board

○ **E.** Check the drive jumpers for correct master/slave relationships

Quick Answer: 228
Detailed Answer: 241

65. Your manager's Windows computer locks up after the graphical user interface starts to load up. However, the computer will boot in Safe Mode. When you access the Event Viewer, you see an entry that states that a driver failed. Which of the following would help you further diagnose the problem?

○ **A.** Run sigverif.

◉ **B.** Enable Boot Logging. Then, in Safe Mode analyze the ntbtlog.txt file.

○ **C.** Disable Driver Signature Enforcement.

○ **D.** Access Debugging Mode.

Quick Answer: 228
Detailed Answer: 241

66. Which of the following commands would be used to fix errors on the system disk?

○ **A.** Xcopy

○ **B.** Tracert /w

○ **C.** Diskpart

◉ **D.** Chkdsk /F

Quick Answer: 228
Detailed Answer: 241

67. A new program is crashing and causing the computer to lock up. What is the best location to check for further information about the cause of the crash?

Quick Answer: **228**
Detailed Answer: **241**

- ○ **A.** System log
- ○ **B.** Security log
- ◉ **C.** Application log
- ○ **D.** Setup log

68. Which of the following versions of Windows 7 can run in Windows XP mode, join domains, and utilize BitLocker encryption?

Quick Answer: **228**
Detailed Answer: **241**

- ○ **A.** Starter
- ○ **B.** Home Premium
- ◉ **C.** Ultimate
- ○ **D.** Professional

69. A customer's computer is running Windows Vista Ultimate 32-bit. The customer would like to upgrade to Windows 7. Which of the following operating systems can the customer's computer be upgraded directly to?

Quick Answer: **228**
Detailed Answer: **241**

- ○ **A.** Windows 7 Professional 32-bit
- ○ **B.** Windows 7 Professional 64-bit
- ◉ **C.** Windows 7 Ultimate 32-bit
- ○ **D.** Windows 7 Ultimate 64-bit

70. You are tasked with copying the entire Users folder and subfolders to a new computer. Which command should you use?

Quick Answer: **228**
Detailed Answer: **241**

- ○ **A.** Xcopy
- ○ **B.** Edit
- ○ **C.** Copy
- ○ **D.** Move

71. You are tasked with disabling services from starting up on a Windows 7 PC. Which command should you run to bring up a window to make these changes?

Quick Answer: **228**
Detailed Answer: **242**

- ○ **A.** SFC
- ○ **B.** Chkdsk
- ◉ **C.** Msconfig
- ○ **D.** GPupate

72. You replaced two 1 GB DIMMs with two 2 GB DIMMs on a Windows Vista 32-bit computer. When you reboot the computer, the BIOS recognizes 4 GB of RAM but the operating system only shows approximately 3 GB. Which of the following is the most likely reason for this?

- ○ **A.** The new RAM is not the correct speed.
- ◉ **B.** Vista only sees 3 GB of RAM.
- ○ **C.** The new RAM is not the correct type.
- ○ **D.** There is a memory hole in the BIOS.

73. What is the most important aspect of using offline files on a networked computer?

- ◉ **A.** Size of the computer hard drive
- ○ **B.** Availability of either a CD or DVD-ROM on the computer
- ○ **C.** Proximity of the computer to the server
- ○ **D.** File server operating system

74. Which of the following is an executable that checks the integrity of an NTFS volume in Windows?

- ○ **A.** NetBEUI
- ◉ **B.** Autochk.exe
- ○ **C.** Convert
- ○ **D.** Regedit.exe

75. In Windows 7, which of the following folders might be stored in a hidden partition by default?

- ○ **A.** \Boot
- ○ **B.** \Windows
- ○ **C.** \Documents and Settings
- ○ **D.** \Bootmgr

76. Jim attempts to plug a scanner into the front USB port of a Windows computer, but the scanner does not power on. What should you recommend to Jim?

- ○ **A.** Use a different USB cable
- ○ **B.** Run Windows update on the computer
- ○ **C.** Upgrade the computer's drivers
- ◉ **D.** Use the onboard USB ports

77. One of your customers has a wireless network that is secured with WEP. The customer wants to improve data encryption so that the transmission of data has less of a chance of being compromised. Which of the following should you do?

    - ◉ **A.** Reconfigure the network to use WPA2
    - ○ **B.** Use MAC address filtering
    - ○ **C.** Modify the WEP key every week
    - ○ **D.** Disable the SSID broadcast

78. Which the following is the difference between a Stop Error (for example, stop C0098xxxx) and a Dr. Watson error?

    - ○ **A.** A Dr. Watson error occurs before the Windows GUI appears.
    - ○ **B.** A Stop error is known as a blue screen and causes complete system failure.
    - ○ **C.** A Dr. Watson error is usually related to a damaged graphics adapter or memory chip.
    - ○ **D.** A Stop error writes the error to a memory dump file before restoring the system to a working state.

79. One of your co-workers just installed a newer, more powerful video card in a customer's computer. The computer powers down before it completes the boot process. Before the installation, the computer worked normally. Which of the following is the most likely cause of a problem?

    - ○ **A.** The video card is not compatible with the CPU.
    - ○ **B.** The monitor cannot display the higher resolution of the new video card.
    - ○ **C.** The computer's RAM needs to be upgraded.
    - ◉ **D.** The power supply is not providing enough wattage for the new video card.

80. A customer states that an inkjet printer is printing streaks on documents. What should you do to resolve this issue?

    - ○ **A.** Replace the printer data cable
    - ◉ **B.** Use the printer's clean option
    - ○ **C.** Print a test page from the printer
    - ○ **D.** Reinstall the drivers

81. Which of the following commands is used to display hidden files?

Quick Answer: **228**
Detailed Answer: **243**

- ○ **A.** dir /o
- ○ **B.** dir /a
- ○ **C.** dir /d
- ○ **D.** dir /?

82. After installing a new video card, the PC loads Windows and continuously reboots. What should you do first?

Quick Answer: **228**
Detailed Answer: **243**

- ◉ **A.** Go into Safe Mode
- ○ **B.** Run Chkdsk
- ○ **C.** Run Msconfig
- ○ **D.** Check the System log

83. You get a complaint from a customer that her computer started receiving pop-up ads after she installed an application within Windows. What is most likely the problem?

Quick Answer: **228**
Detailed Answer: **244**

- ○ **A.** The installed application contains a logic bomb.
- ○ **B.** The installed application is a worm.
- ○ **C.** The installed application is a Trojan horse.
- ◉ **D.** The installed application included adware.

84. What should you do to prepare a mobile device in case it is stolen or lost? (Select the three best answers.)

Quick Answer: **228**
Detailed Answer: **244**

- ○ **A.** Disable Bluetooth
- ○ **B.** Configure remote backup
- ○ **C.** Enable Wi-Fi encryption
- ◉ **D.** Enable GPS
- ○ **E.** Enable Wi-Fi tethering
- ◉ **F.** Configure a pattern screenlock

85. You want your computer to boot off of the network and have the ability to be brought out of sleep mode over the network. Which two technologies should you implement in the BIOS?

Quick Answer: **228**
Detailed Answer: **244**

- ○ **A.** WAP and WPA2
- ○ **B.** RIS and Magic Packet
- ◉ **C.** PXE and WOL
- ○ **D.** Norton Ghost and Unattend.xml

86. Two co-workers share the same file inside a folder. User A works on the file, makes changes, and saves the file. User B then works on the file, makes changes, and saves the file as well. The next time User A attempts to open the file, she receives an access denied error. What could cause this error message?

Quick Answer: **228**
Detailed Answer: **244**

- ○ **A.** The NTFS permissions were changed on the file to allow only execute.
- ○ **B.** The file was set with the system and hidden attributes.
- ○ **C.** The file was set to read only by the Accounts Receivable administrator.
- ○ **D.** The file was moved before being modified and then moved back to the share.

87. A customer brings in a laptop with a non-functioning LCD screen that always remains black; however, when you connect the laptop to an external monitor, the laptop boots to Windows normally. Which of the following actions should you take first?

Quick Answer: **228**
Detailed Answer: **244**

- ○ **A.** Replace the inverter
- ○ **B.** Replace the LCD panel with a compatible model
- ○ **C.** Check the functionality of the LCD cutoff switch
- ○ **D.** Install a different video card

88. You are troubleshooting an issue over the phone and determine that the user has a faulty hard drive. The only information the user can give you is that the computer was bought in the late 1990s and the drive capacity is 40 GB. Which kind of HD should you bring to the service call?

Quick Answer: **229**
Detailed Answer: **245**

- ○ **A.** SATA
- ○ **B.** PATA
- ○ **C.** USB
- ○ **D.** Solid-state

89. In Windows Vista, which of the following commands should be used to verify that a previous system shutdown was completed successfully?

Quick Answer: **229**
Detailed Answer: **245**

- ○ **A.** `ipconfig`
- ○ **B.** `chkntfs`
- ○ **C.** `chkdsk`
- ○ **D.** `sfc`

90. Logging on to a network with a username and password is an example of what?

- ○ **A.** Authorization
- ○ **B.** Identification
- ○ **C.** Identity proofing
- ◉ **D.** Authentication

91. A customer tells you that a networked printer is not printing documents. You successfully ping the printer's IP address. What is the problem? (Select the two best answers.)

- ○ **A.** The printer is low on toner.
- ○ **B.** The network cable is unplugged.
- ◉ **C.** The printer is out of paper.
- ○ **D.** The gateway address on the printer is incorrect.
- ◉ **E.** The spooler is not functioning.

92. Your boss asks you to install a new wireless network. Which of the following should you implement on the wireless network to help prevent unauthorized access? (Select the two best answers.)

- ○ **A.** Install additional wireless access points
- ○ **B.** Use WPA2
- ○ **C.** Broadcast the SSID
- ○ **D.** Use MAC filtering
- ○ **E.** Install a signal booster

93. Ray installs a new 802.11n wireless network adapter in a desktop computer. He tries to connect to an access point but doesn't see any access points in the wireless configuration manager. Why are none of the access points listed? (Select the best answer.)

- ○ **A.** The access points are out of range.
- ○ **B.** No IEEE 802.11n access points are available.
- ○ **C.** 802.11n is not supported on the network.
- ○ **D.** The access points cannot accept any more connections.

94. In Windows 7, which of the following enables administrators to perform administrative tasks that integrate scripts over a network?

- ○ **A.** PowerShell
- ○ **B.** Command Prompt
- ○ **C.** Command-line
- ○ **D.** Windows Script Host

95. Which of the following tools should you use in Windows 7 to migrate user files and settings for multiple computers?

- ○ **A.** Files and Settings Transfer Wizard
- ○ **B.** Windows Easy Transfer
- ○ **C.** User State Migration Tool
- ○ **D.** Profile Transfer Tool

96. Which of the following can be used to kill a running process?

- ◑ **A.** Task Manager
- ○ **B.** Computer Management
- ○ **C.** Control Panel
- ○ **D.** Tasklist

97. Which of the following file systems is suited specifically for USB flash drives?

- ○ **A.** FAT32
- ○ **B.** FAT64
- ○ **C.** NTFS
- ○ **D.** FAT16

98. You have been asked to replace the wireless network adapter in a laptop. After performing the replacement tasks, the laptop cannot locate any wireless signals. What is the most likely cause of the problem?

- ○ **A.** The new network card was not seated properly.
- ○ **B.** The software drivers were not installed.
- ○ **C.** There are no wireless signals available.
- ◉ **D.** The antenna leads were not reconnected.

99. A program has been detected collecting information such as the computer name and IP address and sending that information to a specific IP address on the Internet. Which kind of threat is this an example of?

- ◑ **A.** Spyware
- ○ **B.** Virus
- ○ **C.** Rootkit
- ○ **D.** Spam

100. You are required to <u>stop the Windows Firewall</u> service. How can you accomplish this? (Select the three best answers.)

- ○ **A.** In Performance Monitor
- ○ **B.** With the `net stop mpssvc` command
- ○ **C.** Within Msconfig
- ○ **D.** Within the Task Manager
- ○ **E.** In System Information
- ○ **F.** With Gpedit.exe
- ○ **G.** In Services.msc

And that wraps up Exam C. Take a nice long break before moving on to the fourth and final 220-802 exam.

Quick-Check Answer Key

1. A, B, E, and G	30. C	59. A
2. A	31. D	60. A and C
3. D	32. B	61. A
4. C	33. A and D	62. D
5. A	34. A and E	63. C
6. D	35. C	64. D and E
7. A	36. A	65. B
8. C	37. C	66. D
9. C and E	38. A	67. C
10. C	39. D	68. C
11. A and D	40. B	69. C
12. C	41. D	70. A
13. B	42. A	71. C
14. C	43. B	72. B
15. B	44. A	73. A
16. D	45. B	74. B
17. A	46. D	75. A
18. B and D	47. D	76. D
19. A	48. D	77. A
20. A, C, and E	49. D	78. B
21. C	50. B	79. D
22. B	51. C	80. B
23. C and D	52. D	81. B
24. D	53. B	82. A
25. B	54. A	83. D
26. A and D	55. C	84. B, D, and F
27. B	56. A	85. C
28. C	57. D	86. D
29. B	58. B	87. C

88. B	**93.** A	**98.** D
89. B	**94.** A	**99.** A
90. D	**95.** C	**100.** B, D, and G
91. C and E	**96.** A	
92. B and D	**97.** B	

Answers and Explanations

1. **Answers: A, B, E, and G.** If the computer is receiving power, everything is hooked up properly, and there is no display, then you need to consider what I like to call the big four: motherboard, CPU, video card, and RAM. These are the four components of the computer that could cause a no display issue. The most common is the video card; check if that is seated properly into the expansion slot. You should also check if that card works in one of your test systems. Then check if the RAM and then the CPU are properly installed and compatible. Finally, check the motherboard if necessary. Of course, at the beginning of this process, you should inquire with the customer as to when this computer failed and if anything was modified on the system of late. This might help you troubleshoot the problem. You would question the user during step 1 of the CompTIA A+ troubleshooting process: Identify the problem. As for the incorrect answers: The hard drive won't even be accessed if the system's RAM, motherboard, or CPU fails because the system won't even POST. There will be little to no activity on the HDD LED. Now, if the video card failed, the system might still boot, but without video, and you would see some HDD LED activity. However, some systems will not boot; lack of video will cause the system to stop at POST. The DVD-ROM drive won't cause a no display issue because it is a secondary device. The power supply is not the cause of the problem in this case. The scenario said that the computer was receiving power. If the power supply fails, nothing would happen when you press the computer's power on button. If the SATA data cable is disconnected (and that was the only problem), you would get video; the system would POST (and most likely record a HDD error); and then when the system attempted to boot to the hard drive, you would get a "missing OS" error or similar message.

2. **Answer: A.** The classification of data helps prevent confidential information from being publicly disclosed. Some organizations will have a classification scheme for their data, such as normal, secret, and top secret. Policies are implemented to make top secret data the most secure on the network. By classifying data, you are determining who has access to it. This is generally done on a need-to-know basis. Social engineering is the art of manipulating people into giving classified information. A remote access server (RAS) allows users to connect remotely to the network. To protect the connection (and data that passes through it), an organization might opt to use a VPN or RADIUS server, or both. Wiping a hard drive is vague. How is it being wiped? If it is being formatted, then that is not enough to protect confidential information. You need to perform bit-level erasure with third-party software, degauss the drive, or destroy it to make sure that no one can access the data. The thing is that data is always stored somewhere on a server or NAS device, so properly disposing of a single hard drive doesn't protect any and all confidential information from being publicly disclosed.

3. **Answer: D.** You want to set a new default printer in the OS because he has installed a new printer. This is usually done simply by right-clicking the printer and selecting Set as default printer. You might also see a question with the option to click File (or Printer). This is if you double-clicked the printer to open it and then selected the first menu. Unused printer drivers for older printers should be removed when the older printers are replaced.

4. **Answer: C.** HKEY_LOCAL_MACHINE is the registry hive that stores information about the programs Windows runs when it starts. The actual hives are stored in

\%windir%\System32\Config. But it's okay to call HKEY_LOCAL_MACHINE and the other HKEYs *hives*. Most technicians do it, and you might see them referred to that way on the exam as well. The HKEY_LOCAL_MACHINE hive is the one you will access the most often. You can configure advanced settings for TCP/IP, the GUI of the OS, and lots more from here. HKEY_CURRENT_CONFIG contains data that generated when the system boots; nothing is permanently stored. HKEY_USERS stores the information for each user profile. HKEY_CLASSES_ROOT contains information about registered applications and file associations.

5. **Answer: A.** Internet Explorer (or any other web browser) is normally used to configure a router. It's sometimes referred to as *romming* into the router because the configuration program is stored in the ROM chip of the router. You can type the IP address of the router into the Windows Explorer address bar, but that will simply open an IE (or other browser) tab. The Device Manager is where you enable and disable devices and install, update, and roll back drivers for devices. Msconfig is used to modify how the computer boots and to enable/disable programs and services.

6. **Answer: D.** The first thing you need to supply is the driver for any special SATA drives, SCSI drives, or RAID controllers. That of course is optional. If you have a typical SATA drive, Windows should recognize it automatically. Once Windows knows which hard drive to install to, partitioning, then formatting, and then configuration of settings can commence, in that order.

7. **Answer: A.** Although Windows has the Reconnect at Logon check box selected by default, it could have been disabled. If you do choose to use the net use command, be sure to make persistent connections. This is done by adding /persistent:yes to the command syntax.

8. **Answer: C.** MAC filtering is used to restrict computers from connecting to a network; it is based on the physical Media Access Control (MAC) address of the computer's network adapter. It works with wired or wireless connections. WPA is used to encrypt the wireless session between a computer and the wireless access point (WAP); its key code is required to gain access to the network. DHCP settings simply allow a specific range of IP addresses, and other IP data such as gateway address and DNS server address, to be handed out to clients. The SSID broadcast is the name of the wireless network, as broadcast out over radio waves by the WAP.

9. **Answers: C and E.** If only one computer is connected to the switch, there shouldn't be much activity. Rapidly blinking LED lights might lead you to believe that the computer's network card (NIC) or the port on the switch is faulty. However, it could be that the person is sending a lot of data to himself while you are testing the network, but that would be strange and rare. The server doesn't have anything to do with this, nor does the hard disk.

10. **Answer: C.** What should have been port 143 was probably configured incorrectly if the person can send but not receive e-mail. The Internet Message Access Protocol (IMAP) receives e-mail and uses port 143. The Simple Mail Transfer Protocol (SMTP) uses port 25 by default to send mail but will use port 443 if SSL or TLS security is implemented. Port 110 is the POP3 e-mail port. POP3 also is used to receive e-mail, but not in this question's scenario. By the way, another port that is used for SMTP is 587. This is done to avoid being blocked by ISPs and to reduce spam. Mobile devices such as

Android phones can be a little more difficult to configure e-mail on, as compared to PCs. Be sure to work with mobile devices and go through the steps of setting up e-mail on both Android and iOS.

11. **Answers: A and D.** Check the basics first! Make sure the power cable wasn't disconnected from the computer, and verify that the voltage switch is in the correct position. Kids like to play tricks on lab computers! A standard power strip should not overload with just two computers connected to it, but if it does, press the reset switch on the power strip. The monitor being unplugged could be a separate problem, but it won't cause the computer to not power on. If the second computer works fine, then that tells you the power strip is plugged in.

12. **Answer: C.** Start with the physical! Check for a link light first. This tells you whether there is physical connectivity. Then, if necessary, you can, in order, test the patch cable, reconfigure TCP/IP, install drivers (from the manufacturer's website, mind you), and finally replace the NIC.

13. **Answer: B.** The print spooler needs to be restarted on the computer that started the print job or the computer that controls the printer. This can be done in the Services console window or in the Command Prompt with the `net stop spooler` and `net start spooler` commands, or anywhere else where services can be started and stopped such as the Task Manager. Okay, that was an easy one, but the real exam will have a couple easy ones thrown in as well. Don't think too hard when you actually do receive an easier question.

14. **Answer: C.** Adding the port number and name of service to the Windows Firewall Exceptions list is the correct answer. But I'm going to pontificate more as I usually do. Uninstalling and reinstalling the SP will not help this particular situation. By default, any Windows OS after and including Windows XP SP2 enables the Windows Firewall automatically and won't allow inbound connections from the server to the network application. Therefore, you need to make an "exception." You can access this in Windows XP by going to Local Area Connection Properties > Advanced tab. In Windows 7/Vista, use the Windows Firewall with Advanced Security: Start > All Programs > Administrative Tools. If you decide to add a port, you need to know the port number of the application. For example, RealVNC is normally port 5900 for incoming connections.

15. **Answer: B.** The PC air intakes are probably clogged with cement dust. This will stop fresh, cool air from entering the PC and cause the CPU to overheat. That's why the system won't reboot immediately because the CPU needs some time to cool down. You should install a filter in front of the PC air intake and instruct the customer to clean the filter often. While you are working on the computer, you should clean out the inside of the system and vacuum out the exhaust of the power supply (without opening the power supply of course). If the PC had a virus, that might cause it to lock up or shut down, but you would be able to reboot the computer right away. Plus, there would probably be other indicators of a virus. The CPU heat sink could be an issue and could cause the same results, but it is less likely. Companies often buy computers from popular manufacturers such as Dell and HP; these computer manufacturers spend a lot of time designing their heat sink/fan combinations to work with the CPU. If the power supply was underrated, it would cause intermittent shutdowns, but not lockups. Nothing in the scenario would lead you to believe that the computer uses so many powerful components as to make the power supply underrated.

16. **Answer: D.** `tracert` (short for trace route) can show the entire path between you and a final destination, displaying every router (or hop) in between. A similar command that gives slightly less information is `pathping`. `ipconfig` displays basic information about your network connection. `ping` tests your network connection against other hosts. `nslookup` enables you to look up name servers and run several commands when connected in the NSLOOKUP shell, thereby allowing you to configure and modify a name server.

17. **Answer: A.** The TV tuner is used to enable the Live TV option in Windows 7 Media Center. This is usually the toughest part to configure on an HTPC. This is due to cable company regulations. However, TV tuners are also becoming more popular when used with over-the-air signals including HD, as long as you are within close proximity to a metropolitan area. A modem is used to make dial-up connections to the Internet. Video cards display video signal to a monitor or TV; often, HTPCs will have a video card with an HDMI output. The network adapter (also known as a network card or NIC) is used to connect to the LAN.

18. **Answers: B and D.** The share-level permissions must first be set to enable access to the user. Then the NTFS file-level "user" permissions must also be set; these take precedence over share-level, unless the share-level access is set to deny. Certificates are normally used in Internet or VPN sessions. Local user access is somewhat vague but doesn't apply here because when a user connects to a shared resource, that person does so over the network to a remote computer.

19. **Answer: A.** Use an uninterruptible power supply (UPS) to provide clean power and eliminate the voltage fluctuations—with the stipulation that the printer is not a laser printer! If it's a laser printer, connect it to its own line conditioner. That is because of the load the laser printer puts on the device it plugs into. The question did not specify that this was a laser printer, and most friends of mine have inkjets. It's not outside the realm of possibility, but it will be less likely, and that's what you have to assume when taking the exam. As for the incorrect answers: a multimeter is what you would have used to figure out that the AC outlet was providing dirty power. A surge protector will not condition the voltage that is coming from the AC outlet; it will only protect against surges and spikes. A gas generator is a ridiculous option that would actually work in this scenario. However, it is not wise to keep a gas generator in the house; plus it will cost the friend more in money and maintenance as compared to a UPS.

20. **Answers: A, C, and E.** First make sure that the iPad has a connection to the Internet. Then check that the e-mail settings were entered properly, including port numbers, server names, username/password, and any security settings. Bluetooth can be off while e-mail is being used. GPS tracks where a mobile device is located, and it too can be turned off when accessing e-mail.

21. **Answer: C.** WPA2 is more secure than all the rest. WAP is actually short for wireless access point; don't mix them up! WEP is deprecated and should be avoided unless it is the only option available. The best wireless encryption method on most SOHO wireless access points is WPA2 with AES.

22. **Answer: B.** Tell the customer to use a UPS. This will protect against power fluctuations, dirty power, brownouts, and blackouts. The computer will have a power supply already. A generator is a bit much for the computer in this scenario, but it might be

necessary for the building. Computers normally connect with an IEC power cable; this is a heavy-duty electrical cord. If the computer doesn't have one, you should replace it immediately.

23. **Answers: C and D.** Pictures and e-mail are possibly valuable, and definitely irreplaceable, if there is no backup. The rest of the answers mention things that can be restored or reinstalled from the operating system disc.

24. **Answer: D.** Use Internal SATA hard drive 3 for the page file. By separating the page file from the operating system and the user profiles, you will maximize performance of the system. If the page file was on either of the other SATA drives, the constant accessing of the page file would slow down the OS performance or would slow down the access of user files. SATA hard drive 3 is a better option than the external USB hard drive for a variety of reasons: it will probably be faster; it will have less latency; and in general, internal drives will perform more efficiently than external drives.

25. **Answer: B.** Of all the answers, the only one that deals with the local level is Local Security Settings. All the others require at least one domain controller on the network. The A+ exam does not test you on your knowledge of domain controllers and their security policies, but you should know some of the terms in order to compare them to security options on the local computer. The Local Security Policy can be accessed from Start > All Programs > Administrative Tools.

26. **Answers: A and D.** You should try shortening the distance between the laptop and the printer and make sure that the infrared (IR) ports on each device can see each other. IR can be difficult to work with due to the short range and need for line of sight. This is why Bluetooth or other wireless methods are usually preferred. Repeaters are used in networking as a method of extending a wired or wireless LAN. Most IR devices' power cannot be boosted. Some IR devices' transmission frequency can be changed, but it will be less likely that you will change the channel or boost the power.

27. **Answer: B.** Because each user on the LAN has his own internal private IP address, users are safe from external public IPs. Network Address Translation (NAT) translates all those internal IPs into one external public Internet IP for communication with outside sources. It enables the outside sources to "see" the public IP but not the internal private IPs.

28. **Answer: C.** Though USB is famous for recognizing devices and installing drivers automatically, it doesn't work perfectly all the time. In the instance of barcode readers, you will often have to download the latest driver from the manufacturer's website. That is the best answer, though an OS update might find a compatible driver. With peripherals such as these, it is all the more important to get the driver from the creator of the device. If the computer was able to recognize the device, you can rule out faulty USB cables or too many USB devices being plugged in. Let's face it—at 127 devices maximum, it's tough to have *too* many USB devices!

29. **Answer: B.** In many cases, passwords cannot be reset by the user or by the systems admin. If that is the case, you need to verify the identity of the person first. You might need to do so just as a matter of organizational policy. Telling the person not to do that or that the person should simply remember the password is just rude. If the password could be reset and you are allowed to do so, it should be reset immediately.

30. **Answer: C.** GPS can help to locate a stolen or lost mobile device. There are plenty of third-party programs that allow the user to track the device, as long as it is on and has GPS installed and functioning. If the device is off, the program will display the last known good location. Passcodes are used to secure the device in the event that it is stolen or lost. Auto-erase is used to wipe the contents of the device if lost or stolen. Encryption protects the data in the case that the user no longer has possession of it.

31. **Answer: D.** Of the listed answers, you should recommend fiber-optic cables. Another option would be shielded twisted pair (STP). Furthermore, you could rerun the cables through a metal conduit or reroute the cables around the mechanical room. Chances are in this scenario that the mechanical room's contents are causing interference on the network cables. Electromagnetic interference (EMI) can be prevented with STP or fiber-optic cables. UTP is unshielded twisted pair, probably what the customer is using currently as it is the most common. Plenum-rated cable is used in areas where sprinklers cannot get to. It has a coating that makes it burn much more slowly. 568B is the most common network cabling wiring standard.

32. **Answer: B.** To aid in preventing access to a wireless network, disable the SSID. But only do this when all computers have been connected. If more computers need to be connected later, they will have to connect manually or the SSID will have to be reenabled. While this is an okay security method, it won't keep smart attackers out of your network. MAC filtering and WPA2 encryption will do a much better job at that than disabling the SSID.

33. **Answers: A and D.** Many laptops have a nearly hidden volume knob; you have to search for it. Proper sound drivers are needed to drive the sound in the system. Though Windows will attempt to install a Microsoft driver, you should get the sound driver from the manufacturer's website. Windows Media is built in to Windows. It will play most types of music and sounds without an update. If Windows Media Player doesn't recognize a file format, it will ask to update itself from the Internet. Whether the laptop is on battery power does not affect the speakers by default.

34. **Answers: A and E.** First, remove the computer from the floor. Second, take the computer outside and clean it by removing the biggest dust bunnies (which you will undoubtedly find), and use compressed air and a vacuum. That should fix the problem of noise; there was probably a lot of dust and dirt in one or more of the fans. A clogged CPU fan can also cause the CPU to overheat, resulting in the computer turning itself off. A new hard drive isn't necessary unless you find that it is malfunctioning. The power cord most likely isn't the problem here, but you could always swap it with another one to be sure. Wiping down the outside of a computer with a cloth won't do much to fix the situation, and you wouldn't wipe down the inside of the computer. On a slightly different topic, static electricity could be generated when a person touches the power button of the computer. Combine this with the computer lying on a carpet, and it could cause the computer to short out and shut down. So, it's best to keep the computer off of the floor for a variety of reasons.

35. **Answer: C.** Some of the letters on the keyboard of a laptop are shared by numbers (which are only accessible when the Numlock is on). So, not only do you have to watch out for the Caps Lock when logging on, but also the Numlock. If the keyboard were bad, you would get no response or only a partial response from it. Keyboards are automatically recognized by Windows 7/Vista/XP.

36. **Answer: A.** If you are just setting the time on the computer, use the `time` command. Time can also be set in Windows within the Notification Area. The `net time` command is needed if you want to synchronize the local computer's time to another system or just find out the time on a remote system. `net timer` is not a valid command. The `net time` command uses the `/set` option if you wish to synchronize time to another computer.

37. **Answer: C.** If the laptop gets power when plugged in but won't work when disconnected from AC power, the battery must be dead or defective. A bad transformer means that the AC adapter would need to be replaced. That and a bad AC port would cause the laptop to fail when plugged into the AC adapter, but it should work fine on battery power (until the battery fully discharges, that is). A bad CMOS battery will cause the time, date, and passwords to be reset in the BIOS.

38. **Answer: A.** The Address Resolution Protocol (ARP) command allows you to see which computers your IP address and corresponding MAC address have connected to recently. It displays these computers formatted as IP, and MAC address. `Arp -a` does exactly this. Those connections listed are considered to be "dynamic" because they are temporary. In this scenario there was only one computer that the local system has connected to recently, but it could show more. The command also enables you to create a permanent or static connection to another system via MAC address and corresponding IP address. `ping` tests a connection to another computer's IP address. `Nbtstat -a`, along with a computer name or IP address, will show the NetBIOS name table for the local machine or for a remote computer. It displays core services running on a computer such as the workstation and server services. `Arp` by itself shows the help file for the command.

39. **Answer: D.** The Character Map enables you to copy characters from any font type. To open it in Windows 7 or Vista, go to Start > All Programs > Accessories > System Tools > Character Map. The Language Bar automatically appears when you use handwriting recognition or speech recognition. It can be configured within Region and Languages. Sticky keys is a feature that helps users with physical disabilities; it can be turned on by rapidly pressing the Shift key five times and agreeing Yes. Control Panel > Fonts opens the Fonts folder where you can add or remove text fonts.

40. **Answer: B.** Jailbreaking is the process of removing the limitations of an Apple device's iOS. It enables a user to gain root access to the system and download previously unavailable applications, most likely unauthorized by Apple. Rooting is similar; it gives administrative capabilities to users of Android-based devices. Both of these are not recommended. VirusBarrier is the first AV software designed for iOS; it was developed in response to a particularly nasty jailbreak. Super-admin powers is just a colorful term for what you get when you root or jailbreak a mobile device.

41. **Answer: D.** The Sync Center is located directly within the Control Panel. It allows you to set up synchronization partnerships with external devices and enables you to manage offline files. Quite often, the individual icons within the Control Panel are referred to as *applets*. Microsoft PowerToys is a group of applications that can be downloaded from Microsoft as an add-on to Windows XP. Apps include CD Slide Show Generator, HTML Slide Show Wizard, and the Power Calculator. The command-line–based User State Migration Tool (USMT) is used to move files and user settings from multiple computers at once. Robust file copy is a Command Prompt tool (Robocopy) that is

used to move large amounts of data; it is the successor to Xcopy, though Xcopy is still available in Windows 7 and older OSes.

42. **Answer: A.** Unicode is the code used to represent characters among multiple computers' language platforms. ASCII and EBCDIC are different types of character encoding sets in the English language only. ITU-T deals with standards for telecommunications.

43. **Answer: B.** `ipconfig` is the ultimate command to quickly display the network configuration information. For in-depth analysis, use `ipconfig /all`. `tracert` displays the route from the local computer to a remote destination. `netdiag` is an older command used in Windows XP (and earlier OSes) that helps to isolate networking and connectivity problems. `pathping` is a limited version of `tracert`.

44. **Answer: A.** If the transfer corona wire is not getting power, the paper will not get the positive voltage needed to attract the toner and the pages will come out of the printer with nothing on them. If the primary corona wire is dirty, you might see lines or smearing in the text. This could indicate that the toner cartridge needs to be replaced. If the printer is not plugged into the USB port, it shouldn't output any pages because the print job will never reach the printer. A message should display on the Windows screen concerning this as well.

45. **Answer: B.** New malicious software (malware) is always being created. Because of this, the best place to find information about spyware, a virus, or other malware is at a place that can be updated often and easily: the anti-malware company's website. Operating system documentation will usually not have this kind of information. In addition, the OS documents and the anti-spyware readme.txt file will be outdated soon after they are written. Never trust in what a user has to say about malware. The user is not the person who would remove it—a technician would.

46. **Answer: D.** The network interface card (NIC) must be faulty if everything else checks out. Be careful not to confuse duplex printing (printing on both sides of the paper) with full-duplex networking (transmission of data in both directions simultaneously). If the printer's memory was full, it could cause the printer to stop printing, but the scenario tells us that you can't ping the printer's IP address, which is a telling sign. It's possible that a printer could need a new maintenance kit, but it would stop printing only if something failed, at which point the printer needs more than maintenance—it needs repair.

47. **Answer: D.** Because it happens often, you should school the user on safer web browsing habits such as being very careful when clicking on links brought up by search engines, not clicking on pop-up windows, and being conservative about the websites that are accessed. Also, the browser can be updated, add-ons can be installed to a web browser for increased protection, phishing filters can be enabled, and so on. Deleting temporary files won't stop the user from visiting the same websites that probably caused the problem in the first place. Defragmenting the hard drive will help the drive and the OS to perform better but won't help in the malware department. The computer should have an antivirus solution or, better yet, an anti-malware solution, but it should be set to update automatically every day.

48. **Answer: D.** Connections can be made by sending Remote Assistance invitations by e-mail (Outlook) or via instant messaging (Windows Messenger also known simply as Messenger). These invitations could be to ask for help or to offer help. This is often

implemented in help desk scenarios in which a user invites a technician to take control of his computer so that it can be repaired. It's effectively a virtual service call. The technician doesn't need to come physically to the user's desk, but instead connects remotely. However, you can also take control of a computer without an invitation (and if you are an administrator or a user with permissions); this can be done only if the computer to be controlled has the Remote Desktop feature turned on. Virtual network computing (VNC) is very similar to Remote Desktop; it enables control of a computer remotely. There are several third-party VNC companies that offer free software. Microsoft doesn't refer to its software as VNC though. On the server side Microsoft also refers to Remote Desktop as Terminal Services. Collectively the client software is also referred to as Microsoft Terminal Services Client (MSTSC). Mstsc.exe is the executable.

49. Answer: D. The default folder location for Windows 7 system files is C:\Windows\System32. That is, if the C: is the drive being installed to. You might also see this referred to as X:\%windir%\System32 or simply \%windir%\System32. The X: is a variable meaning whichever drive is installed to. %windir% is a variable referring to the name of the main installation folder (usually Windows). %windir% is also expressed sometimes as %systemroot%. Windows Vista and XP also use this folder for system files. C:\Windows is the systemroot, where the OS is installed to (though it will also inhabit subfolders). C:\Windows\System32\Config is where the registry hives are stored. There is no C:\System Files folder, unless you were to create it yourself.

50. Answer: B. You would use the Android Cloud backup solution so that files can be backed up to a location outside the company. There are several other third-party solutions available as well. iCloud is the Apple solution for file backup, apps, and so on. The Microsoft Cloud has the same types of features in a variety of solutions. A company-based local network-attached storage (NAS) device would go against what you have been asked to do in the scenario. If the NAS was on the Internet or part of a cloud, that would be a different story.

51. Answer: C. Use Notepad. It is a text-based editor that applies virtually no formatting. Text and other information can be copied from a web page, pasted to a Notepad document, and then copied again and pasted into Word; all formatting will have been removed. Notepad is also a great tool for web developers (using HTML) and system administrators (when creating batch files and other configuration files). CMD, or more specifically cmd.exe, is the executable that opens the Microsoft Command Prompt. Excel is a program by Microsoft that enables you to create and modify spreadsheets. The MMC is the Microsoft Management Console. This is a utility in Windows that enables you to work with several console windows within the same program; it saves the last place you were working.

52. Answer: D. The printing subsystem is most likely failing for one of a variety of reasons. The first solution is to end the spoolsv.exe service in the Task Manger or in the Command Prompt with the `taskkill` command. Then restart the computer. If that doesn't work, the system may have to be repaired, restored, or modified in the registry (which could be an in-depth process). It is also possible that a virus has compromised the system. There are viruses that are also called spoolsv.exe; a quick sweep of the system folders with AV software should uncover this...hopefully. If the Windows update was running, it should not take up that many resources—not nearly so. Also, the executable for that is wuauclt.exe. Hyperthreading can be disabled in the BIOS on some systems. This should have no effect on the ability of the system to multitask, though, and multiple processes should be able to run simultaneously without a problem.

53. **Answer: B.** IMAP is the Internet Message Access Protocol, which allows an e-mail client to access e-mail on a remote mail server. Generally the e-mail client software will leave the messages on the server until the user specifically deletes them. So, the user can selectively download messages. This allows multiple users to manage the same mailbox. Real-time messaging can be accomplished by using instant messaging and chat programs. IMAP, like POP3, allows users to download or receive messages, but it does not send messages; a protocol such as SMTP would be used to send mail. IMAP, like POP3, authenticates the user, but again not for sending e-mail—just when receiving e-mail.

54. **Answer: A.** The wrinkled pages are the number one indicator that the fuser needs to be replaced. Random patterns of missing print further indicate that the fuser is not working properly. If you note toner not being fused to the paper, then that is the last clue. The fuser usually needs to be replaced every 200,000 pages or so on a laser printer. If the toner cartridge was defective, either you would get blank printouts or there would be lines or smears, but there wouldn't be any page wrinkles. If the transfer corona wire is defective, it might result in blank paper. Damage to the primary corona wire can also result in black lines or smearing. High humidity could cause the separation pads or rollers to fail.

55. **Answer: C.** Libraries are commonly known as metafolders; they are logical representations of a user's content. For example, one library in Windows 7 is called Documents. The Documents library includes two default locations: My Documents and Public Documents.

56. **Answer: A.** Use the Device manager to disable a component in Windows, regardless of whether it is a laptop or a PC. Use the Task Manager to analyze basic system performance and stop processes. Use Computer (My Computer in Windows XP) to view folders, files, and other computers. Use the Services console (services.msc) to stop and start and enable/disable services.

57. **Answer: D.** A chassis intrusion means that the computer case has been opened. Some BIOS programs have the capability to detect this. This is a security feature that informs the user of a possible breach. As a PC technician, you should check the computer inside and out for any possible tampering. The BIOS program will not detect if the CD-ROM drive is open. If the CPU was loose, the computer would not boot and there would be nothing to display. It is possible that a malicious individual has hacked, or attempted to hack, the system. However, this is not necessarily the case, although you should check just to make sure.

58. **Answer: B.** The most likely reason the computer won't boot and presents the no OS error is that the removable drive is not locked. Removable drives are common in schools and labs. A frame is installed to a 5 1/4" bay and connected to the motherboard via SATA or IDE the way a hard drive normally would. Then, swappable trays are inserted into the frame, each with a different hard drive and a different OS. When the drive tray is inserted into the frame, it must be locked; it is common to forget to

lock one or two. If it isn't locked, the data port will not connect properly and the OS will not boot. If you get a message on the screen, then you know the monitor is working. No operating system or missing OS messages happen before the computer can connect to the network, so have no fear—the lab network is probably not down. If the memory needed to be reseated, you would get a message in the POST or a series of beeps.

59. **Answer: A.** `ping -t` is a continuous ping. It will ping the web server with ICMP echo packets until you manually stop the operation. You can stop the operation by pressing Ctrl+C on the keyboard. When you do so, an average of the ping results will be displayed, as well as the total packets that were sent, received, and lost. `ipconfig /all` displays the configuration of your network adapter. `nslookup` enables you to find out a domain's corresponding IP address, as well as carry out other name server configurations. `ping -l` is a four-packet ping, but the `-l` parameter enables you to modify the size of the packet being sent.

60. **Answers: A and C.** If you can't shut down the application in the Running Services area, then try initiating a soft reset first. On an Android device this is simply pressing and holding the power button, shutting it down, and then restarting it after a few seconds. If, however, pressing the power button doesn't do anything, remove the battery so that the device will have its power supply cut. Replace the battery and reboot the phone! Don't do a hard reset unless it is absolutely necessary. On an Android-based device, this will clear it and return it to factory condition. Removing the memory card in of itself won't fix the problem, but seeing as how many devices store the memory card under the battery, this could indirectly fix the problem.

61. **Answer: A.** The sigverif.exe tool can be used to check for unsigned drivers within your operating system. Unsigned drivers are drivers that have not been verified by Microsoft. If you receive error messages and are troubleshooting, run this command from the Run prompt. When the check is finished, unsigned drivers will be displayed. This list is also stored in a file called sigverif.txt within the %systemroot%. `dxdiag` is short for DirectX diagnostics. It is used to test the functionality of audio and video devices. `ping` is used to test whether or not another host is on the network. Msconfig (the Microsoft System Configuration Utility) is a tool used to troubleshoot the startup process of Windows.

62. **Answer: D.** User Account Control (UAC) is the portion of Windows that asks for confirmation of administrative rights before allowing a user to make system changes or run certain applications. It can be disabled within the User Accounts applet within the Control Panel by clicking the Change User Account Control Settings link. But beware; only users that have administrative rights should even be permitted to turn this off.

63. **Answer: C.** If a "print sub-system not available" message or similar message appears, it most likely means the spooler has stalled. This can be turned back on within the Services section of Computer Management or by issuing the command `net start spooler` in the Command Prompt. If the wrong printer driver was installed, either the user would get a message stating that the printer is not available or the document would print but the information would be garbled. If the printer has not been added, the user would not be able to print any documents to any printers, and therefore should not get an error message. If the printer is not getting power, the user would most likely get a message stating that the printer is not available.

64. Answers: D and E. On older IDE connections you need to make sure that the data cable is oriented properly on each drive and the motherboard (or controller card). Also, make sure that the drives are jumpered correctly. The main drive with the OS should be set to master; the other drive (which probably contains data) should be set to slave. If either of these is incorrect, the hard drive LED could stay on constantly indicating a problem. If the LED light is on, you know that the drive is getting power, so nothing in the power subsystem should be troubleshot. Older BIOS systems allowed you to modify master and slave settings, but newer systems rely on the jumper settings; still newer systems rely on newer technologies such as SATA!

65. Answer: B. Boot Logging can be enabled from the Windows Advanced Boot Options Menu (ABOM); it is generally the fourth option. Once this is enabled, the system will automatically create a file called ntbtlog.txt. Afterwards, you can access the system by booting into Safe Mode, once again from the ABOM. Sigverif is a program that can be run in Windows that verifies whether drivers have been signed by Microsoft. Disabling Driver Signature Enforcement is another ABOM option; you might use this to help fix the issue, but not to diagnose the problem. Debugging Mode is another ABOM option, but in this scenario you don't necessarily need to debug the system, but rather repair the individual driver that failed to load up.

66. Answer: D. Chkdsk /F allows you to fix errors on a disk. It does not fix all errors, but checks for disk integrity, bad sectors, and similar issues. Xcopy copies files and directory trees; Microsoft recommends using Robocopy on newer Windows operating systems. Tracert /w analyzes the path to another computer with a specific timeout per reply. Diskpart is the command-line tool that enables you to make changes to the operating system's partition table.

67. Answer: C. The application log is the location for all events concerning Windows applications and third-party programs. The system log contains information about drivers, system files, and stop errors, but not application crashes. The security log contains information regarding auditing events. The setup log stores information of events that occurred during the installation of Windows.

68. Answer: C. Windows 7 Ultimate can run in Windows XP mode, join domains, and utilize BitLocker encryption. Starter and Home Premium can do none of these. Windows 7 Professional cannot utilize BitLocker encryption. On a side note, Windows 7 Enterprise can also run BitLocker, although it was not one of the listed answers.

69. Answer: C. Windows Vista Ultimate 32-bit can only be upgraded to Windows 7 Ultimate 32-bit. It cannot be upgraded to any other version of Windows 7. As a rule, 32-bit versions of Windows cannot be directly upgraded to 64-bit versions of Windows.

70. Answer: A. Use Xcopy. This is designed to copy entire folders (and all of their subfolders) to a new location. Another option is Robocopy, the successor to Xcopy. Edit is a program in the Command Prompt that allows you to create and modify text files; not all versions of Windows offer this—for example, Windows 7 Ultimate 64-bit. Copy is the original command for copying data from one location to another, but it is not as well-suited to copying large amounts of data as Xcopy or Robocopy are. The move command does just that; it is the equivalent of the *cut* in cut-and-paste operations.

71. **Answer: C.** Msconfig is the only option listed where you can disable services. The key in the question is the phrase "bring up a window". Msconfig runs in a Window, whereas the rest of the answers run as text in the command-line. Msconfig can also be used to modify how the system boots and to enable/disable applications. SFC is the System File Checker; it scans the integrity of protected system files and repairs problems if necessary, and if possible. Contrast this with Chkdsk, which can locate and repair errors on the disk, but not within system files. GPupdate can update user and computer policy settings on the local computer or on remote computers.

72. **Answer: B.** Although Windows Vista 32-bit can technically address 4 GB of RAM, Windows Vista 32-bit (and Windows XP 32-bit) systems and applications can only *use* 3.12 GB of RAM. That is because these operating systems reserve the remainder for devices in what is known as memory-mapped I/O (MMIO).

73. **Answer: A.** The most important factor is the size of the hard drive. This is because the offline files are stored locally. Optical discs are not necessary for offline files to be used. Though the computer is on the network, the network doesn't really play into the offline files on the local computer. Yes, the computer will synchronize files and needs to have proper access to the network and the file server when it does so. But when using offline files, it is all done locally. So the proximity to the server and the type of OS on the file server isn't as important. As long as the client computer can use offline files (7/Vista/XP), it should be able to sync them up with any Windows Server.

74. **Answer: B.** Autochk.exe is an executable (and system process) that checks the integrity of an NTFS volume in Windows. It enables a Windows operating system to revert core system settings to their original state. Autochk is similar to chkdsk but autochk runs during system bootup (after a cold boot), whereas chkdsk will run in the command-line or in the Recovery Console. Autochk cannot run within the command-line. Autochk will be initiated if: 1. Chkdsk cannot gain exclusive access to the volume, 2. If you try to run chkdsk on the *boot* volume, and 3. If the volume to be checked is "dirty". For example, if a system hangs, and has open files, those files are considered to be dirty, and therefore the volume that houses them is also dirty, and is checked by autochk after a hard reset otherwise known as a cold boot. NetBEUI is a network protocol used by older, deprecated versions of Microsoft operating systems such as Windows 95/98, and Windows NT. It stands for NetBIOS Extended User Interface. It uses computer names to identify other computers on the network, does not use IP addresses, and therefore is not routable to other networks. This protocol is outdated and is not often found in networks. The convert command is used to change a FAT partition to NTFS without loss of data. Regedit.exe is the executable in Windows that opens the Registry Editor.

75. **Answer: A.** The \Boot folder can be located in a hidden partition (100 MB in size), by default, which is separate from the C drive. The Windows folder is where the operating system is installed to; it is also known by the variable %systemroot% or %WINDIR% and is located in the C: drive by default. \Documents and Settings is also located in C: by default. Bootmgr is the Windows Boot Manager, which is the Windows loader program; it is a file, not a folder.

76. **Answer: D.** Tell the customer to use the onboard ports. This means the ports that are integrated directly to the motherboard on the back of the computer. It's a quick temporary fix but should work because they are hardwired to the board. The front USB plugs

are part of the computer case; they probably were never connected to the mother-board properly. Now, you should also check if the USB scanner needs to be plugged into an AC outlet. If the back USB ports don't work, then you could try a different USB cable. Software shouldn't affect the USB device getting power. If it has a proper USB connection, it should power up. But, after that, if Windows doesn't recognize it, try updating drivers and Windows.

77. **Answer: A.** The best solution is to upgrade the wireless network from WEP to WPA2, or at least WPA. WEP is a deprecated wireless encryption protocol and should be updated to a newer and more powerful protocol if at all possible. If this is not possible, it would be wise to use a strong WEP key and modify it often. MAC address filtering will not increase the level of data encryption, but it will filter out unwanted computers when they attempt to connect to the wireless access point. Disabling the SSID broadcast will deter new computers from making initial connections to the wireless access point.

78. **Answer: B.** Stop errors are also known as blue screens (BSODs). They are a complete system failure that cannot be recovered from and the system has to be rebooted. Dr. Watson errors (common to Windows XP) occur while the OS is running. They are due to an application or system file failing but do not cause the entire system to crash.

79. **Answer: D.** Today's video cards can be very powerful and might require a more powerful power supply than is in the computer currently. Video cards need to be compatible with the motherboard, not necessarily with the CPU. If the monitor could not display the higher resolution, the operating system would still boot but you would probably see garbled information on the screen. Because a video card comes with its own RAM, the computer's RAM usually does not need to be upgraded.

80. **Answer: B.** Use the printer's built-in clean option. This might be accessible from the display on the printer or from within the printer's software in Windows. Cleaning the cartridges is necessary every once in a while so they don't get clogged. If the clean option doesn't work, you can try physically removing the cartridge, sparingly using a solution of 50% water/50% isopropyl alcohol, and cleaning the cartridge nozzle with a Q-Tip. Streaks on documents are not caused by faulty data cables or bad drivers. A faulty data cable would probably cause complete print failure; bad drivers would cause the printer to print garbled text. Printing a test page will result in the same document streaks.

81. **Answer: B.** dir /a can be used to display hidden files. Specifically, dir /ah can be used to show hidden files only. dir /o deals with various sort orders of files—for example, alphabetical. dir /d sorts files by column in wide format. dir /? displays the help file for the dir command.

82. **Answer: A.** Try accessing Safe Mode first and see if the problem continues. It probably won't, and you will need to roll back the driver and locate, download, and install the correct one. Remember to get your drivers from the manufacturer's website, and don't forget to download the correct driver for your particular operating system. Chkdsk will check the integrity of files and fix them if necessary. Msconfig is used to boot the computer in different ways. While you normally could select Safe Boot in Msconfig, it is not possible in this scenario because the system won't boot into

Windows properly. You could check the System log while in Safe Mode, but it won't explain much except that the system shut down improperly and rebooted continuously.

83. Answer: D. If a computer starts receiving pop-up advertisements after an application has been installed, the application probably included adware. While pop-up ads are not necessarily harmful to a computer, the other answers (including Trojan horse, worms, and logic bombs) will usually be more serious and affect the computer adversely.

84. Answers: B, D, and F. First off, you should configure some kind of remote backup. This way, if the device is compromised, you have the confidential data backed up outside of the device at another location. The other half of this solution (not mentioned in the answers) is remote wipe. Once you are positive that the device is stolen or lost, and you know the data was backed up at some point, trigger a remote wipe to remove all data from the device. Second, Enable GPS on the device so that it can be tracked if it is lost or stolen. Third, configure a screenlock of some sort, be it a pattern that is drawn on the display, a PIN, or a password. A strong password is usually the best form of screenlock and will be the hardest to crack. It doesn't make a difference how Bluetooth and Wi-Fi are configured. They won't help to protect confidential data.

85. Answer: C. PXE and WOL. To configure the BIOS to boot off of the network, you will have to enable the Preboot Execution Environment (PXE) network adapter. To allow the computer to be brought out of sleep mode by another system on the network, you will need to configure Wake-on-LAN (WOL) in the BIOS. WAP stands for wireless access point; WPA2 is the Wi-Fi Protected Access version 2 encryption used on a WAP. RIS is Remote Installation Services and is used on Windows Server 2003 to deploy installations of Windows to remote computers. A Magic Packet is a special packet sent to a computer to wake it up, but it is configured in Windows. Norton Ghost is used to create or install images of operating systems. Unattend.xml is the answer file created for unattended installations of Windows over the network.

86. Answer: D. Most likely User B moved the file to another location outside of the current partition, made the changes (which is possible since User B is the one who moved it), and then moved it back to the original location. Whenever a file is moved to another partition or volume, the file takes on the permissions of the parent folder. However, if the file had been moved *within* the volume, the permissions would have been retained. Tricky. Remember this: If the file is moved within the same volume, it retains permissions, so the permissions don't change. But, if a file is moved to another volume, it takes on the permissions of the folder it is moved into. As for copying, the file's copy always takes on the permissions of the parent regardless of where that copy is placed. On to the incorrect answers: If NTFS permissions were changed to allow execute, then User A should have been able to open the file. If the file was set with the hidden attribute, then User A should not have been able to see the file. Accounts Receivable might or might not set a file to read-only. However, User A should still be able to open the file, but in read-only mode.

87. Answer: C. Check the functionality of the LCD cutoff switch first before opening the laptop and replacing parts. The LCD cutoff switch turns off the monitor when the laptop is closed; these are prone to failure. Although the LCD panel and inverter could possibly fail, it is less common, and because they require a lot of time and effort to replace, they should be checked afterwards. Generally, a laptop's video card is the least common component to fail, although it can be replaced on some laptops.

88. **Answer: B.** You should bring a PATA (IDE) drive. Chances are this older computer currently is using an IDE drive and only has connections for IDE. Indicators include the age of the computer and the capacity of the drive. If you brought a SATA drive, you would have nothing to plug it into, unless you also brought a SATA controller card, but that would be an extra expense for the customer. You can't even be sure that the computer will have USB ports, and if it does, they would probably be very slow version 1 USB ports—not quite feasible for a hard drive. Solid-state drives are typically SATA and are out of the question.

89. **Answer: B.** Chkntfs can check to see if a previous system shutdown completed successfully. Generally, you would check this on the system drive (for example, C:). If the drive is okay and the system did complete the shut down successfully, you'll get a message such as "C: is not dirty." Otherwise, you will get a message telling of the error. Chkdsk checks the integrity of the disk. Ipconfig displays the configuration of your network adapters. SFC scans the integrity of all protected system files and can replace them with the correct versions if necessary.

90. **Answer: D.** Authentication is when a person's identity is confirmed or verified through the use of a specific system. Authorization to specific resources cannot be accomplished without previous authentication. Identification is when a person is in a state of being identified. Identity proofing is an initial validation of an identity.

91. **Answers: C and E.** The printer could simply be out of paper. Or, the spooler could be malfunctioning. If the printer is out of paper, fill all trays and suggest that the user check the trays every couple days or so. If the spooler is not functioning, you should restart the spooler service in the Services console window or in the Command Prompt with the net stop spooler and net start spooler commands. If the printer was low on toner, you would get weak print or completely blank pages. If the network cable was unplugged, you wouldn't be able to ping the printer. Printers don't always use gateway addresses, but if this one did, it wouldn't affect your ability to connect to it (as long as it was on the LAN). The gateway address is used so that the printer can communicate with computers beyond the LAN.

92. **Answer: B and D.** By using WPA2 (the strongest type of encryption on most wireless access points), you ensure a high level of encryption, helping to reduce unauthorized access. Using MAC filtering will filter out unwanted computers by checking their MAC addresses when the computers first try to connect. Additional wireless access points and signal boosters would increase the chances of unauthorized access. Broadcasting the SSID also increases the chance of unauthorized access because any wireless device will see the name of your network. When all wireless devices have made their initial connections to the wireless access point, consider disabling the SSID broadcast.

93. **Answer: A.** Most likely the access points are out of range. 802.11n indoor range is 70 meters (230 ft.), and outdoor range is 250 meters (820 ft.). If Ray is outside this range, the computer will not be able to see any access points in the wireless configuration manager. It is unlikely that no 802.11n access points are available. If Ray installed an 802.11n wireless network adapter, then he must know that there is an 802.11n WAP around. It's a possibility that none exist, but that's remote. Even if 802.11n wasn't supported, an 802.11n network adapter can downgrade to 802.11g or even 802.11b, so it should still be able to connect. Regardless, he should still be

able to see other slower wireless access points in the wireless configuration manager. Finally, if there were access points, but they couldn't accept any more connections, he would again at least see them in the wireless configuration manager program. That answer doesn't explain why he can't see them.

94. **Answer: A.** The Windows 7 PowerShell enables administrators to perform administrative tasks that integrate scripts and executables and can be run over a network. It is a combination of the Command Prompt and a scripting language. The PowerShell is the successor to the Windows Script Host (WSH). The Command Prompt is Windows' version of a command-line. It is not as functional as the PowerShell.

95. **Answer: C.** The User State Migration Tool (USMT) is a command-line tool that can be used to migrate user files and settings for one or more computers in Windows 7 as well as Windows Vista. Windows 7 employs additional features such as AES encryption support and shadow copying of volumes of information. The Files and Settings Transfer Wizard is an older version of Windows Easy Transfer that is used with Windows XP and other older operating systems. Windows Easy Transfer enables you to copy files, photos, music, and settings, but not for multiple computers.

96. **Answer: A.** The Task Manager can end (or "kill") a running process. It is also used to end applications that lock up and it analyzes the performance of the system. Computer Management is the main configuration console window; it contains the Device Manager, Event Viewer, and Services among other things. The Control Panel lists all of the configuration applets available in Windows such as Power Options, User Accounts, and Windows Defender. `tasklist` is a command in Windows that displays a list of the processes that are running. To kill a process in the Command Prompt, first find out the name of the process and/or process ID (PID) with `tasklist`, and then use the `taskkill` command to end the process.

97. **Answer: B.** FAT64 (also known as exFAT) is suited specifically for USB flash drives and many other mobile storage solutions. It is the successor to FAT32 and can format media that is larger than 32 GB with a single partition. Older file systems such as FAT32 and FAT16 are very limited as to the partition size. NTFS can be a good solution for USB flash drives, but exFAT was developed specifically for USB flash drives and is the better solution if you have an operating system that will support it, such as Windows 7, Windows Server 2008, and Windows Vista with SP1.

98. **Answer: D.** The most likely answer is that the antenna leads were not connected, or not connected securely. Wireless network adapters for laptops have antennae that are removable. This way the antennae don't get damaged in transit, which is common for laptops and which is why it is common for the antenna to be forgotten. The laptop wireless network adapter isn't a card like in a PC. It could connect to USB or to a PC Card or ExpressCard slot. It is less likely that the card was not inserted properly; plus, if it was not connected properly, you would wonder why Windows failed to find it automatically. If Windows doesn't install it automatically, it would ask for a driver. So, unless you disregard that message (or install the wrong driver), the drivers shouldn't be an issue. It is rare that *no* wireless signals are available. It is always more likely that something was not installed properly at the local computer.

99. **Answer: A.** Spyware is a type of malicious software that is usually downloaded unwittingly by a user or is installed by third-party software. It collects information about the user and the user's computer without the user's consent. A virus is code that runs on the computer without the user's knowledge; it infects a computer when the code is accessed and executed. A rootkit is software designed to gain administrator-level control over a computer system without being detected. Spam is the abuse of electronic messaging systems such as e-mail.

100. **Answers: B, D, and G.** You can stop a service in a variety of ways. The easiest and most common is to go to the Services console window. This can be done by typing services.msc at the Run prompt. You can also stop services in the Task Manager by accessing the Services tab and right-clicking the service in question. But in the Task Manager you have to know the executable name of the service. The name of the Windows Firewall service is mpssvc. So, the third way (of the listed answers) is to use the `net stop mpssvc` command in the Command Prompt. Performance Monitor, System Information, and GPedit do not allow you to stop services.

CHAPTER TEN

220-802 Practice Exam D

Ready for a hundred more? This final practice exam will be similar to Exam C in difficulty. But just for the heck of it, I might throw in a few extra doozies. Be ready for questions with longer, more in-depth scenarios and more complex answers. This exam is freestyle, meaning the questions are randomized. You can expect questions from any of the four domains, in any order. In this exam I assume that you have a fair understanding of acronyms and basic concepts and do not explain those within the explanations.

If you didn't already, I once again suggest taking a break between exams. If you just completed the third exam, give yourself a full hour at least before you begin this one. If you didn't score 90% or higher on exam C, go back and study; then retake exam C until you pass with 90% or higher.

Write down your answers and check them against the answer key, which immediately follows the exam. After the answer key you will find the explanations for all of the answers. Good luck!

Practice Questions

1. Which type of hypervisor runs operating systems on bare metal?

- ○ **A.** Type 1
- ○ **B.** Type 2
- ○ **C.** Virtual PC
- ○ **D.** Windows XP Mode

Quick Answer: **277**
Detailed Answer: **279**

2. Which of the following relies on PPTP to create a secure tunnel?

- ○ **A.** WWAN
- ○ **B.** WiMAX
- ○ **C.** VPN
- ○ **D.** WLAN

Quick Answer: **277**
Detailed Answer: **279**

3. Which of the following will occur if %temp% is executed from Run?

- ○ **A.** Applications located in the %temp% folder will be executed.
- ○ **B.** The operating system's temporary folder will be open.
- ○ **C.** The current user temporary folder will be open.
- ○ **D.** Applications will be deleted in the %temp% folder.

Quick Answer: **277**
Detailed Answer: **279**

4. A customer has a home office. Which of the following technologies would benefit from the use of QoS?

- ○ **A.** SSID
- ○ **B.** Instant messaging
- ○ **C.** E-mail
- ○ **D.** VoIP

Quick Answer: **277**
Detailed Answer: **279**

5. Which type of device uses an MOV to protect equipment?

- ○ **A.** Power strip
- ○ **B.** Power supply
- ○ **C.** Surge suppressor
- ○ **D.** Multimeter

Quick Answer: **277**
Detailed Answer: **279**

6. Ray used file properties to hide files in his folder and now needs to get the files back. Using a command-line tool, which of the following combination of parameters will make the files viewable once again?

- ○ **A.** Attrib - RV *.*
- ○ **B.** Attrib - A+H *.*
- ○ **C.** Attrib + A+ *.*
- ○ **D.** Attrib -H *.*

7. Which group is best to assign to a home user to prevent software installation?

- ○ **A.** Administrators
- ○ **B.** Power users
- ○ **C.** Remote Desktop users
- ○ **D.** Users

8. Which of the following is the best solution for repairing a hard drive when a computer displays an "NTLDR is missing error" upon booting?

- ○ **A.** Recovery Console with the fixmbr command
- ○ **B.** Recovery Console with the fixboot command
- ○ **C.** Recovery Console with the chkdsk command
- ○ **D.** Recovery Console with the bootcfg /rebuild command

9. A Windows PC is not booting correctly. You need to locate bad sectors and recover information. Which command is best?

- ○ **A.** Chkdsk C: /R
- ○ **B.** Chkdsk C: /F
- ○ **C.** Chkdsk C: /C
- ○ **D.** Chkdsk C: /I

10. Where can a user's Desktop folder be found in Windows Vista by default?

- ○ **A.** C:\Users\%username%\desktop
- ○ **B.** C:\Documents and Settings\%username%\desktop
- ○ **C.** C:\System Volume Information\%username%\desktop
- ○ **D.** C:\Users\System32\%username%\desktop

11. You are called to an office that had a gigabit Ethernet LAN installed six months ago. Everything was fine until a week ago. A few customers at the office report that the speed of the Internet has drastically decreased since a recent network hardware refresh by another technician. What could be attributed to the problem?

Quick Answer: **277**
Detailed Answer: **280**

   - ○ **A.** The DHCP server is not working correctly.
   - ○ **B.** The firewall was not turned back on.
   - ○ **C.** The switches are configured for 100 Mbps.
   - ○ **D.** The cellular repeater installed is interfering with the network speed.

12. A technician is setting up a SOHO and has configured the wireless network adapter on a laptop with WPA2. While the technician configures the WAP, he notices that WPA2 is not listed as an option. What should the technician do next?

Quick Answer: **277**
Detailed Answer: **280**

   - ○ **A.** Install the latest WAP firmware
   - ○ **B.** Install the latest wireless network adapter drivers
   - ○ **C.** Install the latest WAP drivers
   - ○ **D.** Install the latest wireless network adapter firmware

13. A user who is part of a workgroup reports that she cannot print to a new printer. Everyone else in the workgroup can print to the new printer, and the user can still automatically send print jobs to the old printer. Which of the following can fix the problem for the user? (Select the two best answers.)

Quick Answer: **277**
Detailed Answer: **280**

   - ○ **A.** Add the new printer to the user's computer
   - ○ **B.** Clear the print queue on the new printer
   - ○ **C.** Change the user's password and permissions
   - ○ **D.** Set the new printer as the default printer

14. You plug in an external hard drive. A message appears in Windows that says the device can perform faster. What could cause this message?

Quick Answer: **277**
Detailed Answer: **281**

   - ○ **A.** The computer has USB 3.0 ports.
   - ○ **B.** The external hard drive is using USB 2.0.
   - ○ **C.** The computer has USB 2.0 ports.
   - ○ **D.** The external hard drive is using FireWire.

15. Your customer tells you that when trying to synchronize a smartphone via Bluetooth to Windows, a "no Bluetooth device" error
message appears on the smartphone. The computer has a
Bluetooth card installed. Which of the following is the most likely
cause?

- ○ **A.** The 802.11 card is disabled.
- ○ **B.** A BIOS setting is incorrect.
- ○ **C.** The hard drive is faulty.
- ○ **D.** A microwave is interfering with the signal.

Quick Answer: **277**
Detailed Answer: **281**

16. Your organization has an Active Directory domain. One of the
users, Bill, should not have read access to a folder named
Accounting. The Accounting folder is shared on a network server,
on a partition formatted as NTFS. How can you stop Bill from having read access to the folder without impacting any other users on
the network?

- ○ **A.** Remove Bill from all domain groups that have access
to the Accounting folder
- ○ **B.** Deny read access to the Accounting folder for Bill
through local access security
- ○ **C.** Deny read access to the Accounting folder for any
group that Bill is a member of
- ○ **D.** Deny read access to the Accounting folder for Bill
through shared access security

Quick Answer: **277**
Detailed Answer: **281**

17. What are three possible reasons that a laptop's keyboard would
stop functioning? (Select the three best answers.)

- ○ **A.** Stuck keys
- ○ **B.** Bad inverter
- ○ **C.** Loose connection
- ○ **D.** Faulty touchpad
- ○ **E.** Warped keyboard
- ○ **F.** Discharged battery

Quick Answer: **277**
Detailed Answer: **281**

18. A customer tells you that her computer is taking a long time to
save large files. She is currently using an IDE hard drive formatted
with NTFS. What would improve the performance of the system?

- ○ **A.** Reformat the drive with FAT32
- ○ **B.** Install a PATA drive and format it as FAT32
- ○ **C.** Install a SATA drive and format it as NTFS
- ○ **D.** Install a PATA drive and format it as NTFS

Quick Answer: **277**
Detailed Answer: **281**

Quick Check

Quick Answer: **277**
Detailed Answer: **281**

19. Examine the following figure. Then answer the question that follows.

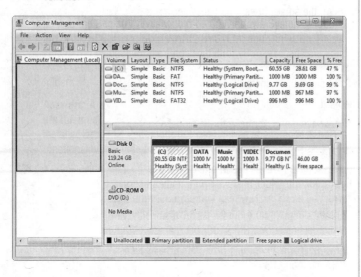

Which portion of Computer Management is being displayed in the figure?

- ○ **A.** Event Viewer
- ○ **B.** Disk Management
- ○ **C.** Disk Administrator
- ○ **D.** DiskPart

20. Which of the following is the correct path if you wanted to disable a service in Windows 7?

- ○ **A.** Msconfig > Settings > Services
- ○ **B.** System Settings > Tools > Services
- ○ **C.** Control Panel > Services
- ○ **D.** Control Panel > Administrative Tools > Services

Quick Answer: **277**
Detailed Answer: **282**

21. What should you do first before removing a paper jam?

- ○ **A.** Turn the printer off
- ○ **B.** Open all the doors in the printer
- ○ **C.** Clear the print queue
- ○ **D.** Take the printer offline

Quick Answer: **277**
Detailed Answer: **282**

22. Which of the following programs in Windows 7 saves problem descriptions and solutions?

Quick Answer: **277**
Detailed Answer: **282**

- ○ **A.** Dr. Watson
- ○ **B.** Problem Reports and Solutions
- ○ **C.** Action Center
- ○ **D.** Performance Monitor

23. A PC's monitor has no display after a power failure. The LED light on the monitor is on. What should be done first?

- ○ **A.** Power cycle the PC
- ○ **B.** Power cycle the peripherals
- ○ **C.** Power cycle the UPS
- ○ **D.** Power cycle the breaker switches

Quick Answer: **277**
Detailed Answer: **282**

24. A co-worker tells you that a work PC has become infected with a virus. What should you do first?

- ○ **A.** Check for system security patches
- ○ **B.** Perform an antivirus program scan
- ○ **C.** Boot the PC into Safe Mode
- ○ **D.** Remove the PC from the network

Quick Answer: **277**
Detailed Answer: **282**

25. What are things you should check when a laptop fails to turn on? (Select the four best answers.)

- ○ **A.** Power LED
- ○ **B.** Sound port
- ○ **C.** AC adapter
- ○ **D.** Inverter
- ○ **E.** Hibernate mode
- ○ **F.** Function key
- ○ **G.** Power button

Quick Answer: **277**
Detailed Answer: **282**

26. A customer reports to you that a newly issued smartcard does not work in a laptop. You try your smartcard in the laptop, and it works without any problems. What will most likely fix the problem?

- ○ **A.** Perform a BIOS flash
- ○ **B.** Reinstall the OS
- ○ **C.** Upgrade the smartcard reader firmware
- ○ **D.** Replace the smartcard reader

Quick Answer: **277**
Detailed Answer: **282**

27. A Windows 7 computer has an Experience Index of 3.8. The technician discovers that the computer has the following:

Performance index RAM1GB4.6Video3D3.8CPU2,4GHz4.2.

The technician upgrades the memory to 2 GB and gets the following results:

Performance index RAM2GB5.0Video3D3.8CPU2,4GHz4.2.

But the Windows Experience Index is still at 3.8. Which of the following can the technician do to improve the performance index?

- ○ **A.** Double the RAM again
- ○ **B.** Upgrade the CPU to 3 GHz
- ○ **C.** Increase the resolution on the screen
- ○ **D.** Upgrade the video card

28. Which of the following commands enables you to copy a file without prompts?

- ○ **A.** Copy /Z
- ○ **B.** Xcopy
- ○ **C.** Copy /Y
- ○ **D.** Copy /A

29. Which of the following is the best Windows 7 utility to back up important system files without requiring external storage?

- ○ **A.** NTbackup
- ○ **B.** Task Manger
- ○ **C.** System Protection
- ○ **D.** Xcopy

30. Examine the following Windows 7 figure. Then answer the question that follows.

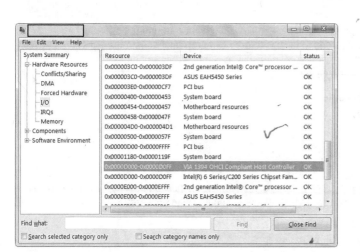

Which window are we looking at, and what is highlighted?

- ○ **A.** WinMSD—I/O setting of IEEE 1394 controller
- ○ **B.** System Information—I/O setting of IEEE 1394 controller
- ○ **C.** Device Manager—I/O setting of IEEE 1394 controller
- ○ **D.** System Properties—I/O setting of IEEE 1394 controller

31. A computer just had a memory upgrade installed. Upon booting the computer, it does not recognize the new memory, even though it is listed as being compatible on the manufacturer's website. What should you do to resolve the issue?

- ○ **A.** BIOS update
- ○ **B.** Adjust jumper settings
- ○ **C.** OS Update
- ○ **D.** New CMOS battery

Quick Answer: 277
Detailed Answer: 283

32. A customer states that the LCD display on a laptop has intermittent lines on the screen. You notice that when the display is moved, the lines appear and disappear again. What is the most likely cause?

- ○ **A.** The display panel is defective.
- ○ **B.** There's a damaged hinge.
- ○ **C.** The video controller is defective.
- ○ **D.** The display cable is loose.

Quick Answer: 277
Detailed Answer: 283

33. Your boss wants to encrypt a hard drive that will be storing critical data. Your boss needs to be able to drag and drop folders onto the volume and have them be encrypted in real-time. Which encryption technique should you suggest?

- ○ **A.** BitLocker
- ○ **B.** PKI
- ○ **C.** TPM
- ○ **D.** Kerberos

34. Dave reports that when a laptop's power button is pushed there is no response. What is the first thing you should try to appease Dave?

- ○ **A.** Replace the battery
- ○ **B.** Close the lid and reopen it
- ○ **C.** Plug in the external power supply
- ○ **D.** Reseat the memory

35. You are tasked with mapping a drive within the Command Prompt to a share named AlbaLonga on a server named Romulus. What is the correct syntax?

- ○ **A.** `net use //AlbaLonga/Romulus`
- ○ **B.** `http://Romulus.com/AlbaLonga`
- ○ **C.** `net use \\Romulus\AlbaLonga`
- ○ **D.** `ipp://Romulus.com/AlbaLonga`

36. Which of the following file extensions will start the program installation process in Windows?

- ○ **A.** *.INI
- ○ **B.** *.CFG
- ○ **C.** *.SYS
- ○ **D.** *.EXE

37. Memory was added to a workstation. When the computer was booted, it reports memory errors. What is the most likely cause?

- ○ **A.** A different brand of memory was installed into bank two.
- ○ **B.** The second memory stick was larger than the first.
- ○ **C.** The second memory stick was smaller than the first.
- ○ **D.** The new memory was installed in the second bank and runs at a lower speed than bank one.

38. One of your department's computers is constantly overheating. The computer seems to work properly but isn't making any noise. What has most likely happened?

Quick Answer: **277**
Detailed Answer: **284**

- ○ **A.** The case fan stopped working.
- ○ **B.** The power supply failed.
- ○ **C.** The heat sink failed.
- ○ **D.** The CPU failed.

39. Your boss asks you to troubleshoot a computer with a virus. What should you do first?

Quick Answer: **277**
Detailed Answer: **285**

- ○ **A.** Run a System Restore
- ○ **B.** Identify the malware
- ○ **C.** Roll back drivers
- ○ **D.** Research malware types

40. Examine the following figure. Then answer the question that follows.

Quick Answer: **277**
Detailed Answer: **285**

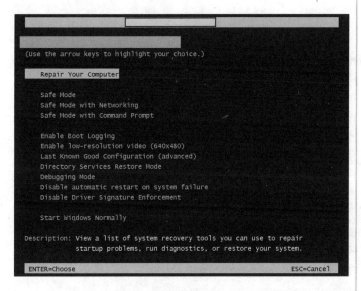

```
(Use the arrow keys to highlight your choice.)

 Repair Your Computer

  Safe Mode
  Safe Mode with Networking
  Safe Mode with Command Prompt

  Enable Boot Logging
  Enable low-resolution video (640x480)
  Last Known Good Configuration (advanced)
  Directory Services Restore Mode
  Debugging Mode
  Disable automatic restart on system failure
  Disable Driver Signature Enforcement

  Start Windows Normally

Description: View a list of system recovery tools you can use to repair
            startup problems, run diagnostics, or restore your system.

 ENTER=Choose                                              ESC=Cancel
```

What are we looking at in the figure?

- ○ **A.** System Recover Options
- ○ **B.** Recovery Console
- ○ **C.** ABOM
- ○ **D.** MSCONFIG

41. User A is part of the Users Group on a Windows 7 Ultimate computer. User A attempts to access files on a UNC path: \\server\fileshare.

Fileshare has the following share permissions:

Administrators—Full Control

Users—Read Only

Guests—No Access

However, the directory on the hard drive where the share is located has the following permissions:

Administrators—Full Control

Users—Change

Guests—No Access

Which level of access will the account User A have?

- ⊘ **A.** Read Only
- ○ **B.** Change
- ○ **C.** Full Control
- ○ **D.** No Access

42. A customer has installed a PostScript driver for a printer that actually only supports PCL. What is the most likely result?

- ○ **A.** The printer will not print at all.
- ◉ **B.** The printer will print garbage or unreadable characters.
- ○ **C.** The printer will process PostScript in the correct way.
- ○ **D.** The printer will print at a decreased resolution (DPI).

43. A marketing employee commonly sends large print jobs to a printer. The employee tells you that during the jobs the printer spontaneously pauses and resumes several times. What is the most likely cause?

- ○ **A.** The toner cartridge is defective. ✗
- ○ **B.** The printer paper tray is not big enough. ✗
- ○ **C.** The printer needs updated drivers.
- ◉ **D.** The printer is overheating.

44. Your boss wants to implement BitLocker on yet a second laptop for traveling purposes. What should you perform before implementing BitLocker?

- ○ **A.** Enable TPM in the BIOS
- ○ **B.** Disable UAC
- ○ **C.** Defrag the hard drive
- ○ **D.** Convert the file system to NTFS

45. Examine the following figure. Then answer the question that follows.

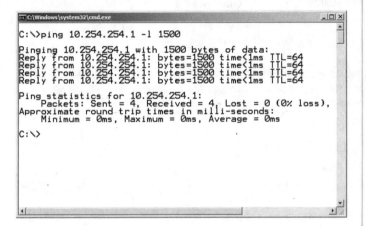

What does the –l switch accomplish in the figure?

- ○ **A.** It pings 10.254.254.1 1,500 times.
- ○ **B.** It pings 10.254.254.1 continuously until stopped.
- ◉ **C.** It pings 10.254.254.1 with four 1,500-byte packets of data.
- ○ **D.** It pings 10.254.254.1 at 1500 MB/s.

46. A computer has a RAID 1 array. SATA Drive 0 failed, and now the computer will not boot. What would most likely fix the problem by allowing the computer to boot again?

- ○ **A.** Replace SATA Drive 1
- ○ **B.** Mark SATA Drive 1 as active
- ○ **C.** Replace SATA Drive 0
- ○ **D.** Reboot and select LKG from the ABOM

Quick Check

47. One of your customers has a defective disk. Which command can
be used to extract readable information?

Quick Answer: **277**
Detailed Answer: **286**

- ○ **A.** Recover
- ○ **B.** Replace
- ○ **C.** Convert
- ○ **D.** REM

48. What is an advantage of Xcopy over Copy?

Quick Answer: **277**
Detailed Answer: **286**

- ○ **A.** The ability to copy files off of a mapped network drive
- ○ **B.** The ability to copy NTFS permissions
- ○ **C.** The ability to copy files and decrypt them
- ○ **D.** The ability to copy entire folder structures

49. One of your customers reports to you that when typing on the
laptop keyboard, the mouse pointer scrolls across the screen.
What can resolve this?

Quick Answer: **277**
Detailed Answer: **286**

- ○ **A.** Reboot the laptop
- ○ **B.** Plug in an external mouse
- ○ **C.** Use an external monitor
- ○ **D.** Disable the touchpad

50. Examine the following figure. Then answer the question that
follows.

Quick Answer: **277**
Detailed Answer: **287**

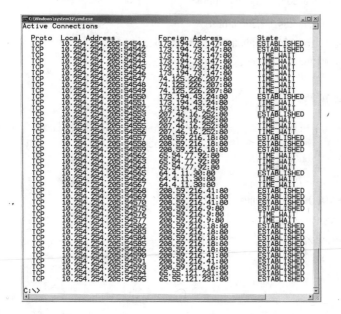

Which command was issued in the figure?

- ○ **A.** netstat
- ○ **B.** netstat -n
- ○ **C.** nbtstat
- ○ **D.** nbtstat -n

51. You are happily working in Windows when you stumble across a dialog box with some unfamiliar terms. What can you do to quickly provide more information?

- ○ **A.** Use the Microsoft Support website
- ○ **B.** Alternate-click and select "More Information"
- ○ **C.** Alternate-click and select "What's This?"
- ○ **D.** Press F1 and search for the term

Quick Answer: **277**
Detailed Answer: **287**

52. An office laser printer is printing lighter in random areas of each page. What is the easiest solution?

- ○ **A.** Clean the fuser area
- ○ **B.** Clean the drum with a computer vacuum
- ○ **C.** Use compressed air on the pickup assembly
- ○ **D.** Replace the toner cartridge

Quick Answer: **277**
Detailed Answer: **287**

53. Which one of the following is fault tolerant, mirrors a hard drive, and allows for disk duplexing?

- ○ **A.** RAID 0
- ○ **B.** RAID 1
- ○ **C.** RAID 5
- ○ **D.** RAID 6

Quick Answer: **277**
Detailed Answer: **287**

54. In Windows 7, which path would a user with the account name Charlie go to in order to view his pictures?

- ○ **A.** C:\Documents and Settings\Charlie\ Pictures
- ○ **B.** C:\Users\Charlie\Libraries\My Pictures
- ○ **C.** C:\Users\Charlie\My Pictures
- ○ **D.** C:\ Documents and Settings\Charlie\My Documents\My Pictures

Quick Answer: **277**
Detailed Answer: **287**

Quick Check

Quick Answer: **277**
Detailed Answer: **287**

55. Examine the following figure. Then answer the question that follows.

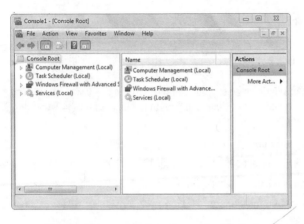

How would you navigate to the application in the figure?

- ○ **A.** Start > Run > Console1
- ○ **B.** Start, right-click Computer, select Manage
- ○ **C.** Start > Run > Computer Management
- ○ **D.** Start > Run > MMC

56. Your friend is playing the latest first-person game on a PC, but the screen is pausing during game play. Your friend has a high-end graphics card and the maximum memory for the motherboard. What should you do to help the situation?

Quick Answer: **277**
Detailed Answer: **287**

- ○ **A.** Upgrade the drivers
- ○ **B.** Reinstall the OS
- ○ **C.** Replace the hard drive
- ○ **D.** Reinstall the game

57. What is the most important reason not to plug an RJ11 phone line into an RJ45 port on a computer?

Quick Answer: **277**
Detailed Answer: **288**

- ○ **A.** PSTN networks are not Ethernet based.
- ○ **B.** Ethernet supports pulse dialing, not tone dialing.
- ○ **C.** Phone line voltages can damage Ethernet equipment.
- ○ **D.** RJ11 connections do not support full-duplex.

58. You have been asked to move data from one laptop to another, each of which has EFS functioning. Which should you perform first?

Quick Answer: **277**
Detailed Answer: **288**

○ **A.** Give the user of the second laptop administrator privileges

○ **B.** Export the user's certificate

○ **C.** Disable networking

○ **D.** Convert the partition to FAT32

59. A technician you work with just finished installing AV software on a PC. What should the technician do next?

Quick Answer: **277**
Detailed Answer: **288**

○ **A.** Update the AV signatures

○ **B.** Remove infected files

○ **C.** Run a full scan

○ **D.** Quarantine infected files

60. A Windows 7 Ultimate computer using IP address 192.168.1.5 on the network serves the bulk of the data to the rest of the six computers within a HomeGroup. Suddenly, though, neither your computer nor any of the other systems can access that Windows 7 Ultimate computer. Which command would you use on your local computer to find out if the Server service is running on 192.168.1.5 and which ID number is the Server service?

Quick Answer: **277**
Detailed Answer: **288**

○ **A.** `netstat` −a and <00>

○ **B.** `nbtstat` −a and <00>

○ **C.** `netstat` −A and <20>

○ **D.** `nbtstat` −A and <20>

○ **E.** `netstat` −A and <03>

○ **F.** `nbtstat` −A and <03>

61. You are troubleshooting what you believe to be a power issue. Which of the following should you test first?

Quick Answer: **277**
Detailed Answer: **288**

○ **A.** Power supply

○ **B.** 24-pin power connector

○ **C.** IEC cable

○ **D.** AC outlet

○ **E.** Circuit breaker

62. A customer's laptop goes into standby mode unexpectedly. What is the most likely hardware component that is causing the issue?

Quick Answer: **277**
Detailed Answer: **289**

○ **A.** LCD cutoff switch

○ **B.** Hard drive

○ **C.** SATA controller

○ **D.** Video card

63. How can you confirm that a new virus definition is authentic?

Quick Answer: **277**
Detailed Answer: **289**

- ◯ **A.** Check the file owner
- ◯ **B.** Check the creation date
- ◯ **C.** Check the file version
- ◯ **D.** Check the hash key

64. No matter how many `ipconfig/release` and `ipconfig/renew` commands you issue, the computer you are troubleshooting can only obtain an APIPA address. What has most likely failed?

Quick Answer: **277**
Detailed Answer: **289**

- ◯ **A.** DNS
- ◯ **B.** DHCP
- ◯ **C.** Network switch
- ◯ **D.** Patch panel

65. This type of malware appears to perform desired functions but is actually performing malicious functions behind the scenes.

Quick Answer: **277**
Detailed Answer: **289**

- ◯ **A.** Virus
- ◉ **B.** Trojan
- ◯ **C.** Spyware
- ◯ **D.** Rootkit

66. One of your customers has a wireless router installed in a home office. The customer complains of issues with signal strength at the opposite end of the house. What is the best option as far as increasing signal strength?

Quick Answer: **277**
Detailed Answer: **289**

- ◉ **A.** Install a wireless repeater at the far end of the house
- ◯ **B.** Install a second wired router at the far end of the house
- ◯ **C.** Install a high gain antenna focused toward the office wall
- ◯ **D.** Run Cat 5e cable to all of the rooms that have poor signal strength

67. A client is attempting to connect a laptop to a TV using an HDMI connector. The person tells you that video works fine, but audio does not. What is the most likely cause?

Quick Answer: **277**
Detailed Answer: **289**

- ◯ **A.** The laptop needs an HDMI application installed.
- ◯ **B.** The HDMI cable is too long.
- ◯ **C.** The speakers are not compatible with the digital connection.
- ◯ **D.** The HDMI audio service has not been selected.

68. The Device Management utility lists a disk as "Foreign". What should you do to make the disk usable?

- ○ **A.** Convert the disk to basic
- ○ **B.** Convert the disk to dynamic
- ○ **C.** Import the disk
- ○ **D.** Set the disk to active

69. How can you reach the System Restore utility in Windows 7? (Select the two best answers.)

- ○ **A.** Start > right-click Computer > Properties > click the System protection link
- ○ **B.** Start > right-click Computer > Advanced
- ○ **C.** Run > type systempropertiesprotection.exe
- ○ **D.** Start > right-click Computer > Properties > click the Advanced system settings link

70. Examine the following figure. Then answer the question that follows.

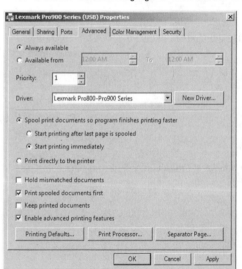

In Windows 7, using individual Control Panel icons, how would you navigate to the dialog box in the figure?

- ○ **A.** Start > Control Panel > Printers > right-click the printer and select Properties > Advanced
- ○ **B.** Start > Control Panel > Devices and Printers > right-click the printer and select Properties > Ports
- ○ **C.** Start > Control Panel > Devices and Printers > right-click the printer and select Properties > Ports
- ○ **D.** Start > Control Panel > Devices and Printers > right-click the printer and select Printer Properties > Advanced

71. Which of the following statements is true?

- ○ **A.** Authentication can be something a user knows such as a smart card.
- ○ **B.** Authentication can be something a user is such as a fingerprint.
- ○ **C.** Authentication can be something a user does such as a PIN or password.
- ○ **D.** Authentication can be something a user has such as signature.

72. You are tasked with accessing a wireless SOHO. The SSID you require does not appear when you scan for wireless networks. What should you do to access the wireless network?

- ⊘ **A.** Enter the SSID manually
- ○ **B.** Change the SSID on the router
- ○ **C.** Change the MAC address on the router
- ○ **D.** Reset the wireless card.

73. This is a type of phishing attack that is directed at the CEO of an organization.

- ○ **A.** Power phishing
- ○ **B.** Vishing
- ⊘ **C.** Whaling
- ○ **D.** Spear phishing

74. This type of data purging standard requires seven full passes or rewrites with bit-level erasure software.

- ○ **A.** Magnetic degausser
- ○ **B.** Low-level format
- ○ **C.** Peter Gutman security method
- ○ **D.** DoD 5220.22-M

75. You are required to implement an organizational policy that states user passwords can't be used twice in a row. Which policy will you configure?

- ○ **A.** Minimum password length
- ◉ **B.** Enforce password history
- ○ **C.** Minimum password age
- ○ **D.** Complexity requirements

76. A customer tells you that the computer runs fine for a few minutes but then freezes. What is the most likely cause?

- ○ **A.** CD-ROM drive is faulty.
- ○ **B.** Power supply failed.
- ◉ **C.** Fans are failing.
- ○ **D.** Memory is not seated properly.

77. You have several computers at your workstation. (Of course you do, you are a master tech!) One of them starts making a loud grinding sound immediately when you power on the computer. However, Windows boots and works fine. The only problem is the grinding that sets your teeth on edge. What is the most likely cause?

- ○ **A.** Bad fan
- ○ **B.** Bad HD
- ○ **C.** Bad power supply
- ○ **D.** Bad CD-ROM

78. You install a fiber-based backbone switch that connects three different departments' LAN switches. Which kind of network topology did you just create? (Select the best, most specific answer.)

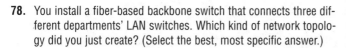

- ○ **A.** Star
- ○ **B.** Hybrid star
- ○ **C.** Star-bus
- ○ **D.** Hierarchical star

79. A user states that the computer monitor is suddenly displaying garbled images and strange colors and leaving cursor trails. The technician determines that the system is using an onboard graphics controller. What is the most likely cause of the display problem?

- ○ **A.** Resolution was set too high.
- ○ **B.** Defective RAM.
- ○ **C.** Outdated firmware.
- ○ **D.** Defective power supply.
- ○ **E.** Fragmented hard drive.

80. Examine the following figure. Then answer the question that follows.

The figure shows the option to set a Passcode in the iOS of an iPad2. How would you navigate to this screen?

  ○   **A.**   Settings > General > Passcode Lock > Turn Passcode On

  ○   **B.**   Settings > General > Turn Passcode On

  ○   **C.**   Settings > Passcode Lock > Turn Passcode On

  ○   **D.**   Settings > General > Passcode Lock > Enable WPA2 Passcode

81. Which of the following switches skips the process that compares directory entries to the file record segments corresponding to those entries, when running the Chkdsk command?

  ○   **A.**   Chkdsk /V

  ○   **B.**   Chkdsk /F

  ○   **C.**   Chkdsk /I

  ○   **D.**   Chkdsk /R

82. You are working on a computer in which you just installed a new hard drive. The system already runs Windows 7. The new hard drive does not appear in Windows Explorer. What should you perform next so that the drive will be recognized by the operating system?

- ○ **A.** Reboot the computer
- ◉ **B.** Initialize and format the hard drive in Disk Management
- ○ **C.** Configure the drive in the BIOS
- ○ **D.** Assign a drive letter to the hard drive in Disk Management
- ○ **E.** Set the drive to active

Quick Answer: 277
Detailed Answer: 292

83. Which utility displays important messages about solving issues in Windows 7?

- ○ **A.** Task Manager
- ○ **B.** Windows Defender
- ◉ **C.** Action Center
- ○ **D.** Problem Reports and Solutions

Quick Answer: 277
Detailed Answer: 292

84. A customer has a computer running Windows 7 Ultimate. The Windows Firewall appears to be causing communications to fail within a certain gaming application even though you set up an exception for the program. You stop the Windows Firewall, but when the computer reboots, the service starts up again. Of the following, which tool should you use to disable the Windows Firewall service?

- ○ **A.** Task Scheduler
- ○ **B.** System Configuration
- ○ **C.** System Properties
- ◉ **D.** Local Security Policy

Quick Answer: 277
Detailed Answer: 292

Quick Check

Quick Answer: **277**
Detailed Answer: **292**

85. Examine the following figure. Then answer the question that follows.

The figure shows a mounted volume. What is the actual mounted volume, and which hard drive folder is it pointing to?

- ○ **A.** F: and GRMCULXFRER_EN_DVD
- ○ **B.** Windows 7 DVD and the Data folder
- ○ **C.** F: and the DVD drive
- ○ **D.** Data folder and GRMCULXFRER_EN_DVD

86. An attacker is constantly trying to hack into one of your customer's SOHO networks. What is the easiest, most practical way to protect the network from intrusion?

- ○ **A.** Disable the SSID broadcast
- ○ **B.** Install an antivirus server application
- ○ **C.** Disconnect the Internet connection
- ○ **D.** Install a firewall
- ○ **E.** Install an IDS

Quick Answer: **277**
Detailed Answer: **292**

87. A CAD/CAM workstation running AutoCAD is displaying rotating 3D images very slowly. The customer needs the images to rotate quickly and smoothly. What should you upgrade on the computer? (Select the best answer.)

- ○ **A.** CPU
- ○ **B.** RAM
- ○ **C.** Video card
- ○ **D.** Hard drive

88. What will happen if a PCIe video card is used in a PCI slot?

- ○ **A.** A PCIe card used in a PCI slot will function properly with a firmware upgrade.
- ◉ **B.** A PCIe card cannot be used in a PCI slot.
- ○ **C.** A PCIe card used in a PCI slot will function normally.
- ○ **D.** A PCIe card used in a PCI slot will function at PCI speeds.

89. One of your customers reports that a laser printer is printing out blurry and smudged pages. What is the most likely reason?

- ◉ **A.** The fuser is not getting hot enough.
- ○ **B.** The toner cartridge is leaking.
- ○ **C.** The toner cartridge is low.
- ○ **D.** The fuser is too hot.

90. Which kind of battery would you find in an iPad, and how long will a full charge last for on the average?

- ○ **A.** NiCd—2.5 hours
- ○ **B.** Lithium—10 hours
- ○ **C.** 16 v—5 hours
- ○ **D.** Lithium-ion polymer—10 hours

Quick Check

Quick Answer: **278**
Detailed Answer: **293**

91. Examine the following figure. Then answer the question that follows.

The figure shows the Computer Name/Domain Changes dialog box in Windows 7. How do you navigate to this window? (Select the two best answers.)

○ **A.** Start > right-click Computer, select Properties > Computer Name tab > Change

○ **B.** Start > right-click Computer, select Properties > Change Computer Name

○ **C.** Run > systempropertiescomputername.exe > Change

○ **D.** Run > systempropertiescomputername.exe > Advanced > Change Computer Name

Quick Answer: **278**
Detailed Answer: **293**

92. One of your customers reports that a computer has no access to the network. You look at the switch and notice that all lights are on and not flashing. The network cables are plugged in, and the computer's network card is functioning properly. What can you do to solve this problem?

○ **A.** Ping 127.0.0.1

○ **B.** Replace the switch's uplink cable

○ **C.** Reboot the computer

○ **D.** Power cycle the switch

Quick Answer: **278**
Detailed Answer: **294**

93. You have a Windows 7 Ultimate computer that you wish to write a batch file for. You want the batch file to turn off the computer after a certain amount of time. Which main command should you utilize in the batch file?

○ **A.** Taskkill

○ **B.** Down

○ **C.** Kill

◉ **D.** Shutdown

94. Which switch of the Robocopy command will copy subdirectories but skip empty ones?

○ **A.** /E

○ **B.** /B

○ **C.** /S

○ **D.** /DCOPY:T

Quick Answer: **278**
Detailed Answer: **294**

95. Examine the following figure. Then answer the question that follows.

Quick Answer: **278**
Detailed Answer: **294**

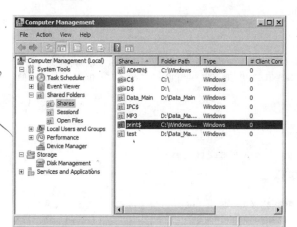

The figure shows the list of shares on a Windows 7 computer. What is the path of the print$ share?

○ **A.** C:\Windows

○ **B.** C:\Windows\System32

○ **C.** C:\Windows\System32\spool\print$

○ **D.** C:\Windows\System32\spool\drivers

96. You need to list all the network shares for a local computer within the Command Prompt. Which command will do this for you?

◉ **A.** Net view

○ **B.** Net use

○ **C.** Net share

○ **D.** Net statistics

Quick Answer: **278**
Detailed Answer: **294**

97. You are now a manager of a technical services team. One of your technicians notices that a printer is jamming just above the printer tray. What should the technician do first to resolve the issue?

- ○ **A.** Clean the feeder rollers
- ◉ **B.** Clean the pickup rollers
- ○ **C.** Replace the fuser
- ○ **D.** Replace the drum

98. A customer is frantic because a mobile device's operating system has crashed. The customer keeps referring to Gingerbread in excited tones but isn't making much sense. Which OS is the customer referring to?

- ○ **A.** Microsoft Windows CE
- ○ **B.** Apple iOS version 5
- ○ **C.** Android version 2
- ○ **D.** Blackberry OS

99. You need to find out which ports are open in the Windows Firewall on a Windows XP computer. Which of the following will allow you to show the configuration?

- ○ **A.** arp -a
- ○ **B.** netsh firewall show logging
- ◉ **C.** netsh firewall show state
- ○ **D.** ipconfig /all

100. You have some DLLs and ActiveX controls that need to be troubleshot. Which command can manipulate these?

- ○ **A.** Regedit
- ○ **B.** Regsvr32
- ○ **C.** ODBC32
- ○ **D.** Regedt32

Well, you made it. Congratulations. Check your answers and read through the explanations carefully!

Quick-Check Answer Key

1. A	30. B	59. A
2. C	31. A	60. D
3. C	32. D	61. C
4. D	33. A	62. A
5. C	34. C	63. D
6. D	35. C	64. B
7. D	36. D	65. B
8. B	37. D	66. A
9. A	38. A	67. D
10. A	39. B	68. C
11. C	40. C	69. A and C
12. A	41. A	70. D
13. A and D	42. B	71. B
14. C	43. D	72. A
15. B	44. A	73. C
16. D	45. C	74. D
17. A, C, and E	46. B	75. B
18. C	47. A	76. C
19. B	48. B	77. A
20. D	49. D	78. D
21. A	50. B	79. B
22. C	51. C	80. A
23. A	52. D	81. C
24. D	53. B	82. B
25. A, C, E, and G	54. C	83. C
26. C	55. D	84. B
27. D	56. A	85. B
28. C	57. C	86. D
29. C	58. B	87. C

88. B	**93.** D	**98.** C
89. A	**94.** C	**99.** C
90. D	**95.** D	**100.** B
91. A and C	**96.** A	
92. D	**97.** B	

Answers and Explanations

1. **Answer: A.** The Type 1 hypervisor is the bare metal, or native hypervisor. It runs directly on the host computer's hardware. Examples include Microsoft Hyper-V, VMware ESX, and Citrix XenServer. This is required for true virtualization workstations. Type 2 hypervisors run *within* another operating system. Examples of this include Microsoft Virtual PC, Windows XP Mode (which runs in a Virtual PC window within Windows 7), and VirtualBox. These do not run nearly as fast as type 1 hypervisors and so are used for limited purposes. For example, if a company wanted to run Windows Server 2008 in a virtual environment but have it be an actual server on the network, it should run in a type 1 hypervisor. But if you are learning how to use Windows Vista—for example, in a lab environment—the type 2 hypervisor would probably be fine.

2. **Answer: C.** Virtual private networks (VPNs) rely on a tunneling protocol such as PPTP or L2TP to create a secure connection between a network and a remote computer or group of computers. WWAN is another name for cellular Internet access. WiMAX is a fast, wireless Internet service used over large geographic areas. WLAN is the wireless LAN that is created when you implement a wireless access point or create an ad-hoc network of devices.

3. **Answer: C.** Typing %temp% in the Run prompt will display a folder with the current user's temporary files. For example, in Windows 7 this would show the C:\Users\%username%\AppData\Local\Temp folder. Nothing will be added or changed. Simply the folder will be displayed in a Windows Explorer window. The operating system's temporary folder is located at C:\Windows\Temp.

4. **Answer: D.** Voice over IP (VoIP) is a streaming telephony application. Streaming applications such as VoIP and online games can benefit from QoS. QoS stands for Quality of Service, which is the capability to provide different priorities to different applications. It guarantees network bandwidth for real-time streaming of the media applications such as VoIP. The SSID is the name or identifier of a wireless network. Instant messaging and e-mail are not streaming applications; therefore, they would not benefit from the use of QoS.

5. **Answer: C.** A surge suppressor (or surge protector) uses metal-oxide varistors (MOVs) to protect against surges and spikes. They protect each outlet and port on the device, but they do not last forever. Most manufacturers recommend that after several years of use you replace them. Power strips do not have these and do not protect against surges and spikes, though the device might have trip functionality and have to be reset in the case of an electrical problem. Power supplies are located within the computer; they do not have MOVs. A multimeter is used to test outlets and wires. An MOV can also be tested by a multimeter by testing its resistance.

6. **Answer: D.** Attrib -H *.* will unhide all of the files in the folder. The attrib command allows you to work with four different file attributes that I like to refer to as RASH. *R* stands for Read-only, *A* = Archive, *S* = System, and *H* = Hidden. Using a minus sign will remove the attribute, while a plus sign will add the attribute. Since the files were already hidden, we needed to use the minus sign to remove the attribute and be able to view the files. *.* means all the files with all extensions within that particular directory. Check out the attrib command in the Command Prompt for yourself by typing **attrib /?**. Ray is always doing interesting things in my books.

7. **Answer: D.** The standard user cannot install software or make changes to the system without knowing an administrative login. Administrators have full control over a system. Power users in Windows XP were able to install programs but are not allowed in Windows 7 or Vista. Remote Desktop users can remote into other machines in order to control them from another location.

8. **Answer: B.** The Recovery Console is a system recovery tool used in Windows XP. There are a lot of different commands that can be issued in this mode. If the NTLDR file has been damaged or is missing, it can be rewritten to the hard disk by issuing the fixboot command while in the Recovery Console. NTLDR can also be manually copied from the CD-ROM disc if necessary. The fixmbr command will rewrite the master boot record of the hard drive. The chkdsk command will check the integrity of the disk. Bootcfg /rebuild can be used to scan for the operating system installations and rebuild that information into the boot.ini file.

9. **Answer: A.** Chkdsk /R will locate bad sectors and recover the information from them. /F fixes errors but doesn't locate bad sectors and recover the information from them. /C and /I skip certain checks of the volume (in this case C:), which ultimately reduces the time it takes to check the volume.

10. **Answer: A.** Every user profile gets a Desktop folder by default. This folder will be located within the user profile folder, which is shown in the answer as a variable %username%. In a standard Windows 7/Vista configuration, the Documents and Settings and System Volume Information folders will be hidden and access will be denied. The System32 folder is inside the Windows folder, not the Users folder. Windows XP used Documents and Settings as the main user folder, but Windows Vista/7 changed that by creating a junction from that folder to the Users folder. Now in Vista/7 the Documents and Settings folder is protected, but you have limited access to the Users folder.

11. **Answer: C.** The switches could have been inadvertently reconfigured to 100 Mbps speed during the recent network hardware refresh. Since the LAN is supposed to be a gigabit Ethernet network, it should be running at 1000 Mbps (1 Gbps). If the network speed is reduced down to 10%, everything will look slower to the customer. The switches should be reconfigured for 1000 Mbps at full-duplex mode if possible. DHCP servers don't have anything to do with the speed of the network or speed of Internet connections. Neither does the firewall. In fact, if the firewall was off, network performance would probably increase when connecting to the Internet, though it would be quite insecure. Nowhere in the scenario is a cellular repeater mentioned. Regardless, a cellular repeater would not interfere with a wireless LAN and definitely wouldn't interfere with a wired Ethernet network.

12. **Answer: A.** The technician should install the latest firmware to the WAP. WAPs don't require drivers; the firmware has all the code they require. On the other hand, wireless network adapters don't need firmware (usually) because they use drivers. But the network adapter is fine because it is already configured with WPA2. It's the WAP we are concerned with; we want it to use the best wireless encryption possible.

13. **Answers: A and D.** If a user cannot print to a brand-new printer, yet everyone else can print to it, you should check if the printer is installed on that user's computer and if it is set as the default printer. If the printer has not yet been installed, there will be no

print queue to clear. However, if the printer has been installed, then the next thing to check would be if the print queue has failed. You could also check the print spooler. If the user was able to print to an older printer that was also shared by other users in the workgroup, then you should not have to change the user's password or permissions.

14. **Answer: C.** This message appears when a device is connected to a USB port; Windows notifies you that the device can run faster than it currently is. It's possible that the external hard drive is compatible with USB 3.0, but the system is not capable of USB 3.0 speeds (5.0 Gbps). In some cases, Windows can't run at those speeds without a driver update or other upgrade software-wise. If the external hard drive was a USB 2.0 device, the message wouldn't appear because everything already runs at USB 2.0 speed. If the drive was FireWire (IEEE 1394), USB wouldn't even be a concern; they are completely different standards and ports. A drive plugged into a FireWire port wouldn't get the message listed in the question.

15. **Answer: B.** Chances are that a computer BIOS setting is incorrect. The card either is not being recognized in the BIOS or is not enabled. Of course, it is also possible that the card has an incorrect driver installed in Windows. 802.11 refers to WLAN (Wi-Fi), not Bluetooth. Disabling the WLAN card will not affect this scenario. If the hard drive was faulty, you would see other indications such as lockups or failure to boot, but nothing dealing with Bluetooth devices. Microwaves are usually not located near a person's computer. Though it is possible for a microwave or other wireless device to interfere with Bluetooth, it is the less likely answer.

16. **Answer: D.** The best option in this scenario would be to deny read access to the Accounting folder for Bill through shared access security. You would not use local access security because the folder is shared from a network server within your Active Directory domain. Also, if you remove Bill from all domain groups that have access to the accounting folder, Bill will probably lose access to other folders as well. If you deny read access to the accounting folder for any group that Bill is a member of, you will probably impact other users on the network negatively.

17. **Answers: A, C, and E.** A keyboard could stop functioning due to stuck keys from overuse or liquid spill; loose ribbon cable connection; and a warped keyboard caused by damage from heavy items, environmental conditions, or misuse. A bad inverter would cause the backlight to fail, and you would just barely be able to see the display. A faulty touchpad is another problem altogether; the touchpad and the keyboard are separate devices on the laptop. A discharged battery would cause the laptop to simply shut off (if using battery power only).

18. **Answer: C.** SATA drives are faster than PATA (IDE) drives, and NTFS is going to be more efficient than FAT32. Plus, if the customer is already using NTFS, you wouldn't want to downgrade the new drive to FAT32.

19. **Answer: B.** The Disk Management component of Computer Management is being displayed in the figure. You can tell because it shows each disk and the volumes within each disk. The Event Viewer houses log information for the system, applications, and security auditing events. Disk Administrator is the predecessor to Disk Management in the old Windows NT days. DiskPart is the command-line tool used to create and modify partitions on the hard drive.

20. **Answer: D.** The correct path is Control Panel > Administrative Tools > Services. Of course, there are lots of other ways to get to the Services console window, but you should know the Control Panel paths for the exam. In addition, there are lots of ways to shut off services; know as many of them as you can, such as in the Task Manager or in the Command Prompt. The path Msconfig > Settings > Services is not valid because there is no Settings option. System Settings > Tools > Services is also an invalid path. Finally, Services cannot be accessed directly from Control Panel.

21. **Answer: A.** You should always turn the printer off and unplug it before putting your hands inside it! Plus, you should wait for about 10 or 15 minutes so that the fuser can cool off. Open the doors after you have turned the printer off. The print queue will be cleared on most printers when you turn them off. Taking the printer offline is not enough; it needs to be shut down to be safe.

22. **Answer: C.** The Action Center in Windows 7 can save problem descriptions and solutions; this is done in the archived messages section. The Action Center could be considered the successor to the Problem Reports and Solutions of Windows Vista, as well as the successor to the older Dr. Watson in Windows XP. Performance Monitor is a program that tracks how much of your device's resources are being utilized—for example, what percentage of the processor is used.

23. **Answer: A.** If there is a power failure, try power cycling the PC. In this scenario it could be that power went out for 5 minutes. When power returned, the monitor was still on (thus the LED) but the computer remained off (thus nothing on the display). Really, in this case you are just turning the computer on. Peripherals should have no bearing on this scenario unless they also plug in. If you power cycle the PC and there is still nothing on the display, try disconnecting the peripherals from the PC, disconnecting their AC power (if they have that), and rebooting the PC. If the monitor has a LED light, you know it is getting power and so the UPS does not need to be power cycled. However, if there was a 5-minute power loss and the UPS didn't keep the PC running, you should check the UPS battery. Turning the breaker switches for the circuit on and off is always fun but would simply cut power to the AC outlets temporarily.

24. **Answer: D.** First thing: remove the PC from the network so that the virus (if there is one) doesn't spread to other systems! Then you can safely go about troubleshooting that system by performing an AV scan while in Safe Mode and checking for system security updates.

25. **Answers: A, C, E, and G.** Check the power LED on the laptop first and see what it is doing. Could be that the user simply wasn't pressing the power button! If it blinks slowly once in a while the laptop might be in a sleep state. Then check the power light on the AC adapter. Make sure the AC adapter is getting power; if it is, check if it is the right adapter. Check if the system is in hibernate mode by pressing and holding the power button. Finally, the power button might be faulty, so make sure it isn't loose. If there is no AC adapter available, you should also check if the battery is connected properly and charged. Make sure the user keeps the AC adapter on hand at all times.

26. **Answer: C.** First, try upgrading the smartcard reader firmware. A smartcard is an intelligent card that authenticates a user. Newer smartcards with more intelligence are constantly being developed. These newer cards might not be readable by a smartcard reader until it is updated. In rarer cases you might have to replace the smartcard

reader. A BIOS flash should be necessary only if the smartcard reader is not recognized. Reinstalling the OS should be avoided at all costs, but it might be necessary if the laptop has a very old version of Windows.

27. **Answer: D.** Upgrade the video card. The Windows Experience Index is based on the lowest component score. In this case that is the video card. You'll note that there is a number after each component. After the RAM upgrade those numbers are RAM: 5.0, Video: 3.8, and CPU: 4.2. The video score is the index. So, the lowest common denominator should be upgraded. Increasing the resolution on the screen won't have an effect, or it will cause the index for video to go down.

28. **Answer: C.** Copy /Y suppresses prompting of overwrite confirmations. Copy /Z copies networked files in restartable mode. Xcopy is used to easily copy entire directories of data to another location. Copy /A allows you to indicate an ASCII text file to copy.

29. **Answer: C.** System Protection is a feature that creates and saves data about the computer's system files and settings. It does this by creating restore points. External storage is not necessary for these; they are automatically stored in the system volume. NTbackup is the Windows XP backup program. The Task Manager is used to view system performance, stop services, and kill processes. Xcopy is used to copy entire directory trees.

30. **Answer: B.** The figure displays the System Information window with the IEEE 1394 (and I/O setting) highlighted. System Information can be accessed from Start > All Programs > Accessories > System Tools or by accessing Run and typing msinfo32.

31. **Answer: A.** You should update the BIOS. If it hasn't been updated in a while, it probably won't recognize newer memory modules. Most of today's motherboards don't have jumper settings for RAM. In fact, the only jumper you will often find is the BIOS configuration jumper, which only needs to be configured if a person forgot a password. The BIOS will have a problem recognizing the RAM far before the OS starts up; no OS updates are required to make RAM recognizable to the system. If the computer needed a new CMOS battery, you would know because the time in the BIOS would reset to an earlier date.

32. **Answer: D.** Intermittent lines are a good indicator that the video cable is loose (or possibly damaged). Remove the keyboard (or disassemble the display), locate the ribbon cable, and connect it securely on each end. This is common with laptops as they are constantly being moved around and jostled; ribbon cables like to come loose! Remember to consider loose connections before guessing at defective parts. A defective display or defective video controller would probably cause a complete lack of video. A damaged hinge would prevent the laptop from closing properly.

33. **Answer: A.** BitLocker is a type of WDE: whole-disk encryption. It encrypts all of the contents that are created on it or copied to it in real-time. It requires a trusted platform module (TPM) on the motherboard or an encrypted USB flash drive. Only Windows 7 Ultimate and Enterprise, and Windows Vista Ultimate and Enterprise, support BitLocker when used in this manner. Other lesser versions of Windows are compatible with BitLocker To Go for reading encrypted documents.

34. **Answer: C.** You should plug in the external power supply. You know that Dave— sometimes he forgets to plug in the power adapter and then the battery goes dead, causing the laptop to be quite unresponsive when pressing the power button. Remember the golden rule: Make sure it's plugged in! Do that first and you will save yourself a lot of hours of your life. However, if that doesn't work, you can move on to checking the battery, checking the type of power adapter being used, the AC outlet you are connecting to, and so on. Some users neglect to charge their batteries, and instead, their laptops are constantly being used at a low percentage of charge. This lessens the lifespan of the battery. So, when you do plug in the AC adapter, sometimes you will find the battery does need to be replaced. Always check to see if it can be charged and if it holds a charge. Recommend to laptop users that they carry a spare battery in the laptop bag. You shouldn't have to reseat the memory unless you get an error message during the POST.

35. **Answer: C.** The correct syntax is `net use \\Romulus\AlbaLonga`. Note the backslashes in use here. You would probably want a persistent connection using a drive letter (such as F:), so you might append that to net use (for example, `net use F: \\Romulus\AlbaLonga` or something to that effect). The universal naming convention (UNC) for mapping drives is \\servername\sharename. The server name is Romulus; the share name is AlbaLonga. It's possible to connect to servers and shares with HTTP but not map a drive to them. Also, the server name is Romulus. Romulus.com is a domain name, something that a server name would be part of— for example, server1 would be the server name (or hostname) of the address server1.davidlprowse.com. The IPP protocol is used to make connections to printers and is often used with IP addresses, not server names.

36. **Answer: D.** *.EXE refers to any file with the .EXE extension. .EXE is short for executable. When you want to run a program, it is usually started with a file that has a .EXE extension. For example, to start Microsoft Word, the winword.exe executable is initiated. And for installing programs, the most common is setup.exe. .INI files are initialization files—for example, Window XP's boot.ini file which has the list of operating systems that can be booted to. .CFG is short for configuration file. These might list commands and parameters for a program. Often, .INI and .CFG files can be manipulated in Notepad because they are text *based* (but not text or .txt files). .SYS files are system files—for example, pagefile.sys. The .SYS extension was used extensively back in the days of DOS, but newer versions of Windows tend to have system files with .dll and .exe extensions.

37. **Answer: D.** For multiple memory sticks to be compatible, they need to run at the same speed. You might be able to get away with one stick being one step slower, if the motherboard supports it, and as long as it is not dual-channel memory. But it isn't worth the chance. If the sticks are not compatible, or if the second stick is not compatible with the motherboard, you will probably get memory errors during POST.

38. **Answer: A.** The case fan is the most likely culprit of the listed answers. If the computer is overheating, it means that the hot air is not exhausting out of the case—the number one offender is the case fan. And if the system is making little noise, you can guess that a fan has failed (although they are making quieter and quieter fans). This is a quick and cheap fix luckily. However, the power supply fan could have failed (less likely), in which case you would have to replace the entire power supply. Heat sinks

are passive and usually don't fail; it is more likely that the CPU fan would fail. If the CPU itself failed, it could be *because* of overheating, but that would cause the system to stop working, which is contrary to the scenario in the question.

39. **Answer: B.** The first thing you should do is identify the malware. (BTW, if the computer is on the network, disconnect it first.) Then, you can research that malware and any possible cures by searching the Internet and accessing your AV provider's website. Rolling back drivers should not be necessary, especially if you find it necessary to run a System Restore at some point.

40. **Answer: C.** We are looking at the Advanced Boot Options Menu (ABOM) screen. This is the screen that comes up if you press F8 while Windows is booting, and it's how you would access Safe Mode and a host of other booting options. The System Recovery Options (WinRE) can be accessed by booting to the Windows 7/Vista DVD and selecting Repair. The Recovery Console is the repair environment for Windows XP; it is also accessed from the Windows disc. Msconfig is a program within Windows that allows you to modify the way the system boots, disable programs, and disable services.

41. **Answer: A.** User A will end up having the Read-Only level of access to the share. Generally, a user gets the more restrictive level of access. The only thing that is different between the share's permissions and the parent directory's permissions is the level of control for the Users group. Normally, a share will obtain its permissions from the parent folder. That is, unless that option is un-checkmarked in the properties of the folder; then, the folder can be reconfigured for whatever permissions an admin wants to set for it. That must be what happened in the scenario. Administrators get Full Control access to almost everything by default. And Guests get No Access to just about everything by default. So the only possibilities for this question were Change and Read Only. Again, in general, the typical user account will receive the more restrictive level of permissions.

42. **Answer: B.** Most likely, the printer will print garbage or unreadable characters (known as *garbled* characters). If you install an incorrect driver for a printer, you risk a garbage printout. You would know if this was the case immediately when trying to print a test page. The incorrect driver could be a printer driver for another printer or one that is PostScript when it should be Printer Command Language (PCL). This won't stop the printer from printing, but you may not like what you see (unless you are into gibberish). The DPI of the printer will not change. A DPI such as 600 cannot be decreased to 300 DPI unless you set that in the printer's Properties sheet in Windows or on the display on the printer. And it can only be increased in the same manner, and only if the printer supports it.

43. **Answer: D.** The printer is probably overheating during these long jobs. Perhaps the fuser is nearing replacement time. The fuser can run as hot as 400° Fahrenheit (204° Celsius), and some printers will pause printing when that temperature threshold is tripped. Once the temperature goes back below the threshold, the printer will begin printing again. If the toner cartridge was defective, you would get blank paper, lighter printing, or paper with lines or smears. As long as there is paper in the tray, the large print job will continue to print (if within operating temperature parameters). Updated drivers are only necessary when the printer will not print the data on the page correctly. Pausing the job in this scenario is not causing any print errors; it's just taking longer to complete.

44. Answer: A. Before implementing the BitLocker solution in Windows, you should enable the trusted platform module (TPM) in the BIOS. This is the chip on the motherboard that includes the encryption code. UAC is User Account Control, a separate security option in Windows 7/Vista that checks if users have administrative permissions before allowing them to carry out administrative tasks. Defragmenting the hard drive is not necessary, but it can't hurt to at least analyze the drive and see if it needs to be defragged. Defragging a drive that requires it can increase performance. BitLocker works on FAT16, FAT32, NTFS, and exFAT partitions, so no need to convert the file system.

45. Answer: C. The −1 switch in this scenario is pinging the host at 10.254.254.1 with four individual 1500-byte packets of data. −1 allows you to change the size of the packet that is sent; it is 32 bytes by default. You can see that the figure only shows four pings total. A continuous ping would keep going until you stop it by pressing Ctrl + C on the keyboard or closing the Command Prompt; that would be performed with the −t switch. A specific amount of pings can be controlled with the −n switch. It is 1500 bytes per packet, not 1500 MB/s, which would be a far greater amount and not one that can be configured with the `ping` command.

46. Answer: B. You would mark SATA Drive 1 as active. If you cannot access Disk Management, you would have to do it by booting the system with WinRE (System Recovery Options), accessing the Command Prompt; executing the Diskpart command; and typing the commands `select disk 1`, `select partition 1`, and `active`. A RAID 1 array is a mirroring array with two drives. The second drive keeps an exact copy of the first drive in real-time. If Drive 1 doesn't take over automatically when Drive 0 fails, you will have to set it to active. Remember that a partition with an operating system must be set to active; otherwise, the computer will not be able to boot to the partition. Replacing Drive 1 is not necessary as it did not fail. Replacing Drive 0 is inevitable if you want to re-create the mirror, but not necessary if you just want to get the system to boot for now. Rebooting to the Last Known Good Configuration will not help; that only reverts system changes back to when the last successful login occurred. It won't fix the failed drive.

47. Answer: A. The Recover command can recover readable information from a bad or defective disk. The disk should be slaved to a working computer to get back the data. The Replace command will replace source and destination files but not recover lost information. Convert changes a file system from FAT to NTFS without losing data. REM records comments in a batch file (.bat) or within config.sys, a root file not typically used in Windows.

48. Answer: B. Xcopy can copy NTFS permissions. Normally, when a file is copied—for example, in Windows Explorer—the file loses its permissions and takes on the permissions of the new parent folder. That is also the case with the Copy command. Xcopy and Robocopy can be used to transcend this rule. Both Xcopy and Copy can copy files off of a mapped network drive and can copy entire folder structures, but neither can copy files while decrypting them.

49. Answer: D. The person's arm or sleeve is probably brushing up against the touchpad, causing the mouse pointer to move. By disabling the touchpad in the Device Manager or elsewhere, you eliminate the chance of that, but the user also loses that functionality. Rebooting the laptop will have the same effect and is not necessary. Using an external mouse alone will not fix the problem; even if there is an external mouse, the touchpad can still be used, unless it is disabled. An external monitor will not help you fix the touchpad issue, but it might be a nice addition to a laptop. In fact, many users who have laptops in an office also use them at home. At the office, and perhaps at home as well, it is best to set them up with a docking station, external keyboard, external mouse, and monitor. It usually results in greater productivity.

50. **Answer: B.** The netstat −n command was issued in the Command Prompt in the figure. −n shows information in numerical format: IP addresses and port numbers instead of computer names and protocol names. netstat by itself would show the same information but by name. Note that the command in the figure only shows TCP sessions. To show both TCP and UDP sessions, use netstat −a. To show both but in numerical format, use netstat −an. nbtstat displays TCP/IP statistics as they relate to NetBIOS over TCP/IP connections. nbtstat −n lists local NetBIOS names.

51. **Answer: C.** Try alternate-clicking and selecting "What's This?" Alternate-click means you are using the secondary mouse button; for right-handed folk this would be a right-click. You could also use the Microsoft Support website or press F1 to search for information within Windows, but they would both take longer. There is no "More Information" option when you alternate-click.

52. **Answer: D.** If the printer is printing lighter in some areas, it is a good indicator that the toner cartridge needs replacement. The fuser need only be cleaned if you see smudges or streaks (you should also check the maintenance schedule and see if it should be replaced). You might clean parts of the printer with a computer vacuum if there was a toner spill (making sure to turn off the printer first), but the drum might be within the toner cartridge, making that impossible. Compressed air is also sometimes used on rollers and separator pads, but it is not usually recommended because it can blow excess toner all over the place—have that computer vacuum handy.

53. **Answer: B.** RAID 1 is mirroring, but if you were to incorporate a separate hard disk controller for each drive, you would then have disk duplexing as well. RAID 1 is fault tolerant because a copy of all data goes to both disks in the mirror. RAID 0 is data striping and has no fault tolerant mechanism. RAID 5 and 6 are both types of striping with parity which are fault tolerant, but only RAID 1 offers disk mirroring with duplexing.

54. **Answer: C.** The path C:\Users\Charlie\My Pictures is where the pictures would be stored. Documents and Settings was used by Windows XP, but as of Vista was redirected (via a junction) to the Users folder. It is possible to access Libraries in Windows 7, but it is a bit easier than the answer listed. Go to Windows Explorer, and then go to Libraries > Pictures > My Pictures.

55. **Answer: D.** The figure shows the Microsoft Management Console (MMC). You can tell because it is given the default name "Console1" and has multiple other console windows within it, including Computer Management. This is accessed by clicking Start, going to Run, and typing MMC. But when it is first opened, it will not be populated with any snap-ins.

56. **Answer: A.** If you see video issues such as pausing during game play, upgrade the video drivers. Make sure that you download the latest video driver from the manufacturer's website. Gamers cannot rely on Microsoft drivers, especially FPS gamers! Sometimes reinstalling a game is necessary but shouldn't be in this scenario.

Replacing the hard drive and reinstalling the OS are drastic and unnecessary measures for this problem.

57. **Answer: C.** Phone lines can carry as much as 80 volts (when they ring), which could possibly damage network interface cards on a computer and other Ethernet networking equipment, so they should be plugged into modems only. Ethernet often uses plus and minus 5 V signals unless you use Power over Ethernet (PoE), which incorporates regular Ethernet but also sends power over the unused wires on the network cable. It's true; the Public Switched Telephone Network (PSTN) is not Ethernet-based. But that only means that a phone line will not work with a standard Ethernet network adapter. Ethernet doesn't support pulse dialing or tone dialing. RJ11 connections are indeed full-duplex; you can talk and listen when having a conversation at the same time.

58. **Answer: B.** The first thing you should do is export the user's certificate from the first laptop to the second laptop. This can be done by clicking Start and typing certmgr.msc in the Search box; then locate and export the correct Personal Certificate. The Certificates console window can also be added to an MMC. The Encrypting File System (EFS) is the standard single-file encryption method for Windows 7/Vista (if the version supports it). Files encrypted with EFS are then displayed as green in color within Windows Explorer. Networking need not be disabled, and we aren't sure which user is being referred to in the answers, but if the certificate has been exported, that user should be able to read the files. Partitions can be converted from FAT32 to NTFS but not vice versa.

59. **Answer: A.** The technician should update the antivirus (AV) software immediately after installing it and set it to automatically check for updates every day. *If* the PC was infected, and the scenario makes no mention of this, the technician should have already removed the system from the network, ran a full scan, and quarantined infected files—in that order. Any other viruses that eluded quarantine would be researched on the AV manufacturer's website.

60. **Answer: D.** Use the `nbtstat -A` command. This allows you to check the name table of the remote computer by connecting to it with an IP address. `-a` connects by computer name (though an IP address can still work if proper resolution methods are available on your network). Note that the options for `nbtstat` are case sensitive. `<20>` is the number associated with the server service, the service that allows the Windows 7 Ultimate computer (IP address 192.168.1.5) to serve data to other systems on the network. If it was functioning, you would see it listed along with the Workstation service `<00>` and perhaps the Messenger service `<03>`. However, if the server service was not running, you wouldn't even be able to connect to the Windows 7 Ultimate computer at all—not with `nbtstat`, by ping, or any other method, until the problem is repaired. *That one might have been considered a "doozie".*

61. **Answer: C.** Check the IEC cable first if you sense that there is a power issue. That is the power cable for the computer; make sure it is connected to the computer and to the AC outlet. Next, check the AC wall outlet. Use a receptacle tester or your trusty multimeter to make sure the AC outlet is wired properly and supplying the correct voltage. If that is fine, you can check the power supply and the 24-pin power connector. Only check the circuit breaker if the power has been cut to an area of the building, and only if you have access to the electrical panels.

62. **Answer: A.** The LCD cutoff switch is normally enabled when you close a laptop. The default action in Windows is to put the laptop to sleep if it senses that the LCD cutoff switch has been engaged (laptop has been closed). If the laptop goes into standby mode unexpectedly without closing the laptop, you will have to repair or replace the LCD cutoff switch mechanism. The hard drive, SATA controller, and video card are put to sleep when the laptop goes to sleep but should not cause the computer to sleep unexpectedly.

63. **Answer: D.** Check the hash key of the virus definition you downloaded against the location that you downloaded from. Other properties of the definition (or signature) file (such as the file owner, creation date, and file version) can all be spoofed. The difference is that the hash key is mathematically contrived and must match the key from the download point.

64. **Answer: B.** If the computer keeps obtaining an APIPA address (an IP address that starts with 169.254), then the DHCP server has most likely failed. Of course, you should check if the computer's patch cable is connected and that the network adapter has a link light. If so, then you can rule out the network switch and the patch panel. DNS resolves hostnames to IP address and isn't part of DHCP.

65. **Answer: B.** A Trojan appears to perform desired functions but is actually performing malicious functions behind the scenes. Trojans are used to access a computer through a backdoor and take control of it. They are the bane of web servers as well. Remote Access Trojans (RATs) are used to take control of Windows clients without the users knowing. A virus is code that runs on a computer without the user's knowledge, infecting files when it is executed. Spyware is malicious software that is unwittingly downloaded and installed. It is usually employed to track the surfing activities of a user. A rootkit is software that is designed to gain administrator-level control over a system.

66. **Answer: A.** Installing a wireless repeater to increase the distance of the wireless network is the easiest and cheapest solution. Of course, you should first ask if the customer would mind *moving* the wireless access point to the center of the home, thus giving broader and more uniform coverage. Running cable is time-consuming, is expensive for the customer, and can be difficult in some houses. Though a second wired router would work, it is a more expensive solution (plus the cabling) than a simple wireless repeater. Plus, it would have to be configured properly. High-gain antennae are usually used outdoors (or in outer space) for long-distance transmissions. They have too much power to be placed inside a home and are an excessive solution.

67. **Answer: D.** On the laptop, enable the HDMI audio service to send audio signal along the HDMI cable to the TV. On DVRs, HDMI is set to transmit video and audio by default. However, on some laptops, the audio software might be set to HDMI video only by default, expecting you to be doing presentations or other things where audio is not required. You can usually change this by right-clicking the sound icon in the Notification Area, selecting Playback Devices, and then selecting the HDMI sound device. Drivers might also be necessary. There is no maximum specified length of an HDMI cable, and the question does not tell us the length, but standard cables are either 5 meters or 15 meters long. If the laptop has an HDMI output, you should be able to modify it in Windows. If the HDMI output is part of a USB device, PC Card, or

ExpressCard, make sure you have installed the latest drivers for the device. The speakers don't come into play here. If the TV with the HDMI output has speakers, those speakers should work.

68. **Answer: C.** Foreign disks that are installed in a computer show up in the Disk Management utility as foreign. They need to be imported by right-clicking them and running through the import procedure. No need to convert them from basic to dynamic unless you decide later that you want to create special arrays of disks or expand/contract the size of partitions. Set a disk to active if it has an OS and you wish to make it bootable.

69. **Answers: A and C.** The correct navigational path to the System Restore configuration utility in Windows 7 is Start > right-click Computer > Properties > click the System protection link. That displays the System Properties dialog box System Protection tab. But you gotta love the other method: Run > type `systempropertiesprotection.exe`. Without touching the mouse, you can bring up the same dialog box: Windows + R > type systempropertiesprotection.exe. Fun! Anyway, Start > right-click Computer > Advanced is not a valid path. Start > right-click Computer > Properties > click the Advanced system settings link is valid, but it brings you to the Advanced tab of the System Properties dialog box.

70. **Answer: D.** The figure is showing the Advanced tab of a Lexmark Pro900 printer in Windows 7. It was accessed by navigating to Start > Control Panel > Devices and Printers > right-click the printer and select Printer Properties > Advanced tab. When you right-click on some printers, you need to select Properties instead of Printer Properties; otherwise, the navigation is the same. The Ports tab displays the physical or logical port being used by the printer and allows you to add, remove, and configure ports and enable printer pooling between two or more printers.

71. **Answer: B.** Authentication can be carried out by utilizing something a user is, such as a fingerprint; something a user knows, such as a password or PIN; something a user has, such as a smart card or token; and something a user does, such as a signature or speaking words.

72. **Answer: A.** If you can't find the SSID by scanning for it, enter it manually in your wireless configuration software. You will also need to know the channel being used and the type of encryption as well as the key. If you were to change the SSID on the router, the rest of the clients wouldn't be able to connect, and you still wouldn't be able to scan for it because SSID broadcasting has obviously been turned off as a security precaution in the question's scenario. MAC addresses are burned into the network adapter of the router; they are usually not modified. Resetting the wireless card is rather vague. You could disable it and re-enable it, but you would be left with the same problem. *Know how to manually enter a wireless configuration in Windows!*

73. **Answer: C.** Whaling is when phishing attacks are directed at CEOs and other powerful entities in an organization. It is a type of spear phishing—a directed phishing attack. Whereas most phishing attacks are performed via e-mail, vishing is carried out over the phone.

74. **Answer: D.** The DoD 5220.22-M standard specifies that a hard drive be properly purged with bit-level erasure software that does 7 complete passes. Compare this to the Peter Gutman security method, which requires 35 passes! A magnetic degausser

is not software at all, but a device that uses a magnetic or electromagnetic pulse to remove all data from a magnetic disk. Low-level formatting can be accomplished by some BIOS programs and third-party utilities, but data can still be reconstructed from data residue (data remanence).

75. **Answer: B.** You should configure the Enforce password history policy and set it to a number higher than zero. This way, when a user is prompted to change her password every 42 days (which is the default minimum password age), that user will not be able to use the same password. Password policies can be accessed in Windows 7 within the Local Security Policy window > Security Settings > Account Policies > Password Policy. Minimum password length is the policy that states how many characters a password must be at minimum. Eight is a decent setting, but to be full-on secure many organizations require 15 minimum. There are several technical reasons for this, but the A+ exam will not go into that kind of depth. Complexity requirements policy, if enabled, forces a user to select a password that meets 3 of the following 5 categories: uppercase characters, lowercase characters, numbers, special characters (such as ! or #), and Unicode characters (not often implemented).

76. **Answer: C.** Most likely a fan is failing somewhere—either the CPU fan or a case fan—causing the computer to overheat and then ironically to "freeze" as the customer put it. What the customer meant is that the computer locked up. The CD-ROM won't cause the system to lock up, but the CD-ROM *driver* could cause a stop error if it failed. If the power supply failed, the system would turn off; it wouldn't lock up. If the memory was not seated properly, the system would probably not get past the POST and you would either hear beep codes or see an onscreen message to that effect.

77. **Answer: A.** A bad fan is the most likely cause. The grinding will most likely come from a dirty/dusty or failing power supply fan or CPU fan. If the hard drive was grinding that badly, you would definitely have problems in Windows. Note: SCSI drives make a grinding sound all the time; it is normal for them. If the power supply was bad, the system wouldn't boot. The power supply can run without its fan. If the CD-ROM was bad, you wouldn't be able to listen to the B-52's (in the case that you wanted to).

78. **Answer: D.** You just created a hierarchical star topology. By taking three current star topologies and connecting them all to a backbone switch, you add a top level of super speed. The backbone switch is at the top of the *hierarchy*. Star-bus is when two star networks' switches are connected with a single bus connection. Both hierarchical star and star-bus are hybrid topologies.

79. **Answer: B.** Defective RAM is the most likely perpetrator in this case. The key in the question is the shared video memory. That means that the video controller relies on the motherboard's RAM memory modules. First, try cleaning and reseating the RAM, and if that doesn't work, make sure they are compatible with the motherboard and with each other (if there is more than one). Then replace the RAM as a last resort. If they fail, video will fail. If the resolution was set too high, the screen would be completely unreadable; you probably wouldn't even see the cursor.

80. **Answer: A.** The path is Settings > General > Passcode Lock > Turn Passcode On. By default, Simple Passcode is enabled, as shown in the figure within the question. This can be disabled on the same Passcode Lock screen.

81. **Answer: C.** Chkdsk /I performs a less vigorous check of index entries. It can be used only on NTFS partitions. /V (short for verbose) displays the full path and name of every file on the disk. /F fixes errors on the disk. /R locates bad sectors and recovers readable information.

82. **Answer: B.** When you add a second drive to a system that already has Windows installed, you will probably have to initialize the drive and format it in the Disk Management utility. Rebooting the computer will not help the system see the drive. You can configure the drive in the BIOS to a certain extent, but that won't help Windows see the drive. When you format the drive, Disk Management will ask you to assign a drive letter. No need to set the drive to active because this drive does not have an OS to be booted to.

83. **Answer: C.** The Action Center in Windows 7 displays important messages about solving issues and security concerns. This is the successor to the Windows Vista Problem Reports and Solutions utility. The Task Manager gives you some basic real-time performance data about the PC and can be used to stop processes. Windows Defender is Microsoft's free anti-malware tool.

84. **Answer: B.** Use the System Configuration tool (Msconfig.exe) to disable the service. Do this in the Services tab. BTW, a cute way to open Msconfig is to Press Start and type **sys** in the search box. Of course, you can also disable services in the Services console window. If you need to stop *and* disable a service, the Services console window is your best bet. That is because Msconfig can disable them but not stop them (plus a restart is required for most Msconfig actions). And the Task Manager can stop them, but not disable them. As to the incorrect answers: The Task Scheduler is used to set a time when particular applications and processes will run. System Properties is the dialog box where you can change the name of the computer, configure System Restore, and set up Remote Desktop. Local Security Policy is where password and auditing policies can be configured.

85. **Answer: B.** The Windows 7 DVD has been mounted. We can tell because the Target is GRMCULXFRER_EN_DVD; that is the name of the Windows 7 64-bit DVD. It just happens to be sitting in a DVD-ROM drive named F:. It is pointing to, or redirecting to, the Data folder on the hard drive (as you can see from the title of the window). This way, if a person clicks on the Data folder, which can be easily shared, he will see the contents of the Windows 7 DVD. This makes it possible to implement advanced networking and security techniques in conjunction with the DVD via the Data folder.

86. **Answer: D.** The most practical way to prevent intrusion to the network is to install a firewall. In fact, if this is a SOHO network, chances are the network is controlled by a multifunction network device that already acts as a switch and a router and probably has built-in firewall technology; it just has to be enabled. Usually these are enabled by default, but perhaps someone inadvertently disabled it, and that's one of the reasons an attacker keeps trying to get into the network. An intrusion-detection system (IDS) is usually more elaborate and costs more money, but it would help to prevent network intrusion. (Some devices combine IDS and firewall technologies, but usually not SOHO multifunction network devices.) Disabling the SSID will help to discourage the average user from accessing the wireless network, but any hacker worth his or her salt will get right past that; plus, the attacker could be trying to connect directly through the Internet connection. Antivirus software, regardless of where it is installed, does not

repel attackers; it locates and quarantines malware. Disconnecting the Internet connection would work—the hacker wouldn't be able to get in, but none of the employees would be able to use the Internet. Not a good compromise.

87. **Answer: C.** The video card should be your first stop on the upgrade express train. Images that do not display properly are usually due to a subpar video card. CAD/CAM workstations require a powerful video card. The CPU will also play into this, especially when rendering images, so that is the second thing you should check. View the Windows Experience Index details to find out what has the lowest score and go from there. The video card will most likely be the lowest. CAD/CAM workstations often require video cards that can cost thousands of dollars. Always read the directions carefully and set up massive ESD prevention techniques prior to installing a card this expensive. RAM is not as important to the CAD/CAM workstation, as long as it has enough to run Windows and the AutoCAD software. The hard drive doesn't play much of a factor while the CAD software is running.

88. **Answer: B.** You can't put a PCI Express (PCIe) card in a PCI slot! That's all there is to it. A card from one expansion bus cannot be used in another. However, if you had a PCIe x1 video card, you could install that to a x1 slot, x4 slot, or x16 slot.

89. **Answer: A.** Blurry and smudged pages tend to indicate that the fuser is not getting hot enough. The fuser lasts for about 200,000 pages of print before it needs to be replaced: a good time to install a maintenance kit. If the toner cartridge was leaking, you might see a lot of toner within the printer that needs to be cleaned properly with a computer vacuum. If the toner cartridge is low, the print would become weaker. If the fuser was too hot, it could cause the paper to become singed and could be a safety hazard. In any case when you need to maintenance the fuser, turn off the printer, unplug it, let it cool, and then replace the fuser.

90. **Answer: D.** iPads and other mobile devices use the lithium-ion polymer battery for its lasting power and its flexibility during manufacturing. It is a step above a standard lithium-ion in that it uses a flexible material that can be shaped into just about anything the manufacturer wants. On the average it lasts for 10 hours of use. Nickel-cadmium (NiCd) batteries were used in laptops during the 1990s and early millennium, but they have all given way to lithium-ion. The iPad uses a 3.7-volt battery. A 16-volt battery would be ridiculous and inefficient, not to mention a real challenge to fit in the device.

91. **Answers: A and C.** You can navigate to the window in the figure by going to Start > right-click Computer, select Properties > Computer Name tab > Change or by accessing Run, typing systempropertiescomputername.exe, and finally clicking the Change button.

92. **Answer: D.** Remember to start with the simple. For PCs, that means check the connections; for networks, that means power cycling the device (and checking connections). If the lights are on and not blinking, it would appear that the switch crashed and needs that reboot! A ping of 127.0.0.1 was probably already done in this scenario. That's how you know the network card appears to be functioning properly. Nothing has been mentioned about the Internet (or other networks), so there is no reason to think that the switch's uplink cable needs replacement. Rebooting the computer should not be necessary because we again determined that the network card is functioning properly.

93. **Answer: D.** Use the shutdown command! It works in the Command Prompt and also works programmatically within batch files (.bat) or beyond. To set a shutdown to occur after a specific time period, use the /t xxx switch. taskkill ends processes from the Command Prompt. down is not a command in Windows, but it has been used by other operating system manufactures to initiate a shutdown. kill is the older Windows NT predecessor to the taskkill command.

94. **Answer: C.** /S will copy subdirectories but will skip any empty ones. /E copies all subdirectories, including empty ones. /B copies files in backup mode. /DCOPY:T also copies timestamps of files and folders.

95. **Answer: D.** The default path of the print$ administrative share in Windows 7 is C:\Windows\System32\spool\drivers. This is an important folder because it contains drivers for different types of printers; it's a folder you might want to access as an administrator over the network. So, the share is hidden as an administrative share by adding a $ to the end of the sharename. The columns were dragged to the left to hide the entire folder path. You can have a folder name with a $ on the end, but that doesn't make it an administrative share; the share itself has to have the $ to make it hidden.

96. **Answer: A.** The net view command will list all of the shares on the computer within the Command Prompt. net use enables you to map network drives to remote shares. net share allows you to create shares within the Command Prompt. net statistics displays information about the server or workstation services.

97. **Answer: B.** The technician should clean the pickup rollers. If they are dirty or oily, they could cause a paper jam directly behind or above the paper tray. The feeder rollers would cause a jam further in the printer. A fuser issue would cause a jam up toward the end of the printing path. The drum (or toner cartridge) will usually not cause a paper jam, but in the rare case, simply replace the toner cartridge.

98. **Answer: C.** Gingerbread is the name of Android version 2. Version 3 is Honeycomb, and version 4 is Ice Cream Sandwich (ICS). Windows CE, Apple iOS, and Blackberry OS don't use such descriptive names.

99. **Answer: C.** netsh firewall show state is a command that can be run in the Command Prompt that will display any currently open ports. The successor to netsh firewall in Windows 7/Vista is netsh advfirewall firewall. Other commands can also show open ports such as netstat -a. However, arp-a will show a table of hosts that the local computer has connected to in recent history; it displays the IP address and MAC address of those remote computers. netsh firewall show logging will display the location of the firewall log, its maximum file size, and whether any packets were dropped. ipconfig /all displays the configuration of your network adapters.

100. **Answer: B.** The Regsvr32 command in the Command Prompt is used to manipulate ActiveX controls and DLLs. For example, to register a sample ActiveX control, you would type regsvr32 sample.ocx. Unregistering requires the /u parameter. This leans more toward the programming side of things, but you should know what the

command does. `Regedit.exe` and `Regedt32` bring up the Registry Editor application in Windows 7/Vista. ODBC is short for Open DataBase Connectivity; it is an interface used within the C programming language to access database management systems. `ODBC32` is not a command in Windows.

CHAPTER ELEVEN

Review of the 220-802 Exam

Great work! You have completed all four hundred 220-802 practice questions. That is a feat in itself. But the real test is yet to come. We'll discuss that in the next chapter.

Now that you have completed the four practice exams, let's do a little review of the 220-802 domains, talk about your next steps, and give you some test-taking tips.

Review of the Domains

Remember that the 220-802 is divided into the four domains, shown in Table 11.1.

TABLE 11.1   220-802 Domains

Domain	Percentage of Exam
1.0 Operating Systems	33%
2.0 Security	22%
3.0 Mobile Devices	9%
4.0 Troubleshooting	36%
Total	**100%**

As you could see while taking the exams, troubleshooting questions are the bulk of what you will see on the exam and are more difficult than the questions from the other domains. You have to place yourself within the scenario and imagine that you are actually fixing hardware and software problems step-by-step.

Even if you are a solid troubleshooter and really know your Windows operating systems, that still leaves a third of the test unaccounted for. So, Security and Mobile Devices become the pivotal domains: without them you could be in trouble; with them, you will have all the tools you need to rule the exam.

Everyone who takes the exam gets a different group of questions. Because it is randomized, one person may see more questions on, say, Window XP than the next person, even though it is over a decade old. Or you might see more questions on Windows security. It differs from person to person. To reduce your risk, be ready for any question from any domain, and study all of the objectives.

Review What You Know

At this point you should be pretty well versed when it comes to the 220-802 exam. But I still recommend going back through all of the questions and making sure there are no questions, answers, concepts, or explanations you are unclear about. If there are, then additional study is probably necessary. If something really just doesn't make sense, is ambiguous or vague, or doesn't appear to be technically correct, feel free to contact me at my website (www.davidlprowse.com), and I will do my best to clarify. Think it through carefully before you do so, though. Many of questions are written in an ambiguous manner to replicate what you will see on the real exam.

Here are a few great ways to study further:

▸ **Take the exams in flash card mode**—Use a piece of paper to cover up the answers as you take the exams. This helps to make you think a bit harder and aids in committing everything to memory.

▸ **Download the A+ 220-802 objectives**—You can get these from www.comptia.org. Go through them one by one and checkmark each item that you are confident in. If there are any items in the objectives that you are unsure about, study them hard. That's where the test will trip you up. There are 20 pages of objectives, so this will take a while. But it really helps to close any gaps in your knowledge, and gives that extra boost for the exam.

▸ **Take the CompTIA A+ Practice Exam**—This can also be found at www.comptia.org. Retake that exam until you get 100% correct. If any questions give you difficulty, contact me at my website so that I can help you understand them.

More Test-Taking Tips

I've mentioned it several times already, but it bears repeating. Take your time on the exam. The thing is, you either know it or you don't. If you know it, you will probably end up with time left over. So there is no rush. Rushing can cause you to miss some key word, phrase, or other tidbit of information that could cost you the correct answer. So take it slow, and read everything you see carefully.

While taking an exam, follow these recommendations:

- Use the process of elimination.
- Be logical in the face of adversity.
- Use your gut instinct.
- Don't let one question beat you!
- If all else fails, guess.

I'll expand on these points in the final chapter.

If you finish early, use the time allotted to you to review all of your answers. Chances are you will have time left over at the end, so use it wisely! Make sure that everything you have marked has a proper answer that makes sense to you. But try not to overthink! Give it your best shot and be confident in your answers.

Taking the Real Exam

Do not register until you are fully prepared. When you are ready, schedule the exam to commence within a day or two so that you won't forget what you learned!

Registration can be done online. Register at Pearson Vue: www.vue.com. They accept payment by major credit card for the exam fee. First-timers will need to create an account with Pearson Vue.

Here are some good general practices for taking the real exams:

- Pick a good time for the exam
- Don't over-study the day before the exam
- Get a good night's rest
- Eat a decent breakfast

- ▶ Show up early

- ▶ Bring ear plugs

- ▶ Brainstorm before starting the exam

- ▶ Take small breaks while taking the exam

- ▶ Be confident

I'll embellish on these concepts in the final chapter.

Well, that's about it for the 220-802 portion of this book. Meet me at the final chapter: Chapter 12, the wrap-up.

CHAPTER TWELVE

Wrap-Up

This chapter provides the following tools and information to help you be successful when preparing for and taking the CompTIA A+ 220-801 and 220-802 exams:

▶ Getting Ready and the Exam Preparation Checklist

▶ Tips for Taking the Real Exam

▶ Beyond the CompTIA A+ Certification

> **NOTE**
>
> This chapter is very similar to Chapter 19 of the *A+ Exam Cram* 6th edition (the Exam Cram study guide). If you also purchased that book, you can use either chapter for your test preparations.

Getting Ready and the Exam Preparation Checklist

The CompTIA A+ certification exams can be taken by anyone; there are no prerequisites, although CompTIA recommends one year of prior lab or field experience working with computers. For more information on CompTIA and the A+ exam, go to:

http://www.comptia.org

Also visit my A+ page:

www.davidlprowse.com/220-801

This page has information, additions, and updated errata that you should check before taking the exam.

To acquire your A+ certification, you need to pass two exams: 220-801 and 220-802, each of which is 100 questions. Although it is possible, I don't recommend taking both exams on the same day, but instead spacing them a week or so apart.

These exams are administered by Pearson Vue (www.vue.com). You need to register with Pearson Vue to take the exam.

It is important to be fully prepared for the exam, so I created a checklist that you can use to make sure you have covered all the bases. The checklist is shown in Table 12.1. Go through the checklist twice, once for each exam. For each exam, place a check in the status column as each item is completed. Do this first with the 220-801 exam and then again with the 220-802 exam. I highly recommend completing each step in order and taking the 220-801 exam first. Historically, my readers and students have benefited greatly from this type of checklist.

TABLE 12.1 Exam Preparation Checklist

Step	Item	Details	220-801 Status	220-802 Status
1.	Attend an A+ course.	A hands-on A+ course can do so much for you when it comes to installing, configuring, and especially troubleshooting. Especially if you don't have the CompTIA recommended experience (12 months), consider an A+ class.		
2.	Review your study guide.	Whatever main study guide (or guides) you used, be sure to review those carefully.		
3.	Complete the Practice Exams in this book.	Take the three 220-801 exams, and review them carefully. On the second run-through of this checklist, take the four 220-802 exams and review them. If you score under 90% on any one exam, go back and study more! If you have any trouble at this stage, consider getting my *A+ Exam Cram* 6th edition study guide, or another study guide of your choice, and read it very carefully.		
4.	Create your own cheat sheet.	See Table 12.2 for an example. The act of writing down important details helps to commit them to memory. Keep in mind that you will not be allowed to take this into the actual testing room.		

TABLE 12.1   Continued

Step	Item	Details	220-801 Status	220-802 Status
5.	Register for the exam.	Do not register until you have completed the previous steps; you shouldn't register until you are fully prepared. When you are ready, schedule the exam to commence within a couple days so that you won't forget what you learned!		
		Registration can be done online. Register at Pearson Vue: www.vue.com.		
		They accept payment by major credit card for the exam fee.		
		(You will need to create an account in order to sign up for exams.)		
6.	Review practice questions.	Keep reviewing practice questions until the day of the exam.		
7.	Take the exam!	Checkmark each exam to the right as you pass it. Good luck!		

Table 12.2 gives a partial example of a cheat sheet that you can create to aid in your studies. Fill in the appropriate information in the right column. For example, the first step of the six-step troubleshooting process is "Identify the problem."

TABLE 12.2   Sample Cheat Sheet

Concept	Fill in the Appropriate Information Here
The six-step troubleshooting process	1.
	2.
	3.
	4.
	5.
	6.
The motherboard form factors you should know	
The three types of DDR and their data transfer rates	
The EP printing process	
Six types of expansion busses and their maximum data transfer rates	

TABLE 12.2   Continued

Concept	Fill in the Appropriate Information Here
Windows 7/Vista startup files	
Windows XP startup files	
Etc.*	

*Continue Table 12.2 in this fashion on paper. The key is to write down various technologies, processes, step-by-steps, and so on to commit them to memory.

Tips for Taking the Real Exam

Some of you readers will be new to exams. This section is for you. For other readers who have taken exams before, feel free to skip this section or use it as a review.

The exam is conducted on a computer and is mostly multiple-choice. You have the option to skip questions. If you do so, be sure to "mark" them before moving on. There will be a small check box that you can select to mark them. Feel free to mark any other questions that you have answered but are not completely sure about. When you get to the end of the exam, there will be an item review section that shows you any questions that you did not answer and any that you marked.

The following list includes tips and tricks that I have learned over the years. I've taken at least 20 certification exams in the past decade, and the following points have served me well:

General Practices for Taking Exams

▸ **Pick a good time for the exam**—It would appear that the least amount of people are at test centers on Monday and Friday mornings. Consider scheduling during these times. Otherwise, schedule a time that works well for you, when you don't have to worry about anything else. Keep in mind that Saturdays can be busy. Oh, and don't schedule the exam until you are ready. I understand that sometimes deadlines have to be set, but in general, don't register for the exam until you feel confident you can pass. Things come up in life that can sometimes get in the way of your study time. Keep in mind that most exams can be cancelled as long as you give 24 hours notice (check that time frame when registering to be sure).

▶ **Don't over-study the day before the exam**—Some people like to study hard the day before; some don't. My recommendations are to study off the Cram Sheet and your own cheat sheets, but in general, don't overdo it. It's not a good idea to go into overload the day before the exam.

▶ **Get a good night's rest**—A good night's sleep (7–9 hours) before the day of the exam is probably the best way to get your mind ready for an exam.

▶ **Eat a decent breakfast**—Eating is good! Breakfast is number two when it comes to getting your mind ready for an exam, especially if it is a morning exam. Just watch out for the coffee and tea. Too much caffeine for a person who is not used to it can be detrimental to the thinking process.

▶ **Show up early**—I recommend that you show up 30 minutes prior to your scheduled exam time. This is important; give yourself plenty of time, and make sure you know where you are going. You don't want to have to worry about getting lost or being late. Stress and fear are the mind killers. Work on reducing any types of stress the day of and the day before the exam. By the way, you really do need extra time because when you get to the testing center, you need to show ID, sign forms, get your personal belongings situated, and be escorted to your seat. Have two forms of ID (signed) ready for the administrator of the test center. Turn your cell phone or smartphone off when you get to the test center; they'll check that, too.

> **NOTE**
>
> If you are a first-time test-taker, I recommend you perform a trial run and drive to the testing center a few days before your exam. This will ensure you know exactly where you are going on the day of the exam.

▶ **Bring earplugs**—You never know when you will get a loud testing center or, worse yet, a loud test-taker next to you. Earplugs help to block out any unwanted noise that might show up. Just be ready to show your earplugs to the test administrator.

▶ **Brainstorm before starting the exam**—Write down as much as you can remember from the cheat sheets before starting the exam. The testing center is obligated to give you something to write on; make use of it! By getting all the memorization out of your head and on "paper" first, it clears the brain somewhat so that it can tackle the questions. I put paper in quotation marks because it might not be paper; it could be a mini dry erase board or something similar.

▶ **Take small breaks while taking the exam**—Exams can be brutal. You have to answer 100 questions while staring at a screen for an hour. Sometimes these screens are old and have seen better days; these older, flickering monitors can cause a strain on your eyes. I recommend small breaks and breathing techniques. For example, after going through every 25 questions or so, close your eyes and slowly take a few deep breaths, holding each one for 5 seconds and releasing each one slowly. Think about nothing while doing so. Remove the test from your mind during these breaks. It takes only half a minute, but it can really help to get your brain refocused. It's almost a Zen type of thing, but for me, when I have applied this technique properly, I have gotten a few perfect scores. It's really amazing how the mindset can make or break you.

▶ **Be confident**—You have studied hard, gone through the practice exams, and created your cheat sheet. You've done everything you can to prep. These things alone should build confidence. But really, you just have to be confident for no reason whatsoever. Think of it this way: you are great...I am great...(to quote Dr. Daystrom). But really, there is no disputing this! That's the mentality you must have. You are not being pretentious about this if you think it to yourself. Acting that way to others...well, that's another matter. So build that inner confidence and your mindset should be complete.

Smart Methods for Difficult Questions

▶ **Use the process of elimination**—If you are not sure about an answer, first eliminate any answers that are definitely *incorrect*. You might be surprised how often this works. This is one of the reasons why it is recommended that you not only know the correct answers to the practice exams' questions, but also know *why* the wrong answers are wrong. The testing center should give you something to write on; use it by writing down the letters of the answers that are incorrect to keep track. Even if you aren't sure about the correct answer, if you can logically eliminate anything that is incorrect, then the answer will become apparent. To sum it up, the character Sherlock Holmes said it best: "When you have eliminated the impossible, whatever remains, however improbable, must be the truth." There's more to it, of course, but from a scientific standpoint, this method can be invaluable.

▶ **Be logical in the face of adversity**—The most difficult questions are when two answers appear to be correct, even though the test question requires you to select only one answer. Real exams do not rely on trick questions. Sometimes you need to slow down, think logically, and really compare the two possible correct answers. Also, you must imagine the scenario that the question is a part of. Really think through step-by-step what is happening in the scenario. Write out as much as you can. The more you can visualize the scenario, the better you will be able to figure out which of the two answers is the best one.

▶ **Use your gut instinct**—Sometimes a person taking a test just doesn't know the answer; it happens to everyone. If you have read through the question and all the answers and used the process of elimination, sometimes this is all you have left. In some scenarios, you might read a question and instinctively know the answer, even if you can't explain why. Tap into this ability. Some test-takers write down their gut instinct answer before delving into the question and then compare their thoughtful answer with their gut instinct answer.

▶ **Don't let one question beat you!**—Don't let yourself get stuck on one question. Skip it and return to it later. When you spend too much time on one question, the brain gets sluggish. The thing is, with these exams you either know it or you don't. And don't worry too much about it; chances are you are not going to get a perfect score. Remember that the goal is only to pass the exams; how many answers you get right after that is irrelevant. If you have gone through this book thoroughly, you should be well prepared and you should have plenty of time to go through all of the exam questions with time to spare to return to the ones you skipped and marked.

▶ **If all else fails, guess**—Remember that the exams might not be perfect. A question might seem confusing or appear not to make sense. Leave questions like this until the end, and when you have gone through all the other techniques mentioned, make an educated, logical guess. Try to imagine what the test is after, and why they would be bringing up this topic, vague or strange as it might appear.

Wrapping Up the Exam

► **Review all of your answers**—If you finish early, use the time allotted to you to review the answers. Chances are you will have time left over at the end, so use it wisely! Make sure that everything you have marked has a proper answer that makes sense to you. But try not to overthink! Give it your best shot and be confident in your answers.

Beyond the CompTIA A+ Exam

CompTIA started a new policy on January 1, 2011. A person who passes the A+ exams will be certified for three years. To maintain the certification beyond that time, you must enroll in the CompTIA Continuing Education Program. This program has an annual fee and requires that you obtain Continuing Education Units (CEUs) that count toward the recertification. For more information on this policy, see the following link:

http://certification.comptia.org/getCertified/stayCertified.aspx

Final Note: I wish you the best of luck on your exams and in your IT career endeavors. Please let me know when you pass your exams. I would love to hear from you! Also, remember that I am available to answer any of your questions about this book via my website at www.davidlprowse.com.

Sincerely,

David L. Prowse